Dissenting Views II
More Investigations into History, Culture, Cinema, and Conspiracy

JOSEPH E. GREEN

ISBN: 0615896405
ISBN-13: 978-0615896403

Cover photograph by Robert Knudsen. Public domain,
from the Kennedy Library collection.

DEDICATION

For
Faith G. Harper
and to the late John Judge. Miss you, buddy.

CONTENTS

Foreword

"The real test of a man is not how well he plays the role he has invented for himself, but how well he plays the role that destiny has assigned him."

-Jan Patocka (1907-1977) Czech philosopher

I first met Joseph Green in 2006 on a sidewalk in front of the Hotel Lawrence, about a block away from Dealey Plaza in downtown Dallas. I was there to film the Coalition on Political Assassinations' annual conference as part of a documentary I was producing. I had shot the conference every year since 2002, and virtually every year since. The numbers of the attendees at these conferences vary from year to year, but one thing that hasn't varied is that almost everyone in the room is a white male over 40.

That's why I was a bit surprised when, during a mid-morning break out on that sidewalk, a guy in his early thirties I had seen in the audience, wearing a Malcolm X t-shirt, strolled up and said, "hey, I'm Joe". He was by far the youngest attendee in years and possessed the calm air of someone with a profound understanding of human nature far beyond his years. And while other conference participants were discussing the finer points of autopsy photos or low-velocity rifle ballistics, we talked about film, fine art, Austin vs. Chapel Hill, and most importantly, whether Henry Rollins ruined Black Flag.

Little did I know that I was speaking with the very future of deep politics research.

An accomplished playwright, novelist, poet and columnist, Joe exemplifies what the next generation of political researcher must be if the search for truth is to flourish in the coming years. This is perhaps what sets Joe apart from every other political researcher I've met over the last 12 years. He has the ability to place the machinations behind major political events in a broader, yet nuanced, cultural context. The mainstream media, timid academics and institutional sycophants might attempt to label Joe and others with the scarlet letter "conspiracy theorist", the death knell for most serious intellectual pursuits. For Joe, the proper label is "institutional and cultural analyst."

Detractors of the research community point out that researchers are obsessed with their own theories and only focus on the facts that support their theories. An esteemed religion professor of mine once said, "there's only one thing I value more than being right: being proved wrong." Joe is one of the few figures in the research community to whom this applies.

In the pages that follow, Joe offers a remembrance of our mentor, leader, research role-model and friend, the late John Judge, co-founder and long-time director of COPA. Joe's chapter sums up the man perfectly; I could only offer a feeble attempt to make a substantial addition.

I first read the above poem just a few weeks after meeting John Judge. I immediately thought of John, and one can't help but realize that Joe is on the same path. In terms of the JFK assassination, most only care about who killed JFK; Joe, as was John, is driven by the unseen hand of destiny to realize JFK's vision of peace, focusing on why he was killed and helping our fellow man understand why it matters. In the pursuit of American democracy, can there be anything more honorable?

The two men will forever be linked in my mind: a generational baton being passed as simply and logically as salt and pepper across a Deep Ellum diner table at 2 a.m.

In my film *The Searchers*, speaking to a crowd on the knoll, John Judge declares, "What died on November 22, 1963, was more than just a president. Truth was killed. Hope was killed. And a government that responded to popular movements was killed. But we in the US are what's left of democracy in the world. We have more potential of any country to make democracy work. We have a strength that the powers in this country are afraid of. But if you want a democracy you have to make it a democracy. And the first step is to take back your history."

    Dissenting Views II epitomizes this spirit. And, as exemplified in the pages that follow, no doubt the reader will agree that there is no one more destined to lead the next generation of researchers on John Judge's march - and to be able to communicate its meaning in a deeper contemporary and cultural context - than Joseph Green.

Randy Benson
Duke University Center for Documentary Studies
Durham, NC
October 20, 2014

For how art thou a king

But by fair sequence and succession?

-William Shakespeare, *Richard II*

JFK & OTHER CONSPIRACIES

2013 marked the 50th anniversary of the Kennedy assassination. The following essays touch on the assassination in varying ways and the media response to it. Also included are a pair of book reviews and essays on something I've been calling the "philosophy of conspiracy," analogous to the philosophy of science of, say, Carnap or Popper. The idea is to stand outside conspiracy theory and observe how it is thought about and what the ramifications are. Thanks to Jim DiEugenio at CTKA, Alex Constantine at The Constantine Report, and Jerry Policoff at Op Ed News for publishing some of these pieces.

REMEMBERING JOHN JUDGE

It was mid-morning under grey skies somewhere between Dallas and Waco, on our way to the Poage Legislative Library at Baylor University. Randy Benson, a filmmaker and professor of documentary studies at Duke, walked alongside me. We trailed two figures walking and talking beside each other: John Judge and Robert Groden.

"This is like being a hockey fan," Randy said, "And we're hanging out with Mario Lemieux and Wayne Gretzky." I agreed.

We all walked into Starbucks and grabbed a table.

I had met all three men during a trip to Dallas in November for the Coalition on Political Assassinations conference. I had decided to go after encountering an article by John Judge called "The Black Hole of Guyana" in a book called *Secret and Suppressed*, edited by the legendary Jim Keith and published by Feral House. It impressed me because - in the first place - the information was incredible. It told a story of the Jim Jones cult suicides utterly at odds with what was conventionally known. No Kool-Aid to be found here. Secondly, however, was the thoroughness of the documentation Judge had used. It was scholarly. It used Guyanese sources rather than standard Western sources, which told a far different tale. There were no suicides at Guyana. The autopsist, Dr. Mootoo, had ruled all of the dead to have been murdered.

I had become interested in so-called "conspiracy literature," which was fascinating but often ill-documented. All too often large claims were based on singular testimony or dubious provenance, so that they didn't always pass rational muster. I was struck by the emphasis on detail and care that went into the article's sourcing. Not long after hearing about the COPA conference and seeing that it was up the road from me in Dallas, I decided I had to meet him.

That first conference I arrived early - about 10 AM - at the Hotel Lawrence, a rickety building with two elevators, one frequently inoperative, but conveniently close to Dealey Plaza. I went up to the 2nd floor breakfast room and saw John sitting at one of the tables, going through some papers and having his breakfast. I walked over, tentatively.

"Hi," I said. "I'm Joe. I know you're, uh, John Judge. Mind if I sit down?"

He agreed and three hours later we parted company and said we would talk later, after the night's speakers. I remember going outside in a bitter wind, barely feeling it because my mind had been blown in so many directions. I had received my first taste of the John Judge experience.

Talking to John could often be like drinking from a fire hose. (WAIT, what did he just say?? And then what?? And wait a minute - what?!?) He flowed from one astonishing fact to another so fast that you couldn't keep up.

I'd get better with practice.

Through John at the conferences I met Robert Groden. Groden was a legend - the man who brought the Zapruder film to popular consciousness along with Dick Gregory on the Geraldo Rivera program, Oliver Stone's research expert on the film JFK (and who had played several roles in the film), author of *High Treason* and *The Search for Lee Harvey Oswald* and creator of the rotoscoped version of the Zapruder film.

Which is why Randy made his remark to me. And it was true - a bit astonishing to be chatting mildly over tea and coffee in some tiny Texas town.

This would become a typical COPA experience.

I attended every COPA conference in Dallas after that, and became more and more involved with the setting up (always to John's specifications) and helping with whatever needed help. In 2008, COPA held conferences in Los Angeles (to mark RFK's death) and Memphis (for Dr. King), which is how I ended up complaining in solidarity with Bill Turner about our LA hotel and having the singular experience of Judge Joe Brown buying me barbecue and listening to

4

stories about the Black Panthers and skiing in Colorado. It is hard to overestimate how amazing the conferences were, in terms of being able to sit around and pick the brains of so many high-level scholars. And it was always brilliant to find that someone you knew had written a book, like T Carter with her *A Memoir of Injustice*, or to find an author you immediately hit it off with, like Lyndon Barsten, Shane O'Sullivan, or John Potash.

And naturally over the years John and I became friends, and he served as a mentor in many ways, helping to guide me through the thickets. My first book, *Dissenting Views*, was dedicated to three people: Ben Rogers, the archivist for the Poage Library, Jim DiEugenio for publishing many of my articles (including my first, "The JFK 10-Point Program") and to John, precisely for his stewardship. I could always check my thinking with him, see if I was on the right track, and though I didn't always agree with him I always respected his agility of mind.

I am sitting on many years of emails, on a huge variety of topics political, philosophical, and personal, and what shines through in them is both his warmth of feeling, his humanity, and his wicked sense of humor. On the phone, I became accustomed to hearing his standard greeting for me: "How are ya, Doc?" or sometimes a booming "Doctor Green, the younger!" (My father is a professor and I grew up around academia, and John always granted me an honorary Ph.D.) And then we'd be off and running about one topic or another. A few years ago, John met a girl. On an internet dating site. And suddenly our conversations changed, and I found myself listening to him wax poetic about a certain Marilyn he'd met and how he wanted me to meet her. The idea is a bit astonishing - looking for a date on a website and winding up with John Judge. But that was John; human, after all, not a walking encyclopedia, a real live person. And he was a happier man for that.

The times that will stay with me forever are the human ones. Eating dinner with him in Memphis and listening to a story about an out of body experience from his days in Ohio. The one conference speech he gave in '09 where he described how dolphins will sacrifice for one another when they know death is imminent for some or all of the group. The late nights with the other techies (Randy, John Geraghty, Tim Plainfeather, and others who came and went) making sure microphones were ready and cameras in place. The one time

John yelled at me (because another "tech" person, Carl, had screwed up the audio on movie night) and after I fixed the problem couldn't help thinking "I just got yelled at by John Judge," and how cool that was. And how we then skipped the movies and went to an all-night restaurant.

The conferences were always 24-7 affairs, and I used to get 3 or 4 hours of sleep per night with everything that needed to be done. This led to a certain level of punch-drunkenness by the time Sunday rolled around, but it was worth it. It was a good exercise for the brain to have astonishing information given to you during the day with so many brilliant speakers, and then work most of the night getting everything ready for the next day.

There have been two conferences in the United States that have been traditional rivals in the JFK community: COPA and Lancer. Many people thought that there were mere differences in opinion between the two, or that it was based on personality disputes. It wasn't. Those close to the situation know what I mean, but I will say that I never regretted my choice of which entity to support, even when COPA was on a shoestring and Lancer appeared to have money coming out of its ears.

Randy and I have since become good friends, and indeed I've made many good friends over the years as a result of the conferences. We're both involved in the making of documentaries about the Kennedy case; his, *The Searchers*, is a brilliant celebration of the original Warren Commission critics. The one I am involved with, *King Kill 63*, is still in post-production but features many things, including the last recorded interview with John, which I conducted. It will hopefully be out before the end of the year, but as anyone will tell you it isn't easy these days.

My hope is that both these films will help preserve the memory of John and the causes he stood for, which were much larger than simply JFK. He was an incredible scholar, a wide-ranging activist whose absence is felt in veteran counseling and in DC schools, a dedicated servant to advocates for change like Cynthia McKinney and Dennis Kucinich, and was a larger than life figure on the research scene. But for me, mostly he was my friend who I admired. I will miss him, his voice, and his sometimes hilarious-if-dark quips. His goal of creating a Museum of Hidden History is a perfect summation of his ideals. He was on a mission to better ourselves, to see and acknowledge the darkness within us, and to try and pull it into the light.

ACCEPTABLE AUTHORITARIANISM

This essay appeared June 29th, 2013, in Op Ed News. John Judge and I talked about a strategy to try to get some COPA people inside the gates, as it were, and we decided to have everybody file on their own and then whoever got in would stage a protest. As it turned out, I qualified for a ticket to attend the 50th anniversary event, but then didn't use it when John failed to get in, since he needed help outside. It was a bitter, rainy, cold day that was brutal for everyone, but we had our event and the moment of silence.

For the 50th anniversary of the assassination of John F. Kennedy, Mayor Rawlings of the city of Dallas has come to a momentous decision. Facing what was likely to be a large-scale protest at the grassy knoll, he and his associates have determined that they will allow 5,000 ticket-holders into their "event." 2,500 will be Dallas residents, and another 2,500 will be for the many thousands of tourists from all over the world.

Their website is at www.50thhonoringjohnfkennedy.com.

This decision is ludicrous, but not as much as the title of the website where applicants can try to screen their way into the lottery. Is it really possible for the city of Dallas to honor John F. Kennedy fifty years after he was murdered on their streets? Did Earle Cabell, then-mayor of Dallas, seize the moment to aggressively pursue Kennedy's agenda at the local level? Did Texas become a place where civil rights are guaranteed and obscene oil profits are renounced? In the last fifty years, has there been any aspect of Kennedy's programs or ideas that have found a home in Dallas?

Just within the last week, the Texas Supreme Court determined, in Salinas v. Texas, that silence can be an indicator of guilt in response to police questioning.

But more on the topic of fascism in a moment.

As is obvious to anyone who looks with clear eyes at the situation, the 50th anniversary is all about public relations for the city of Dallas. City leaders are hoping that once it passes, interest in the case will die down and they never have to deal with the city's shame again. In the meantime, they are going to do their level best to keep out the "crazies" and have a solemn, meaningless event for the cameras. They know the world will be watching and they need to put a good face on the President being shot in the head on a public street.

If Lady Macbeth were alive today, her PR firm would have her endorsing soap flakes.

However, they are not the only ones interested in controlling the message. Some of the agitation comes from the other side, as well. Every year, John Judge of the Coalition on Political Assassinations holds a moment of silence on the grassy knoll on the anniversary of the moment Kennedy was killed. The moment of silence takes place in the context of what is typically a weekend conference, in which people gather to hear speakers on various topics related to political assassination.

Every year, the conference goes well beyond JFK. We discuss the "big four" of 1960s assassinations – the two Kennedys, Dr. King, and Malcolm X – but we also go into more recent political killings and some which are quite obscure even to attendees. In 2011, I myself gave a presentation on the murder of Fred Hampton, a Black Panther leader who was executed by Chicago police in December of 1969. The Coalition on Political Assassinations ends in a plural – JFK is incredibly important, but he isn't the only topic on the agenda.

There are some who disagree. Some people within the movement, including long-time researchers, want to make the 50th anniversary conference all about John Kennedy and nothing else. No one wants to hear about these other assassinations, they say. We should focus only on JFK.

And once again this comes down to what it means to properly honor John F. Kennedy.

I don't believe that Kennedy was some sort of demigod. I know that he had serious flaws. I also know, however, that there were reasons he was shot, and those reasons had to do with being more

concretely democratic than his fellows. There is no doubt that if
Kennedy had remained alive, our country doesn't stay in Vietnam.
Virtually everyone in his cabinet who has spoken out on the matter
has agreed. But in a sense, it doesn't matter how democratic he
actually was. What matters is how those in power perceived him. This
excellent point was made by Michael Parenti in his brilliant study, *The
Assassination of Julius Caesar.* To our eyes, looking back, Caesar may
not have seemed particularly democratic; but to the assassins, he was
a dangerous radical.

Now, having said all that, if we researchers – like the city elders
of Dallas – wish to honor Kennedy, then do we do that by only
discussing his murder? Or does it make sense to continue the study
of all political murders, since they seem to be both (1) related to one
another and (2) related to our rapid slide into what one might call
acceptable authoritarianism?

The Kennedy assassination doesn't happen in a vacuum. The
major assassinations of the Sixties wiped out the political Left in this
country and paved the way for Richard Nixon's ascendance in 1968.
That is the critical point where a button is pushed and democracy
starts to give way to fascism. And it has been accelerating.

Just a few days ago, Nancy Pelosi – the Democratic House
Minority Leader from California – stated that she thought Edward
Snowden should be prosecuted[1] for releasing documents confirming
National Security Agency spying on all Americans. Pelosi, who is
loathed by the political right in this country, considered a leftist
nonpareil, is on the side of NSA! This is a Democrat, ostensibly. To
the people's credit, she was booed when she made these remarks.
They also made comments about this being George W. Bush's
"fourth term," commenting on the fact that the wars abroad have not
ended, and the wars at home – in terms of surveillance and loss of
rights – have continued with alacrity. The people are on the left of
the leadership.

We continue our gradual slide into acceptable authoritarianism. I
call it this because much of the public seems to go along with the
incredible corruption of the state as long as their lives are relatively
unimpeded. To understand this process, one should begin on
November 22, 1963. But unless all the context is studied – the arc of
history whose end never ends, because it continues right up until this

---

[1] http://www.huffingtonpost.com/2013/06/22/nancy-pelosi-booed_n_3484062.html

moment – one cannot understand the assassination. For those interested in understanding how the world works, JFK's murder isn't some true crime story where the point is to revel in the lurid details. It's to reveal the beginning of a series of political murders done for the purpose of changing the world to benefit the few against the many.

As always, it's all about agendas, and controlling the message. Whether this arises from the city of Dallas, desperate to make everyone forget, or certain JFK researchers who want everyone to remember only what they want them to remember.

My personal feeling is that it's bigger than all of us. None of us can grasp the whole thing. But if we're serious about honoring John F. Kennedy, it behooves us to try.

A CONSPIRACY PRIMER

"I must frankly confess that the foreign policy of the United States since the termination of hostilities has reminded me, sometimes irresistibly, of the attitude of Germany under Kaiser Wilhelm II ... It is characteristic of the military mentality that non-human factors (atom bombs, strategic bases, weapons of all sorts, the possession of raw materials, etc.) are held essential, while the human being, his desires and thought - in short, the psychological factors - are considered as unimportant and secondary ... The general insecurity that goes hand in hand with this results in the sacrifice of the citizen's civil rights to the supposed welfare of the state."
–Albert Einstein, *The Military Mentality*

I am not a conspiracy theorist. Sometimes people label me that way. Many of my friends get labeled that way, and some of them might be – but some of them clearly aren't. In order to know for sure, we would have to know what is meant by the term.

Now the term 'conspiracy theorist' is meant to be dismissive, obviously. It's a term used to put borders on thought, to reassure, to identify aberrant patterns in individuals and create distance between us and them. You call someone a 'conspiracy theorist' to put them down or accuse them of being an intellectual outcast without having to think hard about it. Talking heads on television often identify someone as a 'conspiracy theorist' when they want to indicate a clear separation: "Well, that sounds like conspiratorial thinking to me," or "If I may sound like a conspiracy theorist for a moment ..." or "I don't want to get into conspiracy theory, so let's take another topic ..." The term is used, in essence, like profanity. It tends to connote 'stupid,' but also 'outrageous,' and – most importantly – not to be taken seriously. *That idea you just had puts you on the outside. You are being stupid and outrageous. People aren't going to like you if you keep thinking that way.*

CONNOTATION

Let's look at the term profanity. We all know what it means: "bad words." Sometimes we say they are "curse" words, which gives them a slightly magical evocation. So: words that are intended to express strong disrespect or to invite the gods to visit heinous things upon someone. As the Woody Allen joke goes, "I told him to be fruitful and multiply, but not in those words." Bad language. When we visit the origins of the word "profanity," we find that it derives from the Latin "profanus," which means "outside the temple." There is a sense in which anything that is not sacred is profane – that is, not specifically holy – but the broader and more common definition is an insult to that which is sacred. That which cannot be done within the temple.

Now I find that fascinating, and I say that the term 'conspiracy theorist' is a kind of profanity, because it fulfills the precise intent of its original meaning. When you call someone by that term, you are indicating that they are outside the temple. We are inside the temple and holy and sacred, and you are outside with the profane. The term is a psychological attack meant to marginalize the speaker of the improper thought.

However, this is only one-half of the equation. The other half is that the term imbues the speaker with psychological reassurance and power. It is like saying, "By saying what you have said, you have proven yourself to be outside the norm, and I have hordes of people who will agree with me." It is powerful bandwagon thinking. For human beings, whose social instincts are so strong that they carry over into the digital and beyond, this type of thinking is not only motivated but receives immediate reward. It is like being inside the Dallas Cowboys football stadium and making disparaging remarks about the Philadelphia Eagles. The crowd will reassure and happily agree with you in solidarity.

When this power is given over to television networks and beat reporters and those who provide opinions in voice and print, there is an incredible foundation laid to support the 'sacred' premises against the 'profane' ones. This is precisely why symbols are used – the flag itself, "old glory," the "founding fathers," and so on – to promote a dedication to certain ideas that shorts-circuits our reason. We hear certain concepts and are granted a pass from thinking about such unpleasantness. *That guy is a conspiracy theorist.*

If the association becomes strong enough and the evocation powerful enough, the end result can be people dismissing anyone who disagrees with the position of the state. Which is precisely the point. And when this happens, otherwise intelligent individuals can make statements like "I support our troops in time of war," when of course a war means that troops will die. That is the point of war – and indeed, the point of troops, but that is an argument for another day. For the moment, we only need to understand that the term 'conspiracy theorist' has force only in a context of the need for reassurance within the confines of the State.

We also should understand that this state of affairs is in some sense necessary. All over the world, at any given moment, the United States is murdering or torturing people somewhere in the name of democratic ideals. Reading William Blum's *Killing Hope* is one of the most distressing, but important, things one can do for oneself, even if it feels like losing part of one's soul.

In fact, it is one of the bumps on the road to saving it.

If the state did not provide a mythology and a process of identification of what is sacred and what is profane and a clear demarcation between party invitees and those to be excluded, the government – any government, for they tend to act in similar ways – would be untenable for most people. Psychologically, most human beings cannot simply tell themselves, "I value my comfort over the lives of millions of others, no matter how atrocious their conditions, because I can lose myself in electronic distraction and temporary entertainments." They need mythology, even when they recognize it as mythology on some level. I think – and this is pure speculation on my part – that most people are aware of this truth, in the back of their minds, but do not acknowledge it. Ursula K. LeGuin's famous short story "The Ones Who Walk Away from Omelas" deals with this very topic. Those who see the horror that gives them their happiness either block it and remain happy, or are haunted by it and walk away.

"The goal of modern propaganda," writes Jacques Ellul, the

author of the marvelous book *Propaganda,* "is no longer to transform opinion but to arouse an active and mythical belief." Exactly – because belief does not require evidence. One cannot be allowed to question one's own house, one's own fathers, the *paterfamilias.* (And in our Western culture, it does tend to be the father – in a way, Western society as it exists is defined by the devaluing of the feminine, but that is another story.) They know best.

This type of thinking, for example, underlies the present Edward Snowden case. Snowden leaked documents showing, among other things, that the National Security Agency was not only spying on Americans but also on the European Union. This isn't news to anyone who researches this sort of thing, but it has caused a sensation in the media. The reason Snowden leaked the documents was because of the disconnect between having faith in one's country and seeing things that he thought were obviously wrong, by a different standard. That is, he used his intellectual judgment. Democrats John Kerry and Nancy Pelosi, among many others, lined up against Snowden, but some of the most telling remarks came from the Republican Lindsey Graham: "This government has been corrupted. They don't have a real legislature. All institutions of democracies have been diminished in Russia, and when people do that inside their country they are not generally inclined to follow the rule of law outside their country ... Putin's handling of the Snowden issue is only the latest sign that Russia is backsliding when it comes to democracy and the rule of law."

Graham uses the evidence that Russia isn't *immediately doing what the United States wants it to do* in order to denote a failure of democracy. It is the statement of a man who has had so much propaganda rubbed in his eyes he can't see anymore.

In fact, the reason the media take the situation so seriously is that it breaks down one of the walls of government. To quote Mel Brooks' character in Blazing Saddles, "We've got to protect our phony baloney jobs, gentlemen!" Prior to Snowden, anyone who argued that the NSA spied on every American in Orwellian fashion could be successfully labeled a paranoid conspiracy theorist. Not so anymore.

CONTENT

We've talked about how the term 'conspiracy theorist' is really just a kind of profanity, an insult bestowing a separation which protects and reassures the user of the term. And that is one reason I don't like it. There is a secondary reason, however, that has to do with the words themselves: *conspiracy* and *theorist*.

It can't mean anyone who concludes, based on some evidence, that a conspiracy exists, because that would mean every District Attorney in the country is a conspiracy theorist. (They are, by the literal meaning.) So is Vincent Bugliosi, because the book that made him famous, *Helter Skelter,* posits an elaborate conspiracy theory in which Charles Manson was able to control other people to such an extent that they murdered in the name of creating a racial war. (Manson, the most notorious mass murderer in America, was never proven to have physically killed anyone himself.) Bugliosi may have been right, or not; that's a subject for another essay. However, it is unquestionably a conspiracy theory.

But that's not what people mean, really. What people mean, beyond the psychological content discussed before, is an elaborate story: The use of evidence to posit an explanatory description. David Icke thinks that many people, including members of the Royal Family, are a kind of space lizard. He has written many books to that effect. There are many people who believe "the Jews" control everything – mostly Nazi types like Henry Ford, who received the highest award a non-German (the Grand Cross of the German Eagle) can receive from Hitler himself. The head of IBM, incidentally, got one too – see Edwin Black's brilliant book *IBM and the Holocaust.*

So I am definitely not a conspiracy theorist in this sense either. I don't have a particular premise that I am attached to with regard to historical events. One has to look at whatever the evidence suggests and go from there. For example, in the Kennedy case, which is enormously complex, my emphasis has always been on proving the negative. That is, I cannot identify precisely who was the shooter who killed John F. Kennedy. However, I know – to a "moral certainty,"– that it wasn't Lee Harvey Oswald.

The evidence is overwhelming. I've discussed some of it in previous writings, and many others have done brilliant work on the case. Of all the theories of what happened in Dealey Plaza on November 22, 1963, Oswald-as-the-shooter is the least likely. He was a mediocre shot, using a poorly designed low-velocity weapon, with a scope that was offline, shooting through Texas Live Oak trees at a tough angle, missing with the first shot but then deadly accurate the second and third times (just think about that for a second). He also used a bullet that created multiple wounds through skin and bone of two individuals but somehow emerged undamaged. He did all of this, by the way, while failing to leave any fingerprints on the weapon. Once arrested, he proceeded to vigorously protest his innocence before being shot to death by a local hood, Jack Ruby. Ruby, who had ties to the Dallas police and shot Oswald to spare Jackie Kennedy the indignity of a trial for her husband's assassin.

The story is idiotic. And this doesn't even scratch the surface.

Countless books have been written on the subject, some of them excellent, detailing the medical and photographic oddities and all the bizarre contextual information pointing in one singular direction: *Oswald didn't do it.* The only reason you would believe this contrived story – the absolutely only reason you might find it plausible on an intellectual level (that is, you weren't being paid to promote a specific view) – is because of the psychological factors. Oswald-as-shooter is within the temple. Anyone-else-as-shooter is outside the temple.

If this were a question of logic, we would conclude that of course conspiracies exist. High finance would be impossible without them, as would certain government operations. It's a fact of modern life, and anyone who dismisses it is operating within the dichotomy illustrated here. That doesn't mean that everything's a conspiracy. That doesn't mean we should believe everything. It does mean that we go where the evidence takes us, parental controls be damned.

There was a conspiracy in the Kennedy assassination, but I am no conspiracy theorist.

A TEXAN LOOKS AT NELSON: *LBJ MASTERMIND OF JFK'S ASSASSINATION*

It seems like such a natural conclusion. The king is dead, long live the king. If you are studying the Kennedy assassination, and you ask the immortal question *cui bono*, you might first land on the name Lyndon Johnson. From "MacBird" to *A Texan Looks at Lyndon* to Ed Tatro in "The Guilty Men" episode in Nigel Turner's *The Men Who Killed Kennedy*, many people have analyzed Johnson's doings and cried foul.

Into this tradition comes Phillip F. Nelson with a sizable work on the subject, wanting to go further than anyone has before. His view of Johnson is comparable to Sherlock Holmes's description of Professor Moriarty: "He is the Napoleon of crime...He sits motionless like a spider in the centre of its web, but that web has a thousand radiations, and he knows very well every quiver of each of them."[2] Nelson's thesis is in his title: *LBJ Mastermind of JFK's Assassination.*

This particular genre of Kennedy book is admittedly one I find less useful than others. It is possible to see the JFK assassination as a game of Clue, deciding whether you think it is David Morales with the candlestick in the conservatory or J. Edgar Hoover with the lead pipe in the study. To my mind, this tendency often becomes engrossed in the less important details of assassination mechanics and (to my way of thinking) the more important mechanics of how states operate, how that affects us, and how best to combat the forces behind it. But that is my bias, so let the reader be informed. As for Nelson, he makes his intent clear. Noel Twyman, he says, names

---

[2] Doyle, Arthur Conan, "The Final Problem," *The Complete Sherlock Holmes Vol. 1* (Barnes & Noble Classics: NY 2003), 559.

"...Lyndon Johnson and J. Edgar Hoover as having been involved in the plot and in the cover-up, though he failed to determine that Lyndon Johnson was the mastermind of the conspiracy. This book merely adds that last element in a case that has already been proven beyond a reasonable doubt." [3]

Let's see if Twyman's 'failure' is Nelson's gain.

BEGINNINGS

The book is divided into 10 chapters that purport to show LBJ's hand in every aspect of the assassination, from the planning to the execution to the aftermath. It begins, however, by spelling out his basic criteria. Nelson argues that Johnson has motive, means, and opportunity, and that further he was a psychopath who would stop at nothing to achieve power.

The author discusses Johnson's rise to power, the ins and outs of the familiar tale of Box 13, and Johnson's many distasteful characteristics. These are, by and large, taken from Robert Caro. In the first chapter alone, at one point there are 26 consecutive footnotes going back to Caro. To this summary he also sprinkles a few quotes from Robert Dallek, but here also begins his penchant for questionable sources. He quotes from Jack Valenti, Victor Lasky, and Seymour Hersh, just for starters. Now the problematic aspects of using those particular writers – at least without some qualification – is apparent to most Kennedy scholars. I won't explain the nuts and bolts here, but instead direct the reader to Jim DiEugenio's essay "The Posthumous Assassination of John F. Kennedy" for details. But suffice it to say that each of these writers has a rather large axe to grind and a willingness to use any means necessary to grind it.

Now these sources do little harm to the early part of the book because Johnson's character is well-established. He was a low-class sort of a person, prone to whipping out his manhood in front of reporters, peeing on his secret service detail, and employing men like Mac Wallace who were murderous criminals. LBJ does seem like the sort of man who, were it within his power, could have had the president killed and not be halted by any moral barriers.

In Chapter 2, Nelson focuses on Kennedy's relationship with the

---

[3] Nelson, Phillip F., *LBJ The Mastermind of JFK's Assassination* (Xlibris Corporation: 2010), 138.

Joint Chiefs and their disagreements over foreign policy. Or were they disagreements? The author seems confused on this point. On the one hand, he seems to agree that Kennedy wanted peace and Johnson was more accommodating of the CIA and Department of Defense. Nelson describes, for example, how the CIA cut off aid to South Vietnam at a time when he was pondering whether to take this very action. They took the action automatically, following a playbook unknown to Kennedy. "But the larger point was that it was a message the CIA was sending to the president, who was being told who was really in control…it wasn't John Kennedy."[4] He also describes how JFK and the military did not get along: "Over the course of the next two years, those relationships would continue growing even further apart and become so well established that it could be argued that in the larger scheme, Lyndon B. Johnson had assumed the mantle of commander-in-chief."[5]

The last bit seems overstated at the very least. However, that aside, the peculiar part of Nelson's analysis is that he seems to buy into the CIA's version of the Bay of the Pigs. He writes that Kennedy wanted a second set of air strikes but was intimidated into not doing so by Adlai Stevenson. He then goes on to criticize Dean Rusk for agreeing with the president's refusal to provide air cover during the invasion.[6] (He gets all this, incidentally, from Lasky.) To call this version of events simplistic is to be generous; but things only get worse from here.

SMEAR CAMPAIGN

Further going into the Cuban situation, Nelson blithely quotes Alexander Haig as saying that Robert Kennedy ran the hit teams killing innocents, although "…he took care to keep his own name out of most of the documents…" Haig goes on to say that with respect to the Cuban assault teams, "Bobby *was* the President!"[7] (Haig, who is obviously not the most credible witness in this context, gave this interview to Gus 'Single Bullet Fact' Russo.) Once again, this is all OK with our erstwhile author, who doesn't stop to mention that

---

[4] Nelson, 571.
[5] Nelson, 151.
[6] Nelson, 148-149.
[7] Nelson, 156-157.

maybe the sources for this information are even potentially problematic.

Nelson steams ahead, quoting James Angleton's aide Nestor Sanchez as saying that "The buck stops with the President on operations like that...All the other conspiracies of the agency was running amok, that's baloney..." He isn't quoting this to isolate a point of view; he's using Sanchez as a viable witness. He does the same with Sam Halpern and Richard Helms, and then writes that "The Kennedy's campaign to get rid of the Castro 'problem' was doomed from the start..."[8] Just so there is no question, he elaborates: "Documents prove...Bobby Kennedy had authorized the plots..."[9] No one will be surprised to learn that Nelson also got this from Russo, from his asinine book *Live by the Sword*. Readers can take a look for themselves, but be aware that Russo believes in the "jet-effect theory,"[10] (i.e., the desperate attempt to show that Kennedy's violent rearward motion could have happened from a rear shot), claims that Lee Harvey Oswald left fingerprints all over the alleged sniper's nest (!!!), and argues that the backyard photograph (with its obvious chin splice) is genuine.[11] You get the idea.

The *pièce de résistance* of this argument comes with Nelson's assertion that Kennedy was aware of the assassination plots against Castro, but the CIA kept the Joint Chiefs in the dark.[12]

Let the reader judge, but let us say that I find this a tad implausible.

Just for information's sake. Please note the following list of people who testified to the Church Committee that Kennedy had never been informed of any assassination plots against Castro:

Dean Rusk
Maxwell Taylor
John McCone
McGeorge Bundy
Richard Helms

---

[8] Nelson, 171-172.
[9] Nelson, 217.
[10] Russo, Gus, *Live By the Sword* (Bancroft Press: 1998), 298.
[11] Russo, 444.
[12] Nelson, 147.

Bill Harvey[13]

These are not friends of JFK, to put it mildly. David Talbot put it like so:

> In the ideological war to define the Kennedy administration, which broke out soon after the president was laid to rest in Arlington and continues to this day, national security officials insisted that the Kennedy brothers were 'out of control' on Cuba, pushing them to take absurd measures against Castro like the Mongoose folly. This would become the standard version of the Kennedys' Cuba policy in countless books, TV news shows, and documentaries – it was rash, obsessive, treacherous, even murderous. But this is not an accurate picture of the Kennedy policy.[14]

Bill Harvey went so far as to say that he would have been the last person that JFK would have ever put in charge of a Castro assassination venture, even if he had desired it.[15]

HERE WE GO AGAIN

Enough about Cuba. Let's get to the sex!

Nelson reports blandly the same things that Hersh wrote in his discredited hatchet job *Dark Side of Camelot:* for example, JFK tried to get Judith Exner in a three-way, then impregnated her, then told her to go see Sam Giancana for assistance getting an abortion![16] I grant this would make for a very exciting *telenovela* on *Galavisión,* but is dubious at best and has zero to do with Lyndon Johnson. (Remember him?) The author doesn't seem to notice this, instead acknowledging the reader may well be more interested in more prurient detail, but he or she should seek other books for this. The

---

[13] DiEugenio, James, and Lisa Pease, *The Assassinations* (Feral House:Los Angeles CA 2003), 328
[14] Talbot, 100.
[15] Talbot, 111.
[16] Nelson, 197.

first one to read, he sagely recommends, is Ronald Kessler's *Sins of the Father*.[17] Incredible.

It does point out the long-term damage books like these can do, however. My own local public library around the corner has perhaps a half-dozen books on JFK, and one of them is *Dark Side of Camelot*. The name 'Seymour Hersh' is stronger than the book's own infamy, in which the investigative reporter was snookered into buying fake documents.[18]

In any event, please accept my apologies. We were talking about sex. "In the interest of brevity, we will consider further only JFK's relationships with Marilyn Monroe, Mary Pinchot Meyer, Judith Exner, and Ellen Rometch..."[19] In the interests of brevity! Nelson then goes on to discuss these stories with no discernment at all, using as his sources material from Nina Burleigh and Deborah Davis, but also Hersh, Donald Wolfe, etc., without any elaboration about how credible the information is that he's using. From Wolfe he gets the observation that "...Hoover had warned Jack about exposing his affairs with Judith Campbell [Exner] and Marilyn Monroe, so he had resigned himself to give up both, no doubt because there were so many others to replace them."[20] Nelson asserts that Wolfe "made a compelling case" of RFK's involvement in Monroe's death, and brings up rumors that JFK and Mary Meyer used drugs together. There are several astonishing claims made in the text, but here is one of my favorites: "It may be just a coincidence that, concurrently with his affair with Mary Pinchot Meyer and their rumored use of drugs together, Kennedy had become less tolerant of the CIA's intelligence breakdowns and the Pentagon's aggressive provocation for military actions, especially in Vietnam."[21]

OK, let's think about this. Which of these conclusions is more likely?

1.) JFK grew apart from his military advisors because of the Bay of Pigs invasion and the Cuban Missile Crisis, where they

---

[17] Nelson, 203.
[18] There is a quick summary of these events in Thomas Powers' contemporaneous review of the book in the New York Times: http://www.nytimes.com/books/97/11/30/reviews/971130.30powerst.html.
[19] Nelson, 191.
[20] Nelson, 195.
[21] Nelson, 193.

revealed themselves to be prepared to destroy the entire
planet in defense of American interests.

2.) JFK grew apart from his military advisors because he was
toking it up with one of his mistresses.

I am going to go with option 1 myself, particularly since we have no
evidence (2) ever happened.

There is a larger point here, which I will raise now: *What does this
have to do with anything?* We were talking about Lyndon Johnson, right?

And so we are. Sometimes. Phillip Nelson's book is a rambling
one, taking 700 pages to express a claim that he could have made in
200 pages. If you delete material which consists of summaries of
other people's books, you might have as little as 20 pages of original
material. And these 20 pages largely consist of his analysis of the
Altgens photograph. We'll get to that later.

LYNDON'S SCANDALS

Having dealt with Caro's stories about LBJ and Kennedy's
involvement in Cuba and women, the middle section of the book
turns its attention to the scandals that clung to the Vice-President.
Most of these are familiar to anyone who has studied Johnson, and
involve Bobby Baker, Mac Wallace, and the various people Johnson
is alleged to have murdered, including his sister. Much of this
appeared in *The Men Who Killed Kennedy*, although Nelson gets most of
the juicy bits from Barr McLellan and the aforementioned Haley (*A
Texan Looks at Lyndon*).[22]

Any book that posits Johnson's involvement in the assassination
is going to use this material, and whether you buy this or not depends
a great deal on testimony from people who may not be the most
reliable witnesses. Nelson has little to add here, and if you are familiar
with the McLellan book nothing here will be news. LBJ's scandals do
have the virtue of being on-topic.

THE MEAT OF THE ARGUMENT

The last third of the book starts to deliver on some of Nelson's

---

[22] I did find it curious that the book never once mentions Ed Tatro, who is well-
known for his research on Johnson.

conclusions. To this point, the main ideas of the book (that is, the ones that relate to LBJ) could be summarized as follows:

1. LBJ was a scoundrel, hungry for power, and possibly psychopathic.
2. LBJ got along better with the Department of Defense than JFK did. (Although Nelson does, curiously, quote Howard Burris from John Newman's book *JFK and Vietnam*, saying that he didn't believe Johnson had a "very deep" understanding of political issues.) Odd for a "mastermind."[23]
3. LBJ had very possibly committed several murders, or at least ordered them done, had stolen elections, and had generally shown little regard for the law.

Having tried to show all these things, the author has to demonstrate Johnson's mastery. And one must give Nelson his due in this regard – he doesn't mess around. He has Johnson planning the entire assassination and ordering people around who were not used to taking orders.

> The 'Johnson plan' would be based upon the concept that the operational and tactical plans would be carefully kept away from the highest level planners; Johnson and Angleton, possibly Hoover and LeMay as well, consistent with the precepts of 'plausible deniability' and interagency secrecy protocols would protect others throughout the 'hierarchical' chain.[24]

Not only does he plan the assassination, he controls the secret service, [25] putting in orders for the Secret Service to compromise themselves. Nelson has no evidence for this, but it is, in his view, a "reasoned conjecture."[26] We are assured that "Johnson's hand would be kept invisible through his having three levels of staff separating him from motorcade planning."[27]

---

[23] Nelson, 131.
[24] Nelson, 379.
[25] Nelson, 360.
[26] Nelson, 425.
[27] Nelson, 426.

As noted, Johnson is the boss, resulting in some dubious statements. One mid-chapter heading reads:

J. Edgar Hoover: Johnson's Willing Lieutenant[28]

I had to put the book down for a moment upon reading that. Hoover was not anyone's willing lieutenant, and the idea that he would have kowtowed to the big Texan – well, I suppose it's not impossible, but it is awfully hard to imagine. Similar to his saying that Johnson would "...undoubtedly recruit...General Curtis LeMay, who shared many of Johnson's attitudes, especially about the president, whom he regarded as an indecisive coward and avowed socialist."[29] Johnson *recruited* LeMay into the operation? Just so there is no confusion: "Just as Vice President Johnson had been feeding secrets to his friends in the CIA (as noted in chapters 2 and 3), it is a reasonable presumption that he was doing the same with his friends in the Pentagon, probably including General LeMay, who was cut from the same, practically identical, bellicose cloth as Johnson."[30]

This last remark simply isn't true. Even in pro-LeMay biographies, one gets the clear sense that LeMay counseled Lyndon Johnson in full commitment, an immense bombing campaign into North Vietnam, which the latter declined to do. Johnson only kept him on board for a year, listening to LeMay complain the whole time that air strikes were not timely or powerful enough for his liking.[31]

INTERPRETATION

Much of the rest of Nelson's arguments rely upon his specific interpretation of specific events. For example, John Connally was "insistent upon the selection of the Trade Mart," but instead of throwing suspicion upon Connally directly, Nelson writes that "...it suggests the unseen hand of his mentor, Lyndon Johnson."[32]

Nelson tells the story of how Johnson got into an argument

---

[28] Nelson, 346.
[29] Nelson, 125-126.
[30] Nelson, 369.
[31] Cronley, Major T. J., "Curtis LeMay: The Enduring 'Big Bomber Man,'" (United States Marine Corps Command and Staff College Center, Quantico VA 1986).
[32] Nelson, 355.

about wanting Connally rather than Ralph Yarbrough to sit next to him during the assassination. JFK told Johnson that seating arrangements would not be changed and the latter became very upset. To Nelson, this is sinister; his foreknowledge intact, Johnson is trying to keep his buddy Connally out of harm's way. However, Nelson also does note that Johnson hated Yarbrough, so he has another reason to not want to sit next to him. So, one assumes, LBJ would have been upset even if he was not the criminal mastermind behind the operation. [33] That is to say, if you already believe in Nelson's thesis, this becomes further corroborative evidence.

The author also provides the solution to why Lyndon Johnson began crying hysterically on Air Force One shortly after the assassination, as appeared recently in Steven Gillon's book. We must consider the "…likelihood that it was a result of his finally finding enough privacy to allow himself a moment to physically release the built-up tension that he had suppressed for hours – actually days, and weeks of intense anticipation – as he planned the critical action that would save his career: the murder of JFK."[34]

A story that Nelson does *not* use in his book occurs on board Air Force One, when new President Johnson tells Bill Moyers, "I wonder if the missiles are flying." That is, Johnson was aware that certain factions within the national security state were interested in a war with the Soviets, and he thought they might use this excuse to get it. James K. Galbraith, the son of Kennedy advisor John Kenneth Galbraith, felt that Johnson understood that Kennedy and McNamara had been holding them off from blowing up the world, and that LBJ himself thought of the assassination as a potential coup.[35] However, this story obviously does not fit the program.

Since so much of the argument for this book depends upon the author's interpretation of various events, it is fair to ask whether we have what literature professors call "an unreliable narrator." We have already seen, curiously, that he accepts material about the Kennedys promulgated by their ideological enemies. He also seems to buy into a rather facile description of Lee Harvey Oswald.

The author blames Oswald's "…fatherless childhood and his early life with a cold and distant mother…" for his willingness to be

[33] Nelson, 422.
[34] Nelson, 448.
[35] Talbot, David, *Brothers* (Free Press: NY 2007), 252.

used. He quotes his brother Robert about the show 'I Led Three Lives' and how much young Oswald loved Ian Fleming novels. "It is ironic," Nelson writes, "that Oswald shared one thing in common with Lyndon Johnson…a determined obsession with fulfilling the fantasies which he dreamt about as a child."[36]

"Oswald thought that, finally, he would achieve his ultimate lifetime goal: becoming a full-time well-paid spy just like his hero from *I Led Three Lives*."[37] In this day and age, can anyone serious still write this sentence? Nelson's analysis of Oswald is so fatuous it could have come from the pen of Norman Mailer. As most everyone knows who studies the Kennedy assassination for more than five minutes, a mass of contradictions surrounds Lee Harvey Oswald. He was allegedly a Marxist, but his best friend was George de Morenshildt, a much older man, in a higher social class, who was a White Russian. He managed to travel unperturbed from the U.S. to the Soviet Union and back, despite being ostensibly a marine, and also brought his Soviet wife back with him, although she had belonged to a Communist youth organization.[38]

But that's not all. He has this to say about Officer J. D. Tippit: "It remains unclear whether the murder of Tippit had anything to at all to do with Kennedy's assassination: A more likely scenario was that it was simply retribution by the husband of the woman Tippit was known to have been sleeping with."[39]

Curiouser and curiouser.

It should also be noted that Nelson supports, for the most part, the scenario presented in David Lifton's *Best Evidence*. Whether or not this counts in his favor or not will depend on the reader's allegiances, but let us observe that adopting Lifton's premises means a whole other set of problems.

He is wise enough not to assert, as Lifton did in his book, that all of the shots came from the front. This is untenable given the works of people like Don Thomas, for example, who in his recent book finds five shots, with four emanating from behind.[40] Robert

---

[36] Nelson, 385.

[37] Nelson, 493.

[38] Parenti, Michael, *Dirty Truths* (City Lights Books: San Francisco CA 1996), 163-164.

[39] Nelson, 529.

[40] Thomas, Don, *Hear No Evil* (Mary Ferrell Foundation Press: Ipswich MA

Groden, another serious analyst, has four shots, with three coming from the rear.[41] These conclusions emerge from serious examination of the available forensic evidence. (It also ignores the fact that Connally was shot in the *back,* which I don't think anyone disputes.)

However, Nelson claims that there was evidence of body alteration, rather than photographic alteration. The author does try to make a case for it, and again has Johnson directing traffic to his swearing-in ceremony, which is mere cover for the snatching of the body. This was done, in accordance with Lifton's thesis, such that JFK was placed in a body bag.[42] Even if we assume that it is plausible that persons unknown were able to sneak the body away for a time in order to perform this surgery – at *any* point in the swearing-in, the flight, or the arrival home – there are still enormous problems with this scenario.

If Lifton is right, then "…the plot to alter the body was integral to the plot to shoot the President – i.e., that it was planned, as part of the murder, to secretly falsify the circumstances of his death."[43] The mind staggers at this prospect. Why would you plan such a nutty thing? There isn't an easier way to kill a president? Lifton also writes that "…the plotters could know, once they saw the body, how much ammunition was needed, and so could coordinate the planting of bullets with the fabrication of trajectories."[44]

So all the bullets were planted – but they were also planted in such a way as to fool the FBI: "The central fact was that if President Kennedy's body was altered, and false ammunition planted, then *within twenty-four hours* of the murder, the U.S. Department of Justice had been deceived."[45] Deceived? Would this be the same Department of Justice that got a palm print off Oswald's dead body?

As questionable as one might find aspects of Lifton's thesis, it gets even worse for Nelson. Because he has to have LBJ coordinating all this. And he dutifully theorizes: Johnson knows the body can be

---

2010), 604.

[41] Groden, Robert and Harrison Livingstone, *High Treason* (The Conservatory Press: Baltimore MD 1989), 224. Actually, Groden seems likely to revise his thesis in his upcoming book, since he has since found at least one other shot on the Zapruder film itself.

[42] Lifton, David, *Best Evidence* (Macmillan: New York 1980), 680.

[43] Lifton, 346.

[44] Lifton, 359.

[45] Lifton, 362.

stolen, and he also knows "…that a 'special' autopsy would be necessary, one that would obliterate any evidence that Kennedy was shot anywhere but from behind…"[46] The chapter in which this appears is entitled 'A More Plausible Scenario.' A less plausible scenario can hardly be imagined.

(Lifton, for his part, seems to have recently gone over to the LBJ-did-it scenario.)

AND, FINALLY, THE ALTGENS PHOTOGRAPH

Nelson spends many pages claiming that Lyndon Johnson cannot be seen in, and is therefore ducking in, the Altgens photograph.[47] He claims that this is smoking-gun evidence that cannot be ignored. It has been sitting in front of all of us this whole time and we've missed it. How can LBJ be ducking so early? He must have known what was coming. It should be noted that Penn Jones had pointed to this almost fifty years ago.

Except I can see LBJ in the photograph, as can most others.

Nelson realizes some might argue this. However, he thinks people who see Johnson in the photo are lying to themselves.[48]

TOWARD A MORE COHERENT SCENARIO

We know, thanks to Hoover's famous comment, that someone was impersonating Lee Harvey Oswald years prior to the Kennedy assassination. And we know that the CIA repeatedly tried to distance itself from Oswald, despite all evidence to the contrary. A couple of good questions in this regard were asked by Gerald McKnight: "Why did the supersensitive SIG have a file on an ex-marine defector? Why did the CIA wait for a year before opening a file on Oswald after learning about his defection?"[49] To this let me add a third question: Is it because Lyndon Johnson said so? And another: Why would the CIA cover for Johnson? In the House Select Committee investigation, Robert Blakely made a pact with the Devil in allowing the CIA to vet the final report pre-publication. Investigator Gaeton

---

[46] Nelson, 546.
[47] Nelson, 501.
[48] Nelson, 507.
[49] McKnight, Gerald, *Breach of Trust* (University Press of Kansas 2005), 308.

Fonzi at first thought Blakely was being too careful, then began to harbor thoughts that Blakley was cooperating with the CIA for other reasons. [50] It was the CIA, for example, that classified the Lopez Report. [51] Why would they do this? What interests are they protecting if LBJ and the Del Charro cronies did it?

But even better questions emerge when we realize that *Dallas wasn't the original choice for the assassination location.* Did Johnson also arrange the Chicago plot, exposed by Edwin Black in his article? If they had killed him in Chicago, Thomas Arthur Vallee would be the "lone nut." Would we then have theories that Mayor Daley was the mastermind of the Kennedy assassination?

Good questions, all.

If you want to be serious about it, you can make a better case for Allen Dulles being the mastermind of the assassination than Lyndon Johnson. His oil ties, for example, are actually stronger than Johnson's. The Dulles brothers had worked hard to destroy the antitrust suit filed against Standard Oil of New Jersey all the way back in 1953.[52] Dulles was a key planner in the overthrow of Mossadeq; under the latter's rule, the Anglo-American Oil Company suffered huge losses. The company was a client of Dulles's firm, Sullivan & Cromwell.[53] Nor was Dulles a stranger to Cuba. Woodrow Wilson's Secretary of State was Allen and John Foster's uncle, Robert Lansing. Allen, on behalf of Sullivan & Cromwell clients losing money (some $170 million) due to a leftist revolt, appealed to his "Uncle Bert." Wilson intervened on their behalf to "protect American property and interests."[54] Also, Dulles had been involved in the recruitment and first interviews of General Reinhard Gehlen, the Nazi-turned American spy.[55]

As Jim Douglass points out:

Dulles got Prouty to create a network of subordinate

---

[50] Fonzi, Gaeton, *The Last Investigation* (Thunder's Mouth Press: NY 1993), 257.

[51] Fonzi, 267.

[52] Lisagor, Nancy, and Frank Lipsius, *A Law Unto Itself* (William Morrow and Company: New York 1988), 203-204.

[53] Lisagor and Lipsius, 210.

[54] Prussen, Ronald W., *John Foster Dulles: The Road to Power* (The Free Press: Macmillan: New York 1982), 21-22.

[55] Mosley, Leonard, *Dulles* (The Dial Press/James Wade: NY 1978), 477-478.

focal point offices in the armed services, then throughout the entire U.S. government...The consequence in the early 1960s, when Kennedy became president, was that the CIA had placed a secret team of its own employees through the entire U.S. government.[56]

According to Nelson, LBJ was afraid he was going to lose his job and go to prison – but Dulles had already lost it. LBJ was a wildly ambitious man who would do nothing to stop at getting power – but Dulles was head of the CIA, arguably a more powerful position than President. LBJ was a sonofabitch – but so was Dulles. He was a different kind of sonofabitch, sure, but his whole life Dulles had been making decisions that got people killed, and he exhibited nothing more than a dry sense of humor about it. There are some psychopaths in government; it's one of the first things you learn when you start doing research into this stuff.

Now all that being said, am I going to write the book *Allen Dulles: Mastermind of JFK's Assassination*? Of course not. The operation is bigger than any one man, even people like Dulles or James Angleton. The head of the snake is the snake.

FINAL REMARKS

Fidel Castro had a much deeper and insightful analysis of the situation than anything in this book:

> I haven't forgotten that Kennedy centered his electoral campaign against Nixon on the theme of firmness toward Cuba. I have not forgotten the Machiavellian tactics and the equivocation, the attempts at invasion, the pressures, the blackmail, the organization of a counter-revolution, the blockade, and above all, the retaliatory measures which were imposed before, long before there was the pretext and alibi of Communism. But I feel that he inherited a difficult situation; I don't think a President of the United States is ever really free, and I believe

---

[56] Douglass, Jim, *JFK and the Unspeakable* (Orbis Books: NY 2008), 86.

Kennedy is at present feeling the impact of this lack
of freedom, I also believe that he now understands
the extent to which he has been misled, especially, for
example, on Cuban reaction at the time of the
attempted Bay of Pigs invasion.[57]

Lyndon Johnson was a bad guy. It would not necessarily be
surprising, in the abstract, if he had foreknowledge or tacit approval
of the assassination. He might even have been directly involved,
although one can argue that. I do not think, however, that at this
date, given the documentary evidence, an explanation which ignores
the larger political forces of the national security state can be taken
seriously.

It is less important, ultimately in my view, to understand *how* he
was killed than *why* he was killed. This is not addressed when one says
'LBJ did it for power,' or 'Allen Dulles did it for revenge.' Again I
quote Douglass:

> Those who designed the plot to kill Kennedy were
> familiar with the inner sanctum of our national
> security state…The assassins' purpose seems to have
> encompassed not only killing a president determined
> to make peace with the enemy but also using his
> murder as the impetus for a possible nuclear first
> strike against that same enemy.[58]

JFK's fateful decision was to go against the same system that
profited his family and assisted his rise to power, and lead with his
conscience. The decision literally killed him. Our whole form of
government, and indeed our entire consumer society, depends
entirely on suppressing our consciences and destroying our empathy.
Our economic and political system is devoid of it – for good reason.
If we allowed ourselves to feel empathy for all the people in the
world who suffer on our behalf, the system could not be maintained.

That is why there is a constant stream of anti-Kennedy books,
shows, and films, and why that fervor slides into seemingly irrelevant
places like Nelson's current book. The major media is desperate to

---

[57] Douglass, Jim, 197.
[58] Douglass, 242.

tear down the Kennedy legacy – to make him a criminal, a cad, or a dope fiend. "He was like all the others," the Victor Laskys of the world will tell us.

He might have been when he came in (although frankly, that is arguable as well). But in any event he clearly changed.

This is the key point. The essence of the Kennedy assassination is the state destroying conscientious leadership like white blood cells killing a virus; understanding this fact changes the assassination from a puzzle to be solved to a cause to be championed. Anything less is an insult to his memory and a disservice to ourselves.

A PERSONAL JOURNEY INTO THE JFK MURDER: JOSEPH McBRIDE'S *INTO THE NIGHTMARE*

It has been nearly fifty years since the assassination of John F. Kennedy became the baptismal event for the sickness that burnt the American dream like a draft card. Vietnam followed, Malcolm fell, then Martin, and Bobby, the left got old and turned right, and somewhere along the line many lost the taste for fighting back. Meanwhile, the media have been stacking skeletons ever since, but that closet grows ever more full, stale, and rotten. Still, the pretense continues: In our age, most mainstream journalism has become a kind of exercise in organized non sequiturs, like artless Beckett, farce without wit.

The premise is objectivity, we are told. Fair and balanced, we are told. Modern investigative reporting, by the available evidence of television and print media, often seems to regard objectivity as reporting all issues as if they have two sides – no more and no less, and to draw no conclusions regardless of how inane one side's claims may be. This seems frequently to be true even in trivial matters, but it gets worse the more controversial the issue. Network news seems to take its cues from intelligent design activists who just want schools to Teach the Controversy.

This context makes Joseph McBride's new book *Into The Nightmare* a jagged reminder of old-school reportage. Going against the grain, he asks difficult questions and tries hard to answer them. And even if every question cannot be answered satisfactorily, much compelling information surfaces throughout.

One of the many unusual things about this book is that McBride is, on the surface, a resolutely mainstream figure. A longtime journalist with numerous publications to his credit, including *The New York Review of Books*, *Cineaste*, *The Los Angeles Times*, *Sight & Sound*, and *The Nation* magazine, *Into The Nightmare* is his 17th book. Included in his previous works are biographies of Steven Spielberg and Frank Capra, as well as a soon-to-be-reissued long-form interview with Howard Hawks, *Hawks on Hawks*. However, he been leading a double life. In the background to his work in film and as a college professor, he has literally spent a lifetime researching this case, having worked for the Kennedy campaign in 1960 at the age of 12. The shock of the president's murder three years later drove him to question the initial reported facts of the case and grow to understand the terrible reality of our times. Hence the nightmare – deeply personal for the author, but deeply relatable for anyone interested in truth.

McBride is already known to the JFK research community as, among other things, the man who discovered the Hoover memo, which has been written about and referenced many times over the years, particularly in Gaeton Fonzi's superb *The Last Investigation*. Russ Baker also made the Hoover memo a central part of his investigation into the Bush family, *Family of Secrets*. The Hoover memo is, of course, the peculiar document dated November 22, 1963, sent by the FBI leader in which a "Mr. George Bush of the Central Intelligence Agency" is noted to have been debriefed on the matter of the assassination.

THREE ACTS

The book, like a well-crafted screenplay, is broken up into three acts. The first section covers McBride's personal history as a young man and his involvement as a Kennedy supporter. Included is a photo of the president taken by the author himself during a campaign visit to Wisconsin, as well as a thank-you letter from Kennedy after achieving the presidency. It goes into his early interest in journalism, his initial shock at the murder, and finally his disbelief in the story and pursuit of the trail leading to this book fifty years later.

The second section of the book is a kind of survey of the evidence. McBride has done his homework, both in terms of familiarity with the published work on the case, the internal documents themselves, and direct interviews with many of the involved parties. He cites many of the best works in the genre –

Fonzi, Peter Dale Scott, James Douglass, John Armstrong, and others, but also makes it clear he follows the John Simkins forum[59] and other similar sites. In short, he has seemingly been following every available lead in his off hours.

The third and longest section of the book largely concerns his deep investigation into the murder of J. D. Tippit. The general public is typically not aware that Lee Harvey Oswald was never arraigned for the murder of the president, but rather for allegedly killing a police officer called Tippit. McBride has done excellent work in this area, and included in this book are excerpts from interviews done with Tippit's father, as well as his wife Marie and his mistress Johnnie.

Part memoir, part investigative journalism, part cultural analysis, McBride uses well lessons learned in his long and successful career in media. One of the real strengths of the book is how smoothly written it is, a difficult task when writing about the complexities of the Kennedy assassination. Like Jim Douglass's *JFK and the Unspeakable*, the book will have appeal to general readers as well as research specialists, and the style has a great deal to do with it. Armed with a cultural knowledge not generally employed in JFK books, McBride sprinkles in allusions and connections that aid understanding and even occasionally startle. In addition, it is the work of someone who has seen the assassination not as a singular incident in our nation's history, but as part of a context and continuum of understanding. McBride employs a wide scope to bear in his analysis, bringing in literature, cinema, as well as a journalist's understanding of how history as it is recorded can differ from history in fact – indeed, how it must be so. This gives his work a breadth that is sometimes missing in the dry, even when notably incisive, work of researchers whose focus is narrower. For example, he writes about the strange and peculiarly American refusal to look at the past as it was:

> The effect is a pervasive atmosphere of unreality
> surrounding postwar American history, a willed
> decision by most citizens (even some who know
> better) to live in a fantasy America rather than the far
> messier place we actually inhabit. The fact that none
> of the official explanations for all the major events in

---

[59] http://educationforum.ipbhost.com/index.php?showforum=126

modern American history – the assassinations of John
F. Kennedy, Robert Kennedy, Malcolm X, and
Martin Luther King, Jr.; the Vietnam War; Watergate;
Iran/contra; the Gulf War; 9/11; and the Iraq War –
makes sense when the evidence is examined with care
should be enough to make even the most trusting
American citizen realize he or she is being duped by
our own government. (136)

He does not back away from making specific criticisms within
the community as well. For example, his assessment of Mary Ferrell
is that she was a disinformation agent, based on his personal dealings
with her. Ferrell, of course, personally disliked Kennedy despite
colleting an enormous quantity of information about the
assassination, which survives as The Mary Ferrell Foundation.[60]
McBride also believes that Ferrell's release of the audio tape to the
House Select Committee on Assassinations (HSCA) near the end of
their run was done so only to provide a kind of escape hatch for
Robert Blakely to suggest a conspiracy without being forced to
investigate its origins. He relates that the first-generation researcher
Penn Jones told him to "stay away from her." (218-221)

In general, McBride does an excellent and thorough job of
giving the reader a sense of the complications in the case without
getting bogged down in relentless detail. As far as where he stands on
some of the more controversial issues in the case, he is with David
Lifton and Doug Horne on body alteration and believes that John
Armstrong has effectively proved his two-Oswald thesis in *Harvey &
Lee*. (100) One of the strengths of the book, however, is that McBride
reports, rather than polemicizes; even if one disagrees with aspects of
his view on the case, one can hardly fault the approach.

He also calls attention to what is still one of the greatest pieces
of investigative journalism ever in the Kennedy case, Edwin Black's
article on the Chicago plot[61] (see APPENDIX A). As McBride points
out, the parallels are incredible. In this case, a designated patsy named
Thomas Arthur Vallee filled the bill as Oswald-style patsy to an
amazing degree. Vallee "was a thirty-year-old-ex-Marine who had
been assigned to a U-2 base in Japan, had been diagnosed as a

---

[60] www.maryferrell.org
[61] http://thechicagoplot.com/The%20Chicago%20Plot.pdf

paranoid schizophrenic by military doctors, and later had trained anti-Castro Cubans to assassinate Castro. Vallee had a job in a warehouse overlooking Kennedy's planned motorcade route." (307) He also points out a remarkable 'coincidence' – had Kennedy not cancelled the November 2, 1963 Chicago visit, in part because of an anonymous tip called in by someone identifying himself only as 'Lee' – he would have possibly been murdered in Chicago *on the same day* that the Diem brothers were being murdered in Vietnam.

INTERVIEWS

One of the advantages of McBride's position in the mainstream media is that he was able to secure interviews not only with peripheral people related to the assassination, but also with notable public figures. Who among us would not like to ask Donald Rumsfeld about George H. W. Bush's appointment to head of the CIA? McBride notes that Rumsfeld, in that 1988 interview, "deflected my questions for eleven minutes with the seemingly befuddled language for which he would later become notorious..." (357) McBride asked television talking head Cokie Roberts about the death of her father, Hale Boggs. Boggs, a known dissenter who served on the Warren Commission, had died in 1972 when his plane went down under somewhat mysterious circumstances. "I have no conspiracy theories about my father's death," she answered him. (164) He also spoke to Senator Ralph Yarborough, who spoke candidly about Lyndon Johnson's comportment the morning before the assassination (worried about the hearings going on about him at that very moment) and some odd remarks about the Secret Service behavior that day. (385)

One fascinating "get," which is reproduced at length, is an interview with Dallas homicide detective Jim Leavelle. Leavelle, of course, was the man in the white hat in one of the most famous photos in history – the shooting of Lee Harvey Oswald by Jack Ruby. Jim Leavelle's description of what they should have done in the Tippit murder is astonishing. "The one thing that we didn't do that we should have done – and this is an afterthought, and I didn't, and I'm responsible for that...what I should have done was canvass those door-to-door like I have done in other murder cases and gettin' evidence. But I had a good, clear-cut case, as far as I was concerned."

(243) This is an astonishing admission. I worked as a private investigator myself and have done neighborhood canvasses many times, sometimes in criminal cases. It is absolutely standard procedure and the idea that he didn't bother to have this done boggles the mind. Together with the other crazy violations of procedure – the Dallas police not recording Oswald's interrogation or even bothering to take notes, FBI agent James Hosty burning his notes on Oswald, and Dr. Humes burning the notes on Kennedy's autopsy – a reasonable person begins to conclude these things go well beyond incompetence and into cover-up.

However, in addition to these interviews, McBride, in his long Tippit investigation, was able to get previously untapped people on the record. For example, in 1992 he spoke with Edgar Lee Tippit, the father of J. D. Tippit. This enables him to fill in some background on the young J.D., and also the crucial observation by his father that he was a fine shot, conflicting with his police service records which suggest he was mediocre. Combined with his personnel file, McBride draws the conclusion that Tippit, among other things, may have been suffering from post-traumatic stress disorder (PTSD) from his war experiences.

Into The Nightmare has the most detailed and constructive analysis into Tippit of any book I have seen thus far, with considerable legwork behind it. In the last section of the book, McBride floats his theory of Tippit's connection to the Kennedy assassination, placing him nearer to the center than previously imagined. It's an interesting thesis, one which is somewhat weakly supported in my view, but it hardly matters in the overall context. Just as one need not believe Armstrong's *Harvey & Lee* thesis to recognize the vitality of the research between its covers, so it is with *Into The Nightmare*.

Also weakly supported, based on the evidence provided, is his assessment of Kenneth O'Donnell as a possible figure in setting the parade route. McBride suggests that O'Donnell was instrumental in choosing the famous hairpin turn that morning, but the quotes he uses tend to show him as acquiescing to the wishes of Governor Connelly, if anything. (541-542) It also follows Gerald Blaine's *The Kennedy Detail* in wishing to spread blame onto O'Donnell, a thesis which is argued against very cogently by Secret Service specialist Vince Palamara in his review[62] of that book. McBride also relies in

---

[62] http://www.ctka.net/reviews/kennedydetailreview.html

part on Seymour Hersh's extremely dubious *Dark Side of Camelot* to establish the possible scandals in O'Donnell's life that might have led him to betray the Kennedys. The problems with Hersh's work[63] have been well-documented, beginning with his willingness to believe phony documents that were taken out of his book only just prior to publication.

McBride's book, taken as a whole, relies on much better sourcing that this particular discussion. Having no specific feelings one way or the other about O'Donnell myself, it is hard for me to say what is going on in this section. In any event, it's a minor issue compared to the wealth of information in the rest of the work.

THE MEDIA

The strongest part of the book, in my estimation, is the analysis of the media. McBride has had direct experience with the walls thrown up by publishing institutions. When he started publishing articles about the Hoover memo in *The Nation* magazine, editor Victor Navasky had an another editor, Richard Lingeman, rewrite sections of the article. McBride reproduces one of the passages deleted from his original article, which concerned Bush's prior involvement with the CIA and his direct quote, "I'd come to the CIA with some general knowledge of how it operated." (Hilariously understated, that.) Although he did not know it at the time, McBride later found that Lingeman had served in the U.S. Army Counter Intelligence Corps in the fifties and had become friends with Navasky as a young man in Yale Law School. (349-354) Another unnamed *Nation* staffer also attempted to defend Bush from CIA association by eliciting quotes from Richard Helms and William Colby, two of the least believable sources imaginable. (353)

Unfortunately, this sort of thing is not at all unusual in our corporatized media. As McBride points out, not only had *Life Magazine* publisher C. D. Jackson served in the Eisenhower administration as a CIA-Pentagon liaison, but had a background in psychological warfare. This made his interest in the Zapruder film, which *Life* purchased shortly after the assassination, something less than innocent, particular considering his boss was the notoriously

---

[63] http://www.buzzfeed.com/jamiekirchick/seymour-hersh-assassination-of-jfk-was-form-of-l-55m2

CIA and Pentagon-cooperative Henry Luce. (97)

Many of us who write about sensitive subjects on a regular basis have experience with the sort of thing on a smaller scale, but it is fascinating to read about how it operates at this level. There are many more details in the book concerning these experiences, and it makes riveting reading. Armed with these experiences, it also lends weight to McBride's more general analysis of the state of reporting in our country. He correctly notes that, for example, longtime CBS anchor Dan Rather "owed his career to the Kennedy assassination and it keeps paying dividends for him, because he has long been a leading figure in the coverup. In an unusual display of candor...Rather described the Kennedy assassination as having been 'the answer to my prayers.' (69). Rather is far from the only one, but is perhaps the most prominent.

McBride also writes brilliantly in observing that the JFK assassination was also the birth of narrative news. Stories have always been shaped, but now of course we get wars with their own theme music and embedded reporters who sell believability from beneath their Army helmets. Jerry Mander had seen this back in the 1970s in his classic *Four Arguments for the Elimination of Television*, but McBride sums up the situation very well:

> What we experienced in front of our televisions that weekend was, in effect, a remarkably sophisticated four-day docudrama about the assassination, the first of many attempts to shape and package the chaotic events into a manageable dramatic and ideological form. The spectacular television extravaganza, a live drama on an unprecedentedly outsize canvas and duration, offered a shockingly violent opening featuring the 'unexpected' death of the protagonist, suspenseful twists and turns, a lurid cast of characters, and most importantly, a simplistic, neatly tied-up conclusion, including the death of the antagonist on the third day and the reassurance by the ending of the fourth that the state, although wounded, would survive. (72)

One key point made by McBride is the way the media plays with language. Oswald, according to all mainstream sources, has always been the assassin, despite the fact that he denied all the charges and never lived to see a trial. "This posthumous verdict was a serious breach of journalistic ethics, showing the *Times* to be more an organ of government propaganda than a disinterested seeker of truth…the "paper of record" has kept calling Oswald the 'assassin' ever since. The word 'alleged' rarely appears in conjunction with Oswald's name in the mainstream media." (111) This is absolutely correct and occurs with other assassinations and situations which the government has an interest in covering up. I found this same phenomenon, in an opposite direction, when writing an article called "The Open Assassination of Fred Hampton." Using only articles from the *New York Times* (in order to demonstrate how obvious it was that Hampton was murdered in cold blood, without provocation, by the police), I found that twenty years later, the *Times* still insisted on using language congenial to the state. For example, it described the scenario as a "shootout" despite the fact that hundreds of bullets went in but no bullets were ever proven to go out, and that Hampton was asleep, drugged, at the time of the murder. In other words, opinions on the incident, just like with Lee Harvey Oswald, froze at a certain point in time and became impervious to evidence.

This situation is bad for all of us and drives the many movements to take back our media. *Into The Nightmare* is an excellent example of doing precisely this, as well as being a superb entry into the Kennedy assassination literature. McBride's work should go on the shelf of books that contain information that cannot be found elsewhere – like Armstrong's book and Barry Ernest's *The Girl on the Stairs* and so many others where there is tremendous legwork involved. It is the summation of a fifty-year effort at assessing the truth, and although one may disagree about one point or another within the work, it is an honest and creditable work. *Into The Nightmare* serves as a solid introduction for the uninitiated and a wonderful new source for the researcher.

LOGIC AND HISTORICAL EXPLANATION

For historians ought to be precise, truthful, and quite unprejudiced,
and neither interest nor fear, hatred nor affection, should cause them
to swerve from the path of truth, whose mother is history, the rival
of time, the depository of great actions, the witness of what is past,
the example and instruction of the present, the monitor of the future.
            -Pierre Menard[64]

    Try this on:
    Abraham Lincoln, by acclamation our greatest president,
freed the slaves via the Emancipation Proclamation and held together
a splintering Union. A great moralist and meditative thinker (as
W.E.B DuBois, among others, have characterized him), he set an
example for the world in declaring equality for all races to live in
harmony in a unified America. He was murdered by a lunatic who
was part of a (very limited) conspiracy of Confederates who were all
later hanged, except for the assassin John Wilkes Booth himself, who
was shot.
    Or this:
    Abraham Lincoln, by all accounts our greatest president, or
certainly one of the greatest, preserved the Union by taking a moral
stand against Confederate separatists. Although admittedly the
Emancipation Proclamation freed the slaves only in "rebel territory"
(think about that for a minute) it was still a great political statement
for all times. He was killed by a small band on conspirators who may
have had some connection to European banking houses who disliked
his policy of printing "greenbacks."

---

[64] Or perhaps Cervantes. See *Ficciones* by Jorge Luis Borges.

Or perhaps this:

Abraham Lincoln, a pragmatic man if nothing else, fought the Civil War to force the Confederate states to remain in the Union. He gave the Emancipation Proclamation as a political gesture to prevent Great Britain and France from recognizing the Confederacy as a separate entity. He also hated black people to such an extent that he constantly used the N-word, told nasty jokes in private, and was so seemingly obsessed with the subject that documents exist at the time from people speculating that Lincoln had a bizarre mental fixation on people of color. Lincoln also favored the *deportation* of African-Americans, not assimilation. The Civil War was essentially geopolitical in scope, with British troops amassing in Canada at the same time the Frenchman Maximilian was installed in Mexico – a war that was won largely because Lincoln solicited and received help from the Russian navy. He was murdered by a conspiracy that may have included his Secretary of War Edwin Stanton (Mary Todd Lincoln went to her grave believing such was the case) and his death was almost certainly at the hands of the bankers that Lincoln most feared.

All of these variable positions, and many more, on the subject of Abraham Lincoln are available and can be found in books by scholars of varying repute. Although variations of (1) and (2) find purchase within the public mind and most academic scholarship, there is does exist documentary evidence – much of it ignored by historians – for (3). For more on the racist aspect of Lincoln, for example, see Lerone Bennett's *Forced into Glory*.

So which version is true?

One can always be led to the wishy-washy and academically respectable "elements from all three versions and many others are true to some degree" answer.

One could take Michel Foucault's answer and say that this is simply the wrong way to think about historical problems, and that these are situations emerging out of their specific contexts and should be analyzed within their respective housing structures. In fact, they cannot be analyzed any other way.

However, it seems to me that historical questions are all related to epistemology. That is to say, like any question about the nature of perception, it is a question of what the best evidence is that can be amassed and fitted within a coherent context provided by all our senses. The rational person sees something move in the shadows; she imagines a mouse, not the boogeyman. One sees a small animal flying at night and assumes it is a bat rather than the Batman. (Of course, if one gathers enough evidence, one could come back to the more radical thesis. David Hume pointed out that extraordinary claims demand extraordinary evidence; but if such is presented, we should be open enough to receive it.)

What I mean to say is this: *All* fact questions are philosophical investigations into the nature of reality.

The present narrative does not purport to be an example of revisionist history. The term 'revisionist' carries an implication that the set of facts that detail any given historical situation is infinitely malleable; taken to its logical extreme, it nestles comfortably with deconstructionist philosophy or anti-realism. And while one can always observe that any event may be described with different emphasis or be subjected to differing interpretations, quite often the attitude behind such nomenclature is a passive one. By 'passive' I mean that one can find historians divided up into their preferred emphases, *often without regard as to whether one particular individual may be closer to the truth than another.*

What does this mean? It means that Howard Zinn, for example, is taken to be the standard example of a leftist historian. Therefore (so the reasoning would go) Zinn's analyses will bear a certain intellectual bias, most famously that Christopher Columbus is not the legendary hero he has long been taught to be. However, this process of categorization has a way of simultaneously dismissing the historian as well; when everyone is simply telling *their* truth, rather than *the* truth, then the entire enterprise becomes a potentially infinite, as well as ineffectual, discussion. One thinks of Nietzsche's remark that there is always contempt in the act of speaking.

What I would like to do in this study is to have the reader accept, even if only on a provisional basis, that it is in principle conceivable to find out the actual truth about any given historical event. In other words, that although one can align a set of facts in one direction or another, there is such a thing as truth, and that it is possible to try and approach it. The other request I make to the reader is to accept that it is at least theoretically possible for the actual truth to conflict with popular established belief. In other words, one might find that a particular fact remains so despite the left-wing or right-wing biases of a particular human being trying to interpret it.

I would like to briefly sketch out what may be a useful metaphor in our search for historical accuracy. It is based on two philosophers, one of whom is often described as the most important philosopher of the 20th century (despite his affiliation with the Nazi Party). The first is Edmund Husserl, (1859-1938) a German academic who described a type of epistemology referred to as Phenomenology. The second is his follower Martin Heidegger, who broke with Husserl on a key element of his thought.

Husserl's basic contribution to epistemology, which is the study of perceptual reality, lies in his description of how human beings process the outside world. For centuries, philosophers have been concerned with how human beings come to learn things from the outside world. This has always been problematic, since it is surprisingly difficult to describe a mechanism through which this happens, without succumbing to skepticism and/or solipsism. Husserl's solution was to note that every human being's thought is 'directed' – that is to say, all of our thinking is processed in such a way that one can later remember it, or have beliefs about it, and so on. He called this directedness *intentionality*, and the content of one's mind is thus *intentional content*.

This is where an important realization came to him. For the purposes of the directed mind, it is irrelevant whether any given object of perception exists in reality or not, because it *does* exist as intentional content. Husserl's process is referred to as the 'phenomenological reduction.' It is the recognition that, although human beings do *not* have direct access to reality, they do have access to direct reality as it is perceived and processed by his intentionality.

An example may be helpful. Husserl could, using this method, derive what might be called the 'bracketing' of all human reality. Therefore, let us take a simple statement of fact – as I write this, there is a small dog sleeping underneath the table my computer is on. I might make a statement about this:

I see a small dog under the table.

From an epistemological standpoint, this statement might be doubted because the dog could be an illusion, or perhaps I am drunk, or perhaps the dog is actually a cat, and so on. However, if we perform the phenomenological reduction, then we get:

[I see a small dog under the table.]

That is, as Husserl recognized, a hard *fact*, in the sense that I cannot be wrong about the second statement. Without a doubt, *I* take it that *I* perceive a small dog under the table. This can be taken as true for all types of perceptions, and therefore philosophy can now move on to other lines of inquiry, since we can take all perceptions of a fundamental nature – that is, that there is such a thing as a world and we are alive and so on, to be true.

Heidegger made an observation about Husserl's philosophical move in his book *Being and Time*. He noted that, while Husserl's analysis may well be correct as far as he goes, that it was essentially a second-order analysis. That is to say, Husserl, by describing epistemological reality in terms of bracketing the universe, was actually buying into a subject-object reality that did not accurately reflect our real-world experience. Husserl, Heidegger says, would claim that there is a self, which perceives the dog, then interprets it, then has feelings about it, and so on. This, however, does not depict what human beings actually experience. Instead, we take in an entire immersive world at once, and move about in the world often without *any* specific directed thought. Take driving, for example. One drives, and hums a tune, and listens to radio or talks on the phone, and there is not an orderly subject-object relation to any of this experience. Instead, one experiences the *doing;* one is in the 'flow,' so to speak, of continuous unbroken action. When Immortal Technique strings together a set or words straight from his consciousness into a microphone, set to a beat and rhyme, he is in the moment, for there is no time to stop and recognize the subject-object relationships in the world. And in fact the word for this in hip-hop *is* 'flow.' The fact is that we don't relate to the world in a subject-object manner. The only time, in fact, we do behave in the subject-object model is when something occurs to shock us out of our total immersion.

For example, suppose one is trying to get out of an unfamiliar house, and finds that the doors are all locked. At that point, we do 'slow down' and become the rational subjects in search of objects to perceive, because we are attempting to methodically track down a solution to the current problem.

Heidegger's solution to the epistemological problem is to propose that human beings – at least most of the time – are a kind of 'situation,' one to which he gives the name *dasein*. The German word means, simply, 'existence,' although it also means 'being there.' It is a recognition that in order for human beings to make their way in the world, they must accept – and be absorbed in – a fully articulated and interrelated world of being. There is a sense in which Heidegger sees past the 'bracketed' universe to come to a conclusion that lies beyond the simple subject-object relation.

What am I on about?

The reason I bring up this somewhat esoteric business is because it seems to me that Husserl's analysis of reality has some application to the historical situation I mentioned earlier. There are a great many statements that are taken to be true at a second-order level and then simply forgotten about. We all take them to be either trivially true, or do not process them at all. I find this 'bracketing' of reality to be a useful metaphor in regard to describing the historical and political experience of most human beings.

In other words:

[There are two prominent political parties in the United States, the Democrats and the Republicans, and they represent different interests.]

[The great success stories in America derived from hard work and honest effort.]

[There are no political assassinations in the U.S.]

[There are no class conflicts in the U.S.]

[There has never been a coup, attempted or otherwise, in the U.S.]

[The interests of the rich and powerful are often countered and balanced at the highest levels of government.]

[The U.S. only pursues its own interests in foreign policy as they pertain to stopping Communism or assisting impoverished countries.]

[The average American can make a killing in the stock markets.]

And so on. I think that these statements are in fact bracketed by most Americans, in order to avoid certain unpleasant realities about their respective situations. What I want to do is to remove the brackets from these ideas, and see if the facts bear out the strength of people's belief in them. This is not to say that one can achieve some kind of universal Truth that everyone agrees with; I am not so utopian. However, in an effort to be 'objective' or to 'moderate' it is easy for academic historians, as well as those in the general populace, to overlook certain obvious facts. Sometimes these facts do not coincide neatly with our ideas – and the resulting dissonance can prove educational.

Now every piece of information we receive arrives on a background – the collected ideas, experiences, and exposure to the world that makes up our intelligence, our psyche. Each new idea is held up and compared to the next, instantaneously, to fit into what we have previously learned. At the most basic level, our mental processing ensures that we have enough spatial recognition to walk forward, make turns, or even (for a privileged few) receive a basketball at a dead run and leap into the air for a dunk. By the same token, when we receive information – a set of facts, figures, or what have you – we make judgments based on comparisons. Sometimes, depending on how that information is received, our judgments can be influenced in one direction or another. In the famous Kennedy-Nixon debates, television audiences generally sided with Kennedy, while those who merely listened on the radio felt Nixon had the upper hand.

A *New Yorker* article from January 2004 discussed the explosion of sport utility vehicles in America, and how people manage to come to precisely the wrong conclusions based on their instincts. The story explored the "mixture of bafflement and contempt" automakers feel toward consumers for liking S.U.V.s. According to "...internal industry market research...S.U.V.s tend to be bought by people who are insecure, vain, self-centered, and self-absorbed, who are frequently nervous about their marriages, and who lack confidence in their driving skills." They also request changes to the vehicle which made zero logical sense, but support their feelings:

> ...Car buyers felt unsafe when they thought that an outsider could easily see inside their vehicles. So Chrysler made the back window of the PT Cruiser smaller. Of course, making windows smaller – and thereby reducing visibility – makes driving more dangerous, not less so. But that's the puzzle of what has happened to the automobile world: feeling safe has become more important than actually being safe.[65]

---

[65] Malcolm Gladwell, "Big and Bad," *The New Yorker,* Jan. 12, 2004.

My background is in philosophy, so when I think about how people process information, my mind naturally turns to epistemology. Epistemology is the study of knowledge, and the processes by which we make judgments about what will constitute knowledge. In mathematics, truth is readily verifiable (except in certain complicated situations) within the system. That is to say, $2 + 2 = 4$, as long as we all agree what each term means. In the outside world, truth is not so easily construed; people disagree about certain fundamental claims, and often these claims are in dispute because of different backgrounds. For example, if I am agnostic, and a theist proposes that she believes in an almighty, loving, personal God because she has direct experience of God's immortal spirit, we arrive at an impasse. Since I cannot access her direct experience, we have different (and perhaps equally valid) points of view.

This egalitarian situation, however, will not always be the case. Some disputes arise out of one person having information that the other does not. In this case, the dispute arises out of simple education. Theoretically, the resolution can be found by educating the one who lacks information. While this would work if human beings were always rational, such is hardly the case. For example, a Fundamentalist Christian proposes that every word in the Bible is true. This is a demonstrably false belief (the Bible contradicts itself at numerous points) but Fundamentalists reform their world view to accommodate the new information. Either excuses are made – "we cannot know the mind of God, but my faith tells me it is so" – or else they deny that the contradictions exist.

I use Fundamentalist Christians as my base example, because even most believers don't take the literal truth of the Bible seriously. For example, one has trouble with the fact that Jesus told his followers that the End Times was nigh. He says:

> Luke 9:27
> But I tell you of a truth, there be some standing here, which shall not taste of death, till they see the kingdom of God.

Obviously Jesus was not perfect, because this prediction turned out to be false. There are more egregious textual examples, but that will take us far off the road I wish to pursue. The point is that human beings will often reinterpret or ignore new facts to satisfy the requirements of their background. This, of course, is not limited to religious concepts.

This is not to say that information processing can always be trusted when it arrives on a scientific, rather than religious, set of assumptions. It is more reliable, if and when its dictums about controls and unbiased collection of information are observed, but of course they aren't always followed. In fact, scientists are human, which is what an author named Thomas Kuhn pointed out.

When Kuhn's *The Structure of Scientific Revolutions* first appeared, some greeted it as proof that science was just as subjective as any other discipline. This was reading too much into Kuhn's thesis (indeed, he began distancing himself from this interpretation almost immediately) but he did demonstrate that science, like anything else, operates from large paradigms. Certain ideas do become entrenched, so that dissent becomes difficult; if you go through the literature of those theorists who propose a Steady-State rather than a Big Bang explanation for the universe, you will find complaints along these lines. In John Horgan's book *The End of Science*, Kuhn is quoted as saying, "For Christ's sake, if I had my choice of having written the book or not having written it, I would choose to have written it. But there have certainly been aspects involving considerable upset about the response to it." He meant precisely the idea that science is fundamentally irrational. "If they had said 'arational,' I wouldn't have minded at all."[66]

The Structure of Scientific Revolutions proposes that science is simultaneously creative and destructive, as new theories replace old theories, often for – and this is the controversial part – political reasons. That is to say, science is not immune to subjectivity. In fact, Kuhn goes as far as to say that different "interpretations of the [same] data" constitutes "metaphysics." Knowledge is itself subjective, at all levels. (Kuhn excludes mathematics from this, arguing that one can achieve truth – systemic truth, anyway – but without any effect on the natural world.)

It's probably true that we can never make 100% factual statements about the natural world, if only because such statements

---

[66] John Horgan, *The End of Science,* p. 41-42.

would imply perfect information. Since we do not operate under the conditions of a closed system, we will never have perfect information. However we can, I would argue, have good information. We can have enough information to make a rational decision.

At every moment we are engaged in inductive reasoning about the world; that is to say, we are assessing probabilities. If I cross the street at this moment, will that truck hit me? No, we think; the truck is quite far enough away. Sometimes we make misjudgments. We're not infallible. But regarding our person, and movement, and getting about in the world, we're usually right. If we weren't, we would be constantly falling down and wrecking our cars and such. The fact that we live another day verifies our success.

Once again, this information comes out of our background. We are used to busy streets and crowded highways; we assess vehicle distance and speed each time we drive or walk in the city. If I were suddenly dropped into the jungle, I would, no doubt, make all sorts of mistakes. I might be killed due to my lack of knowledge, but also my background, which includes instincts. My instincts, unfortunately, have no practical experience with tigers and snakes.

This background, or *Weltanschauung*, extends to my ideas about politics, or literature, or music, or history. We believe, in general, what we are taught in schools. We believe in schools. We accept money in the form of colored paper – talk about metaphysics! As John Searle pointed out in *The Construction of Social Reality*, the act of paying a waiter for a drink in a small café has staggering metaphysical implications. We accept all of them in an instant, without question.[67] We learn the normal beliefs of our fellows and go along with them, in principle. We get jobs and function in society. We accept that people should get "jobs" and that we should, in general, "function" in society. We also invent words that become new paradigms – the "dysfunctional family," for an example. What, precisely, is a "functional family"?

Even when we rebel, we rebel in the accepted manner. As Heidegger illustrates in *Being and Time*, human beings generally do not do things that are considered spectacularly inappropriate. For example, one does not strip naked and jump into a field of flowers. That would be "inappropriate." The only way a person would do such a thing is if society changed and this behavior became

---

[67] John Searle, *The Construction of Social Reality,* p.

appropriate. In the 1980's, teens wishing to show rebellion might get a Mohawk. That became a 'sign' meaning 'rebellion'; so that everyone would now understand, "I am in the presence of someone who is a rebel." However, teens in the 1980's did not show rebellion by refusing to wear clothes at all times. Such a person becomes "insane" and is taken to an institution, because they cannot grasp the accepted norms. As Michel Foucault once said, "normal" is "a process of coercion."

The citizenry of the United States is, in general, very poorly informed. Michael Parenti quotes some depressing statistics about the state of education:

> The most comprehensive federal survey, released by the U.S. Department of Education, finds that nearly six in ten high school seniors lack even a rudimentary knowledge of American history. A survey conducted by the Gallup Organization shows that 25 percent of college seniors cannot come within a half-century of locating the date of Columbus's voyage...Most cannot describe the differences between World War I and World War II...Another Gallup poll finds that 60 percent of adult Americans are unable to name the president who ordered the atomic bomb to be dropped on Japan, and 22 percent have no idea that such an attack ever occurred. A 1995 survey in the New York Times reports that only 49 percent of U.S. adults knew that the Soviet Union had been an ally of the United States during World War II, with the rest either having no opinion or thinking that the Soviets were noncombatants or on the enemy side.[68]

We are used to such statistics. And while one may argue the impeachability of the numbers, the point remains that a large portion of the population does not have even the bare beginnings of what would be required to question what is given to them. The rest of most of us, however, still accept the basic background, as it is given in history books and the media. For example, we believe that there is

---

[68] Michael Parenti, *History As Mystery*, p. 6-7.

a process in the United States of free and fair elections, and that individual votes count for something in these elections. We might argue to what degree, and range from the optimistic to the cynical, but in general we agree that elections mean something. We believe that America does not generally try to destroy other countries, that we do not favor dictators, that we desire democracy for all and stand for freedom and justice. Again, there are levels of assent to this picture, but an educated American who buys *The Wall Street Journal* and *Newsweek* would be expected to agree to these basic premises.

If someone comes along that seriously questions the structure of American society, rather than merely criticizing some aspect of it, then we often react like Fundamentalist Christians. We make excuses, or else we just pretend we didn't just hear that bit of information.

A good example of this is the reaction to James Bacque's book *Other Losses*. Bacque's research led him to collate eyewitness accounts and primary-source documentation showing that the United States maintained death camps for German soldiers after World War II. Roughly 1 million prisoners died. Bacque describes the situation in an article: "In the Eisenhower camps, starting in April 1945, most of the prisoners were given no shelter at all, very little food, and – for long periods – no water. They were simply herded through the barbed-wire gates, deprived of their pay-books and ID discs, and left to starve in a field under the open sky."[69]

Bacque was initially assisted in publication by the (in)famous American historian Stephen Ambrose. Ambrose, by Bacque's own admission, was vital in the latter stages of compiling the manuscript of *Other Losses*. Ambrose, however, was torn. "This book destroys my life's work," he said, referring to his biography of Eisenhower. He wrote Bacque a letter that expressed some of his inner conflicts: "You really have made a major historical discovery...Many will curse you; many will denounce you, many will argue with you; most will try to ignore you..."[70]

Eventually, despite making supportive public statements, Ambrose changed his mind about the book, and about Bacque. He became convinced that Eisenhower could not have been responsible for the camps, and began to state publicly his opposition. "Ambrose and the Ike-minded virtually admitted that they were suppressing the

[69] James Bacque, "A Truth So Terrible," *Abuse Your Illusions,* p. 262.
[70] Ibid, p. 261-264.

story. Ambrose had begun his 1988 letter to me with the admission that the story "can no longer be suppressed." He and his cohorts often admitted that they had no facts to rebut the book, then rebutted away, regardless. They said that they preferred their estimates to the documents in the archives."

Bacque also describes one of his critics:

> Sir Michael Howard, writing in the Times Literary Supplement, admitted that he was an "innumerate historian" not qualified to judge the statistical analysis in *Other Losses*. He develops a "criterion" to help him along. This is "the criterion of inherent probability," which relieves him not only of the need to do research but also of the need to understand research set plain before him. Howard writes, "Which is in fact the more probable explanation; that a million German prisoners quietly died in American hands in 1945 without anyone noticing, or that the American authorities...made mistakes in their initial figures...?" Which of course not only gets him out of having to understand research, but also cynically ignores that a million and a half Germans had never come home from Allied captivity. For Howard, the fate of these people is as nothing compared with the need to defend the flightless swans of academe from the terrorist raid that *Other Losses* represents to them.[71]

This "criterion of inherent probability," I think, is a very useful phrase naming the process by which most people reach decisions. They compare it to their background, and decide if it fits. Since replacing the background is an exhaustive enterprise, requiring a great deal of cognitive effort, they discard the pieces which don't fit for reasons that have little to do with rational principles. Like the Edward G. Robinson character in Double Indemnity, many people abide by the rumblings of the "little man who lives in my stomach. He's never wrong." Of course, unlike E. G. Robinson, people's stomachs are often wrong. It is reminiscent of the "argument from personal incredulity" that Richard Dawkins draws attention to in *The*

---

[71] Ibid, p. 266.

Blind Watchmaker. The "argument from personal incredulity," affects much of Creationist literature, according to Dawkins. It relies on statements of the form, "It is hard to believe that..." the human eye could evolve, for example.[72]

If one reflects for a moment just how difficult it is to replace one's framework, the effort required can seem daunting. To get an idea of what is required, Malcolm X provides an excellent example in his *Autobiography*. After his pilgrimage to Mecca, Malcolm comes to realization that the White Man is not "the Devil." Some of them are, some of them are not; virtue is neither excluded from nor conferred upon any given race. The intellectual realization was greater, of course, in his case, given his many public statements to the opposite – he had to make an equally public conversion.

In any case, the Bacque example is instructive in that some professional historians were given to dismiss *Other Losses* solely on the basis of its subject matter. Its thesis could not be true a priori, because the idea interfered with their background. There are many such ideas which are not well-received. One idea was the former "conspiracy theory" that Franklin Roosevelt (or, at least, officials within the Roosevelt government – this becomes debatable at a certain point) had been aware of the attack on Pearl Harbor before it happened, and allowed it to occur in order to force America's entry into World War II. Documents obtained under the Freedom of Information Act and published in the book *Day of Deceit* have shown this "conspiracy theory" to be precisely correct. Interestingly, the author, Daniel Stinnett, agrees with the government's motivation (the U.S. populace was so isolationist that only such an act would allow American involvement in the war, necessary to halt the Nazis.) However, the fact remains that the information only arrived in printed form sixty years after the fact, and provided to a populace that isn't sure if the Russians were "good guys" or "bad guys" during the war.

A key component of conventional historical thinking is a preference for psychological explanations of the general public, of the leaders of foreign nations, and anyone who is not in a position of bureaucratic or corporate power over the American people. This preference disappears when it comes to explanations about key

---

[72] Richard Dawkins, *The Blind Watchmaker*, p. 38.

events in American history. A few examples should help clarify what I mean.

Let's first take how the public is handled and described in terms of public media, news programs, and historians.

In the first place, the American is manipulated by television commercials during the 20 hours the average American spends in front of the TV set. Many people believe that they aren't influenced by commercials and will tell you so. This is obviously false, since corporations wouldn't waste billions of dollars on them if they were not efficacious. Almost all commercials are mini psychological experiments in association. Sleek modern automobiles are associated with sex because of the models driving them or standing next to them. Beer commercials frequently assert that beer should be a replacement for sex – they depict situations in which men find ways to avoid their women, who either want attention or otherwise take them away from their true love, beer. That is to say, no commercial ever attempts to make a rational argument in favor of its product. It simply tries to bypass the rational part of the brain and go straight to the associative to make you believe a product is sexy, or cool, or necessary.

At the same time, news programs endlessly speculate about the nature of the 'public.' Will the public accept a given position from the President on abortion? Will they continue to buy useless goods and services and thus keep the economy going? In fact, consumer confidence is itself a unit of measure in contemporary economics. The public is outraged by Janet Jackson's breasts. The public isn't interested in health care if it means going to a socialist system. The public rallies around the flag. The public is gearing up for campaign season.

Historians do the same thing. Pick up any general history book used in academics and you will find the people willing all manner of activity. 'In 1947, the Greek populace demanded intervention by the United States to aid them from the Communist insurgent threat' or 'People, weary of crisis and war, turned to conservatism to end conflict in 1968 when they elected Richard Nixon to high office.' Mass psychoanalysis is the historians' prerogative.

Indeed, when it comes to certain aspects of history, the psychological explanation is taken to be definitive. For example, Hitler is frequently analyzed as a sociopath, or a twisted version of the charismatic personality, or a medicated schizophrenic, as if these explanations were sufficient to explain the Hitler phenomenon. At the same time, historians tend to ignore the financing of Hitler, without which he would have been a sociopathic charismatic schizophrenic with no power whatsoever. In a sense, historians limit themselves to aesthetics in dealing with a personage such as Hitler, in describing the innate nuances of the man, but never arriving at the *efficient* part, the part which actually made him a world figure. This is because anyone who explores Hitler's funding is going to find that he was created by the British with the help of American corporate executives like Henry Ford and Irenee du Pont, and this leads us down a very dark road indeed. For we find the same British and American financiers behind the Communist Revolution, and after a while we may find ourselves asking just what is going on here. This is once again dangerous territory, so historians limit themselves in endless psychoanalysis when not simply describing the content of various battles and so on.

At the same time, it is also safe for American writers to speculate about the particular psychological motives of the current leaders of other nations. For example:

> A harsh law on nongovernmental organizations that Russia's President Vladimir Putin and his Kremlin coterie are pushing through a docile Duma shows Putin's true colors. This is the move of an antidemocratic ruler acting on the paranoid belief of his security services that foreign human rights, educational, and medical organizations are disguised tools of Western intelligence agencies plotting to orchestrate a popular uprising in Russia like those that toppled corrupt regimes in Georgia and Ukraine.[73]

There are literally millions of examples of editorials and assessments like this written about foreign leaders in the American papers throughout history. What is positively *not* allowed, if one is to remain in intellectual currency, is to reason from specific facts to

---

[73] "Putin's Power Grab," Boston Globe editorial, 1 December 2005. http://www.boston.com/news/globe/editorial_opinion/editorials/articles/2005/12/01/putins_power_grab/

possible motivations of *American* leaders. So if one were to reason in the following fashion:

(1) Jack Kennedy beat Nixon in a stolen election in 1960.
(2) Jack Kennedy is assassinated in 1963 by a crazed gunman.
(3) Nixon decides to run again for President in 1968. Bobby Kennedy enters the Democratic primaries rather late in the process, but gains momentum and emerges as an overwhelming threat to win.
(4) Bobby Kennedy is assassinated in 1968 by a crazed gunman.
(5) Nixon wins the election.
(6) In the 1972 election, George Wallace emerges as a Southern Democratic threat to Nixon in the primaries.
(7) In 1972, George Wallace is shot and crippled by a crazed gunman.
(8) Nixon wins the election.

Therefore, crazed gunmen do the bidding of Richard Nixon.

Of course, I am oversimplifying. However, to even point out the fact that Richard Nixon's road to the presidency was laid with bullets is to get into dangerous territory, and to actually have the temerity to even *suggest drawing any conclusions* from that fact is to invite public scorn and outcries of 'paranoia.' This, despite the lessons of European history, which are a constant chronicle of poisonings, stabbings, and even less pleasant means for aspirants to the throne to do away with one another. Many of these events are recorded in the history plays of Shakespeare.

It's quite simple. A woman is murdered. She's married. Who is the prime suspect? Her husband. A child is killed. Who killed him or her? Odds are it was the parents, who are vastly more likely to murder their children than anyone else. The same goes for molestation and rape. Strangers don't generally hurt one another – typically when they do violence it is those within their own circle. This is known to every criminal investigator in the world as a fact of life. It is internalized by most Americans, who have at their fingertips a dizzying number of police-procedural television shows which depict this on an hour by hour basis.

And still the inference is improper.

What all this suggests is a peculiar kind of schizophrenia in which American historians are able to mentally separate what they know of how people behave in the rest of the world and how they behave in the United States. We 'don't do that sort of thing.' American is the land of fair play, in which some men – such as Nixon himself – are wild aberrations from the norm, but in the main we have merely bloodless transfers of power. Any genealogist can tell you that in any presidential election, the man with the bluest blood almost always wins. Should we try to draw conclusions from this? Heaven forfend.

The breakthroughs from this sort of thinking do not often come from academics, and for good reason. However, they do occasionally come from artists.

A THEORETICAL MODEL FOR INTERPRETING
CONSPIRATORIAL EVENTS

I used to be a private investigator. I worked cases all over the state of Texas and all over the greater Los Angeles region, from Mulholland Drive to Florencia Street in South Central. As a result of my job, I spent a good deal time visiting county jails and going inside police stations, large and small, to chase down reports, interview officers, and obtain video information in theft cases.

One thing that struck me in virtually every police station is that somewhere in the building would be a plaque proudly stating what Freemasonic Lodge the officers served in. When police officers talk about the thin blue line and state that they are a Brotherhood, this is what they mean. They swear oaths of fealty to one another in Masonic rituals.

Exaggeration?

In 2011, the Daily Telegraph ran an interesting story about John Tully, head of the Sine Favore temple lodge, who gained publicity by fighting against David Cameron's attempts to cut funding. The details of how the lodge operated were described as follows:

> Masonic rules require members to do all they can to
> support each other, to look after each other and to
> keep each others' lawful secrets.
> New members of the so-called Brotherhood are
> blindfolded, a hangman's noose placed around their
> necks and they are warned their throat will be slit and
> their tongue torn out if they break their oath. Critics
> argue this could put them at odds with discharging
> their duty to serve the public.[74]

While most of us these days have to sign non-compete agreements and the like to obtain work, I think we can agree that this is a bit extreme. And it has real-world effects, as when officers refuse to testify against their brethren and cover up one another's crimes.

Is this a conspiracy? We have people meeting in secret, pledging allegiances to one another that contradict the public good and their official capacities.

I happen to think this is a question worth asking.

In recent years, the police have become militarized and the number of heavily publicized unwarranted police shootings has risen dramatically, such as in Ferguson. One thing that is generally avoided by the media in talking about such issues is how difficult it is to get police officers indicted of anything, much less convicted. Part of this is because of the institutional protections brought on that come from the state, and the police establishment itself.

This brings up a key point. A conspiracy, in addition to being established by a chain of evidence, posits more than just the specifics of relationships. To say that any particular event or occurrence is a conspiracy is to make a claim about *human nature*. That is, we asserting that the evidence points to a specific motivation.

This may seem obvious, but it's quite important. When investigators look into the homicide of a man, and it turns out that his wife had taken out an enormous insurance policy on him two weeks before, the event becomes suspicious because suddenly we have a concrete motivation for her to kill him: she benefits. "Cui bono?" goes the Roman question. The fact doesn't establish that she killed him, but it provides an important logical (rather than causal) link. She might have been *motivated* to do it.

Anyone who spends any time researching historical events realizes that history as it is formally taught in public schools consists of nonsense and deceit. Virtually all the premises of high school history are false, especially the concept of evolutionary progression, in which the United States is presented as marching through time in a

---

[74] The Daily Telegraph, 20 August 2011, by Jason Lewis, "Freemasons in the police leading the attack on Cameron's riot response," http://www.telegraph.co.uk/news/uknews/law-and-order/8713343/Freemasons-in-the-police-leading-the-attack-on-David-Camerons-riot-response.html, accessed 19 February 2013.

continuous procession with occasional setbacks.

We know there are reasons for the deception. Just as movies require audience identification with the protagonist in order to work – we imagine ourselves as Indiana Jones having adventures in the course of a film – academic history tells a story in which the students are invited to see themselves in a continuum. And, as John Taylor Gatto has pointed out, schools are essentially laboratories cooked up by rich elites for the purpose of control. Hence the Prussian basis for our schools (that is where we get the term *kindergarten,* "garden of children") and the Pavlovian bells signaling the ends of classes, inspired by behavioral scientists.[75]

Academic history at university allows more flexibility, and indeed in the standard process of demarcating those at the top from those in the middle, some are allowed to unlearn what they gleaned in high school and gain some insight. But even that is proscribed, and in academic circles one can go perhaps as far as Howard Zinn in *A People's History of the United States* or James Loewen in *Lies My Teacher Told Me.* Embarking on taboo subjects further out than that is to endanger one's career. A good example of this is Marxist historian Michael Parenti, who has written about power relationships much of his adult life and dares discuss the Kennedy assassination, and has therefore found his academic career troubled and sporadic.

The same is true in the sciences, as Thomas Kuhn pointed out:

> Scientific education makes use of no equivalent for
> the art museum or the library of classics, and the
> result is sometimes a drastic distortion in the
> scientist's perception of his discipline's past…he
> comes to see it as leading in a straight line to the
> discipline's present vantage. In short, he comes to see
> it as progress.[76]

What's interesting about Kuhn's perspective here is that he imagines that if science had the equivalent of a shared history known

---

[75] There is more – much more, including the "Rockefeller Occasional Letters" and other astonishing documentation which prove his thesis – in Gatto's book *The Underground History of American Education.*

[76] Thomas S. Kuhn, *The Structure of Scientific Revolutions* (University of Chicago Press: 1962), 167.

to scientists, there would be fewer illusions. Of course, we know that is absolutely false, since historians themselves have in many cases created broad stories that – even when the text itself insists otherwise – give the illusion of progress.

DEVIL IN THE DETAILS

You might remember that after the 9/11 attacks on the World Trade Center and the Pentagon, in the days and weeks following there were a number of anthrax attacks that took place using the U.S. postal service. It would later turn out that those anthrax samples came from domestic labs – in particular from a place called Fort Detrick, in Maryland.

Fort Detrick was started by a man named Dr. Cornelius Rhoads. He worked for the Rockefeller Institute of Medical Research. In 1911, a prominent physician named Dr. Hideyo Naguchi, working for this same institute, deliberately injected 146 children with syphilis in an experiment. Twenty years later, Rhoads gave cancer to a group of people in Puerto Rico, thirteen of whom died. He later wrote in a letter that Puerto Rico should be wiped off the face of the Earth. Rhoads became so notorious for his racism and alleged murder of Puerto Ricans that his name was stripped from an award given by the American Association of Cancer Research.

Fort Detrick was created in 1942 as the domestic home for biological warfare research. The U.S. Army Biological Warfare units were established and directed by the Dr. Rhoads himself.

The individuals targeted during the anthrax attacks were curious. For example, not a single Republican was targeted, despite being the ruling party at the time of the 9/11 incident. Instead, the editor of a national tabloid that had run stories on the drunken escapades of the George W. Bush daughters was killed by anthrax, and spores turned up in the mail of Ted Daschle, who had expressed relatively mild objections to the upcoming Patriot Act. There are a number of oddities within this situation, but let's ask just these three questions:

(1) Why did the White House begin anthrax inoculations beginning on *the evening* of September 11, 2001? No one had received anthrax letters yet. Judicial Watch, in fact,

filed suit against the government to release files about this very issue.[77]

(2) How is it that the anthrax spores, of the Ames strain, originated from a military source – specifically Dr. Rhoads' own Fort Detrick, Maryland?

(3) Why did the FBI destroy the bank of anthrax samples that would have aided the investigation? Also, why was the biological weapons facility at Fort Detrick demolished in December of 2002? Why is it that the company hired to destroy and clean up the Fort Detrick site was the same one used to clean up the Oklahoma City bombing and the World Trade Center itself (Controlled Demolition Incorporated)?

No matter how you feel about what happened on 9/11, these are all reasonable questions to ask. Now I have no particular axe to grind with regard to the 9/11 situation and have not done sufficient work on the subject to say anything with certainty about it. But did you know these things? Are they part of the narrative in the same way that Osama bin Laden survived for a dozen years despite being on kidney dialysis in the remote caves of Afghanistan, before then being assassinated by a brave team of U.S. Special Forces hitmen (later celebrated in the film *Zero Dark Thirty)*?

SPORTS

One interesting thing about conspiracies in the modern media is that they will believe in them when foreign potentates are involved. Newspapers will freely speculate, for example, about whether Vladimir Putin had his rivals put to death en route to power. They would never run a similar story on, for example, whether Mike McConnell, a hacker who figured in the "stolen election" stories arising from the 2004 presidential race, was murdered because he knew too much.[78]

---

[77] http://www.mail-archive.com/ctrl@listserv.aol.com/msg92769.html. Accessed 20 February 2013.
[78] http://markcrispinmiller.com/2012/02/new-details-on-bushcheneys-stolen-re-

For some reason, however, conspiracies *are* allowed in sports.

Jess Passan, in writing about the baseball team the Florida Marlins, and their then-owner and president Jeffrey Loria and David Samson, openly states in an article that they were involved in a conspiracy to dupe the public and make millions from their ownership of the team. He asserts, essentially, that Loria was undermining his own team so that he could move the team to another city, while getting the city to pay for a stadium that ultimately cost more than $2 billion. (This is a bit like the plot of the comedy film *Major League*.) He invokes the very specific notion of conspiracy that most people are familiar with:

> This is not some Roswell, black-helicopter, second-shooter conspiracy. This is very real. This is three rich, powerful men getting together and using their influence and business acumen to affect dealings that hurt the sport and help their bank balances. This is an insult to those who care about baseball. And we know this all because this isn't the first time it's happened.[79]

This kind of charged language is very rare in American newspapers and would almost never be applied to the kind of deals that go on every day in high finance or the halls of government. This language is allowed if the topic is sports.

The NBA is rife with conspiracies that nearly all fans know and many believe. It is widely believed, for example, that the NBA rigged the 1985 lottery for the New York Knicks in allowing them to draft Georgetown star Patrick Ewing. "Everyone knows" that Michael Jordan's decision to play baseball for two years in the middle of the greatest career in basketball history was due to his gambling situation being out of control and forcing the Commissioner's hand in "suspending" him off the record.

One reason sportswriters may be able to accept these ideas (or at

---

election-and-what-looks-like-the-murder-of-mike-connell/, accessed 19 February 2013.

[79] Yahoo News, 14 November 2012, by Jeff Passan, "Marlins trade is a baseball tragedy, and Bud Selig deserves his share of blame," http://sports.yahoo.com/news/marlins-trade-a-baseball-tragedy-bud-selig-deserves-blame.html, accessed 20 February 2013.

least argue for them provisionally in a way that say, journalists on a political beat would not) is that sports *don't matter.* Additionally, sports have concrete results that are posted to a scoreboard. If sportswriters were forced to write about sports the way newspapers and television reported on political events, you would see headlines like

STEELERS ALLEGE SUPER BOWL VICTORY; CARDINALS DISSENT

Because of the way media typically reports stories of political importance, the facts don't carry any weight. One authority can cite a fact about a particular topic, and another authority can say something crazily untrue in response, and the news will report the event as a controversy.

However, if you could assign point totals to ideas, it would become clear very quickly who has the facts and who doesn't. If we assigned point totals to the Conspiracy and Lone Nut ideas in the Kennedy assassination, the score would be something like 98 to 2 in favor of Conspiracy.

KNOWN CONSPIRACIES

A number of conspiracies have already happened in the United States. Every historian accepts them. They may not be *labeled* as such, but the meet the parameters we are starting to define. Let's look at a few of them.

BLETCHLEY PARK

The project went under the code name ULTRA. During World War II, a group of mathematicians, philosophers, and a motley core of bookish eccentrics were brought together at a place called Bletchley Park in Buckinghamshire in England. Beginning in 1938, they were brought together to break the codes produced by the famous Enigma machine, which was a machine that generated coded messages to disguise the transmission from the Nazi High Command. After the Pearl Harbor incident in 1941, the Americans got involved, sending one of the great geniuses of the 20th century, Alan Turing, in to help.

The result of these workings, in effect, produced the first programmable computer, a machine known as Colossus. The solutions to the Enigma-encoded messages were printed out by Colossus on IBM machines – something of a bitter irony since IBM had also taken on the contract to build the machines which generated the numbered codes tattooed on Nazi death camp prisoners.[80]

The whole thing was protected by and provided for by Winston Churchill, who kept the inner workings of the Bletchley Park secret even in his biographical accounts of the war.

In point of fact, most of the operations of the group were kept absolutely secret until the mid-1990s. There came a book, and later a film written by Tom Stoppard, called *Enigma*.

This was a conspiracy, of course. It was essentially a *benign* conspiracy, from the point of view of the Western world and against the Nazis, but it functioned the way high-level conspiracies are supposed to operate. It went all the way to Churchill and kept secret until nearly a *half century* after the war.

Is it possible to keep government secrets under the conditions even of war? It appears the answer is yes.

THE MANHATTAN PROJECT

Starting in about 1939, but really getting going in 1942, a collection of American, British, and Canadian scientists grouped together to create the atom bomb. This would later become famous as the Manhattan Project. Led by the theoretical physicist J. Robert Oppenheimer, the group produced "Fat Man" and "Little Boy," the test bombs at varying levels of power. Although the group at Los Alamos became most famous scientists tackling the problem, in fact the Manhattan Project was coordinated through and conducted experiments at numerous locations all around the United States and Canada. Some 130,000 people were involved in some way or another.[81]

When the scientists conducted the famous Trinity Test in March 1944, they weren't sure how big the explosion was going to be. Some scientists speculated that it would set off a chain reaction in the

---

[80] See *IBM and the Holocaust* by Edwin Black.
[81] Richard Rhodes, "Why Robert Oppenheimer's Atomic Bomb Still Haunts Us," Newsweek, 15 May 2013. http://www.newsweek.com/2013/05/15/why-robert-oppenheimers-atomic-bomb-still-haunts-us-237382.html.

atmosphere and destroy the planet. Knowing the risks involved, they performed the test anyway.

Of course, in 1945 the bombings of Hiroshima and Nagasaki exposed the Western control of the Bomb to the world, but secrecy had been well maintained up until then. Indeed, only a handful of people had known the actual import of what they were working on; successful division of labor meant that engineers and laborers could work on aspects of the project while thinking they were working on ordinary munitions.

Once again, this was a successful conspiracy, operating precisely the way conspiracists claim they do. It arguably wasn't sinister, but it was a large-scale government-overseen project with thousands of employees which operated in complete secrecy. So when somebody says, "How can the government keep a secret with so many people involved?" We know it *can* happen because it *has* happened.

Bottom line: the idea that large-scale conspiracies could not operate *in principle* is demonstrably incorrect.

A MODERN COINTELPRO

All right, so we might acknowledge the existence of these 'benign' conspiracies. But what of those that are not so benign?

In early 2014 a document leaked to the press that included information related to the FBI's assessment and plan for handling the Occupy movement. Having been formed in the wake of the incredible financial scandals and subsequent bailouts ordered from the Obama administration, Occupy did precisely that, taking over huge swathes of property around Wall Street and at prominent places around the country. Occupy, as an organized movement, did get a fair amount of press coverage and did create difficulties for these same financial centers. The FBI, it seems, took notice.

> On October 13, 2011, writer sent via email an excerpt
> [redacted] regarding FBI Houston's [redacted] to all
> IA's, SSRA's and SSA [redacted]. This [redacted]
> identified the exploitation of the Occupy Movement
> by [redacted] interested in developing a long-term
> plan to kill local Occupy leaders via sniper fire.[82]

---

[82] FBI Situational Information Report, documents released under FOIA, p. 68.

The FBI sent no warnings to any of the Occupy leaders or publicized the plots in any way. *Sniper assassinations?*

The documents reveal a consistent pattern of treating Occupy protesters as terrorists:

> The Federal Reserve of Richmond, Virginia had its own private security surveilling Occupy Tampa and Tampa Veterans for Peace and passing privately-collected information on activists back to the Richmond FBI, which, in turn, categorized OWS activities under its "domestic terrorism" unit. The Anchorage, Alaska "terrorism task force" was watching Occupy Anchorage. The Jackson, Mississippi "joint terrorism task force" was issuing a "counterterrorism preparedness alert" about the ill-organized grandmas and college sophomores in Occupy there. Also in Jackson, Mississippi, the FBI and the "Bank Security Group" – multiple private banks – met to discuss the reaction to "National Bad Bank Sit-in Day" (the response was violent, as you may recall).[83]

Now one can quibble about whether Occupy is worth supporting or not, but this is essentially duplicating certain aspects of the FBI's COINTELPRO program, right down to the targeted assassination of leaders. Once again, we are dealing with what one might ordinarily call a "conspiracy theory" – but the documentation from the source itself shows that it actually happened. To put it another way, as Dr. Cornel West once said, "I don't believe in conspiracies. I do believe that there is coordinated activity performed in secret, but I don't believe in conspiracy."

Conspiracies are an unfortunate part of our society, and if we don't even acknowledge their existence, we will be unable to account

---

See http://www.justiceonline.org/commentary/fbi-files-ows.html.

[83] The London Guardian, 29 December 2012, by Naomi Wolf. "Revealed: how the FBI coordinated the crackdown on Occupy," http://www.guardian.co.uk/commentisfree/2012/dec/29/fbi-coordinated-crackdown-occupy.

for and properly explain much of the modern world. And that means allowing human beings to be human and allowing them to have normal human motivations.

AND AFTER ALL, WE'RE ONLY ORDINARY MEN

The societal paradigm prevents drawing certain conclusions in a formal or public context. And, if you think about it, this makes sense.

Human beings are tribal creatures. In hunter-gatherer societies, it made sense to form small bands to protect one another against the elements, fierce animals, and of course other bands. It's an instinct that is shared with our closest animal neighbors, monkeys and apes. Such groups trained themselves to look *outward* for danger, to divide the world into *us* and *them* for quite sound reasons.

In modern society, we are encouraged to continue thinking and behaving in such patterns, as listening to any sports talk show will attest. "We [i.e., my sports team] need to cut payroll in order to try and sign Lebron James," a fan might declare. The identification becomes total when a fan wears a shirt of a particular player. The same fan identifies with other fans, and rejects others who support other teams. There are also rivalries for which one has a specific enmity – Yankee fans despising Red Sox fans, for example.

In extreme examples, these frivolous conflicts can turn to violence. In May 2008, a female Yankees fan became enraged when a Red Sox fan screamed "Yankees suck!" at her. She ran over him with her car, killing him.[84]

Right-wing politicians have been taking advantage of this primitive tendency for years. It was the basis for the Southern Strategy that took advantage of Democratic social policies to flip the Southern states into becoming Republican.[85] Although the party represented interests not their own in most cases – the South, as

---

[84] Mike Underwood, "Cops: Sox fan hit, killed over Yankees rivalry," *The Boston Herald,* 6 May 2008.
http://news.bostonherald.com/news/regional/general/view.bg?articleid=1092028&srvc=home&position=recent
[85] Take it from the man himself: Kevin Phillips, *American Theocracy* (Viking: New York 2006), 179-181. Phillips is virtually the inventor of the Southern strategy.

always, was largely poor and rural and unlikely to benefit from Republican policies – the overriding hatred of blacks and immigrants drove the South away from the Democratic Party. The same dynamic is in place now in driving hatred of gays and Middle Eastern foreigners.

Social approval is a powerful force. Pierre Choderlos de de Laclos described how the acceptance of one's circle can literally become a life and death matter in his 18th century novel *Les Liasions Dangereuses*. The novel dissects the decadent leanings of the *ancien régime* just a few years before the French Revolution, and it depicts the Marquise de Merteuil's ultimate downfall as ostracization, which to her is worse than death. And of course anyone who has attended public school is aware of the countless stratifications and complex social structures dividing young people into small contiguous bands.

Another good example comes from calculus and the famous dispute over priority between Isaac Newton and Gottfried Leibniz. Although Leibniz's notation was better, and likely his invention first, Great Britain nonetheless defended Newton. "[They] used Newton's notation rather than that of Leibniz, which proved bad for them since the rest of the Western world adopted the latter's notation. Civic pride overrode considerations of scientific efficiency."[86] Of course; Newton was an *us* rather than a *them*.

This tribalism even comes into play in the dinner party, as Howard Bloom discusses. He points out that much of communication takes place between human beings is done with subtle body signals of approbation or disapprobation that drive behavior. The effect is familiar to us all:

> If we run into a gathering of friends, spring a tantalizing bit of information on one of them, and everybody else edges over to hear it, we fell invigorated…If, on the other hand, we spring a piece of gossip that, to us, seems irresistible, and the people near us immediately march away, we become discouraged…Like the bee arriving with unwelcome food, we aren't motivated to deliver more of a tidbit no one seems to want.[87]

---

[86] Jason Socrates Bardi, *The Calculus Wars* (Thunder's Mouth Press: New York 2006), 234.

This seems to me to be a key insight.

The unwelcome food, in this case, is any realistic discussion of the motives of the internal structures of power, because in this discussion we have to face ourselves. Just as family members may suffer for years with one or more violent parents, and even defend them to outsiders, so people feel about their government and the *concept* of the United States. Some people become so enamored with the fantasy elements of the romanticized United States that they prefer to live in a world of flags and other symbols rather than look squarely at the facts. Or else, presented with uncomfortable information, they present false choices: "You wouldn't rather live in Russia, would you?" Or they attack the information without addressing the content: "Well, that's just another statement from the Blame America First crowd." These meaningless responses reveal how deep such information pokes into their psyches. It ceases to be rational.

And, as we have seen, it *isn't* rational. It is inculcated both from a natural-born kin altruism and fostered by an educational system obsessed with grouping, teams, and hierarchical assessment.

INTERPRETING HISTORICAL EVENTS

It should not be surprising, then, that the most taboo subjects in our culture – or any given culture – concern the motivations of those in power. These are paternal figures ("the heads of state," they are sometimes called) who are called upon to lead, or so their speeches claim. Human beings have a powerful psychological motive not to accept deceit among their leaders; it disturbs their comfort. It throws into question the structure of the society in positing that the *us* might also be the *them*.

This is just the opposite of what is usually argued in the major media. Frequently, such people will argue that conspiracists are actually psychologically driven to see conspiracies, and that they find them comforting! A typical observation was made by Patrick Beach in an Austin-American Statesman article on the 40th anniversary of

---

[87] Howard Bloom, *The Lucifer Principle* (The Atlantic Monthly Press: New York 1995), 142.

the Kennedy assassination: "There's also an allure to conspiracy that's at once comforting, empowering and thrilling. No wonder some people, in an impotent rage, fall for it like swooning schoolgirls: It's one-stop shopping for those who ever felt their life's progress impeded by an unseen hand."[88]

This is, of course, a barking proposition and exactly the opposite of the truth. It would be much more comforting to believe in progress, and the essential humanity of our leaders, and that they make mistakes but basically have their hearts in the right place. Unfortunately, any serious study of the facts tells us this is not so.

However, psychological explanations often make their way into the major media. Let's take a look at a few of the possible means for interpreting history.

One type of historical interpretation is often referred to as Methodological Individualism. It has been highly influential from Max Weber, through his student Joseph Schumpeter, and in F.A. Hayek and Karl Popper under a slightly different form. According to Weber, social activity originates from individual actors whose intentions provide an explanatory framework. Collectivizing opinions into group motivation ignores the individual context of each action and is thus to be avoided – and, perhaps most importantly, contrasted with historical materialism. Weber explains it like so:

> A correct causal interpretation of a concrete course of action is arrived at when the overt action and the motives have both been correctly apprehended and at the same time their relation has become meaningfully comprehensible. A correct causal interpretation of typical action means that the process which is claimed to be typical is shown to be both adequately grasped at the level of meaning and at the same time the interpretation is to some degree causally adequate.[89]

One example from his work might be his linkage of rationality and economic capitalism as an outgrowth and opposition to the Church.

---

[88] Patrick Beach, "A conspiracy among us," *The Austin-American Statesman* (23 November 2003), page 1 of the Sunday Insight section.
[89] Max Weber, *The Theory of Social and Economic Organization* (Oxford University Press: New York 1947), 99.

Weber addresses the issue of, for example, usury, which was considered unethical until the dawn of rationalism, where it was recognized what economic growth was possible under the capitalist system. But, as he points out, it's not a question of a simple transformation – instead, Weber analyzes a whole structure of subtleties in charting Protestant Capitalism.[90]

His pupil Joseph Schumpeter eventually expanded this idea into a larger defense of capitalism as a whole in a theory that came to be known as "creative destruction." Schumpeter emphasizes that in a democratic system there is a watering-down process by which the political will gains traction, pushing radicalism to the corners. He notes the balance between the Parliament's cabinet ministers and the Prime Minister in working with one another to stabilize the country and prevent total shutdown.[91] (And indeed, it was effectively satirized in the British television program "Yes, Minister," in which an idiot is elected Prime Minister because he offends no one particularly.)

There is also Historical Materialism. This is the view that history proceeds as a dialectical process in which one idea (thesis) is dominant, another idea (antithesis) rises in opposition, and finally the result is synthesis. This synthesis becomes a further thesis and the process continues again. It is associated with the German philosopher Hegel and, of course, Karl Marx, who borrowed Hegel's idea for his own Dialectical Materialism.

Historians and journalists often prefer purely psychological explanations for motives. These explanations frequently make generalizations about the will of a given populace or the broad intentions of a government. These same people will tend to avoid discussing specific psychological motives of intent if they indicate self-interest distinct from the general will.

Let's take a concrete example: the Mexican War of 1846. A popular textbook asserts that James Polk, the U.S. President at the time, tried to buy land from Mexico "at a good price" but the Mexicans were "too proud to sell." This same textbook then goes on to state that Mexican troops went north of the Rio Grande, thus

---

[90] Max Weber, *The Protestant Ethic and the Spirit of Capitalism* (Charles Scribner's Sons: New York 1958), see especially 71-76.
[91] Joseph Schumpeter, *Capitalism, Socialism, and Democracy* (HarperPerennial: New York 1942), 278.

instigating war.[92] A different textbook tells much the same story, although it does bring Zachary Taylor into the equation:

> President Polk sent Zachary Taylor with American troops clear down to the Rio Grande; that is to the farthest edge of the disputed area. A fight resulted between American and Mexican troops. Then President Polk sent a message to Congress saying that Mexican soldiers had invaded American territory and killed American troops on American soil. He asked Congress to declare war on Mexico.[93]

In the first example, we have broad reasons given about the general will, including the interpolation that Polk's offer to buy land from Mexico was in good faith and at a good price, while Mexican pride soured the deal. In the second example, we have individual motives carefully excised from the proceedings, with only declarative statements which are all true in of themselves; true, but insufficient. What is unspoken in both cases is the fact that the U.S. agitated the border situation with the Mexicans precisely in order to obtain the land. In fact, Polk had first gone to the Texas hero Sam Houston to instigate the war by falsely claiming the Mexicans attacked after riding near the border. Sam Houston declined, so Polk turned to Zachary Taylor, who agreed. Taylor rode down, executed the plan, and when American blood was shed the newspapers trumpeted the fact that the Mexicans had invaded. The War of 1846 was on.[94]

The textbooks selected in this example are old; but little has changed. For example, take a look at what PBS has to say on the subject:

> The United States, fueled by new technological breakthroughs and inspired by the concept of "Manifest Destiny," confidently expanded its

---

[92] Casner and Gabriel, *Exploring American History* (Harcourt Brace: New York 1938).

[93] Tryon, Lingley, Morehouse, *The American People and Nation* (Ginn and Company: New York 1943).

[94] Glenn W. Price, *The Polk-Stockton Intrigue*, (The University of Texas Press: 1967).

territories westward. The young country was regarded
as a "go-ahead" nation, looking forward to a future of
seemingly endless possibilities for itself and its people.
Meanwhile, Mexico struggled to maintain control
over the vast expanses of land it had inherited from
Spain following its long war for independence.
Lacking the resources to settle much of its territory
and suffering from deep internal political divisions,
Mexico looked to the past for its sense of meaning,
back to a time when "New Spain" had once promised
to be the continental power of the New World.[95]

I hardly know what to say about such an incredibly facile analysis. It
reads like parody.

This example reveals that we must be careful about our analysis.
Historians may prefer psychological motivations or structural
motivations for historical events depending on the situation, but the
important thing is to be wary of the available information. When the
subject is Adolf Hitler, you can find thousands of books
encompassing psychological explanations of one kind or another.
What was the source of Hitler's madness? Various answers are given
– medication, self-hatred, knowledge that he himself may have been
of partial Jewish descent, his failed aesthetics, and so on. What is
universally ignored by mainstream historians is the issue of Hitler's
backers (because these were British and American) and the occult
aspects of the Third Reich (presumably because these are too bizarre
and too similar to certain aspects of the American and British
governmental structures.) So here the psychological explanation is
preferred.

On the other hand, especially for the Left, a structural analysis of
the JFK assassination is adopted without fail. The issue of individual
motive is utterly stricken from all discussions of the matter, as if this
could never be an issue in the murder of a President. Arguing
otherwise is too Machiavellian, as Walter Cronkite once observed.
Mental states, so important in understanding the motivations of the
Third Reich, are eliminated entirely from the main parties involved in
the assassination. They only become important again when analyzing

---

[95] http://www.pbs.org/kera/usmexicanwar/prelude/

the sanity of *those investigating the murder,* as asserting possible motives in the JFK case is *a priori* evidence that one has lost one's grip.

One good example of this is in Michael Shermer, editor of *Skeptic* Magazine. He adopts a dichotomy that precludes interpreting historical events in any other way but his own. He notes the difficulty of historical interpretation and then defines conspiracy out of existence: "This turns out to be an impossible task because historical events are highly *contingent,* by which I mean *a conjuncture of events occurring without design.* Contingencies, in turn, interact with *necessities,* or *constraining circumstances compelling a certain course of action.*" (Italics in the original.)[96]

Well, conspiracies definitely don't exist then, since historical events are by definition occurrences without design! He doesn't back down from this statement; later in the book, he states that a modern historian will be interested in "contingency (unplanned conjunctures of events)" and "necessity (constraining forces and trends compelling certain actions)" for *every* event.[97] One wonders how anything ever gets done, given that people are always deterministically reacting to random events.

It has been shown time and again that such views eventually serve to limit thought, and to constrain people's thinking into paradigms, which grow ossified and immovable over time. This is despite (or perhaps because of) the fact that many of the world's greatest intellectual achievements have occurred outside academic circles. Einstein, as everyone knows, was a patent clerk. Leon de Foucault, inventor of the famous pendulum that moves in alignment with the Earth's rotation, was soundly rejected by the world's scientific community when he first presented his ideas. At the time of his invention he was a mere lab assistant. The fact that he had done something none of the mathematicians he served stunned and embarrassed them.[98]

ADOPTING A FRAMEWORK

---

[96] Michael Shermer, *The Borderlands of Science* (Oxford University Press: 2001), 72.
[97] Ibid., 304.
[98] Amir D. Aczel, *Pendulum: Leon Foucault and the Triumph of Science* (Washington Square Press: New York 2003), 104-110.

What we need then, it seems to me, is a rough framework for interpreting events as they happen. All of us who do research have had the experience that, as soon as a story is announced, we immediately realize that the story is either false or a cover for something else. This happened to me recently in the case of the alleged New York terror cell, which I will discuss in a moment.

The reason researchers are frequently able to "see through" what I am calling "conspiratorial events" (CE) is because they have internalized a framework that enables them to do so. The most important thing to realize is that it isn't ideologically driven, unlike, say, Schumpeter; it tries to best accord with the facts, given what one knows about historical reality.

Further, conspiracies occur for precisely the opposite reason that Shermer gives. Those who are in power have more influence over historical events than those not in power, and they tend to behave in typically human, self-interested ways. Machiavelli explains this perfectly:

> I maintain that one finds in history that all
> conspiracies have been made by men of standing or
> else by men in immediate attendance on a prince, for
> other people, unless they be sheer lunatics, cannot
> form a conspiracy; since men without power and
> those who are not in touch with a prince are devoid
> alike of any hope and of any opportunity of carrying
> out a conspiracy successfully.[99]

He goes on to spell out why this is so: (1) If men without power try to form a conspiracy, they can't let it go on without an informer destroying the group. This is an extremely valid point which is obvious, for example, from viewing the war on drugs. The truly powerful movers and shakers within the system of illegal narcotics remain in power and, indeed, frequently appoint themselves to investigate. Meanwhile street dealers are knocked out left and right, because they have no power. (2) Men in power (and it does tend to be men) have access to the person they are conspiring against. This should be obvious; only those with direct access to John Kennedy,

---

[99] Niccolo Machiavelli, *The Discourses* (Penguin Books: New York 1998), 402-403.

for example, could influence the path of the limousine in Dallas to take the hairpin turn and slow down to a speed where the shooting became feasible. (3) Such men are the primary beneficiaries of a change in power, with regard to ownership of property or whatever the infringing prince is doing to create the desire for removal, and they therefore perform a cost-benefit analysis for an overthrow.[100] Certainly relevant to the Kennedy assassination is that he had angered many different segments of the aristocracy, including *nouveau riche* Texas oilmen, banking elements, and various representatives inside the military-industrial complex.

We know that hard-edged reasoning occurs in business. Pfizer, in a famous example, decided from an actuarial standpoint that it made more sense to kill people by giving them faulty artificial hearts rather than fix the problem with the hearts. It was a simple cost-benefit analysis which caused the corporation to murder roughly 300 people.[101] When we know corporations can behave in this manner, is it insane to believe that governments can follow suit?

Not at all.

In fact, we know that governments (that is to say, people, the leadership in governments) frequently behave as sociopaths. Anyone who has studied the Vietnam War or lived through it, or analyzed Henry Kissinger's reasoning for the bombing of Cambodia, knows that such behavior is possible. Anyone who has read the Operation Northwoods documents (presented to Kennedy by Lyman Lemnitzer, and proposing that the U.S. kill John Glenn, among other things, to blame it on Cuba) or has witnessed George Bush's Charlie McCarthy smile when announcing that the Iraq War was over when it clearly wasn't, understands this. We should therefore not rule out government involvement *a priori* in any event. We have to look at the facts of each individual case.

Machiavelli tells us that in cases of conspiracy, the men in charge of the conspiracy appoint themselves to investigate it.

In the Kennedy assassination, of course, this was the Warren Commission, which was in large part directed by former CIA

---

[100] Ibid., 403.
[101] "Lawsuit Settled Over Heart Valve Implicated in About 300 Deaths," *The New York Times*, 25 January 1992, http://www.nytimes.com/1992/01/25/us/lawsuit-settled-over-heart-valve-implicated-in-about-300-deaths.html

Director Allan Dulles and Nazi enthusiast, Rockefeller lawyer, and presidential advisor John J. McCloy. In the case of the 9/11 Commission, this was directed by Executive Chairman Philip Zelikow, who co-wrote a book with Condi Rice and produced untrustworthy transcriptions of the Cuban Missile Crisis in order to downplay and hide JFK's opposition to the Joint Chiefs.[102]

Any theoretical model is defined by a particular set of characteristics. The one I am proposing as the following set of attributes:

(1) We assume that, when it comes to large-scale events that have some impact on the globe, it is unlikely the whole truth will be transmitted by the major media, owing to their allegiances. We therefore will be on the lookout for incongruous evidence, often presented in the earliest reports of an event, tending to go against the official narrative.

Examples:

In the Kennedy assassination, there were confusing reports that the weapon found in the Sixth Floor had been either a British Enfield[103] or a 7.65 German Mauser.[104] Only later did it become a Mannlicher-Carcano. However, in this instance, the identification of the Mauser, which was actually documented by the officer who found the weapon, makes more sense than the Carcano, since it is a high-velocity weapon whereas the latter is not. The incongruities didn't end there; the rifle found by Eugene Boone and Seymour Weitzman had a barrel that extended 3 to 4 inches further than did Oswald's Mannlicher-Carcano.[105]

During the 9/11 attacks, it was immediately reported on the major networks that Osama bin Laden was the culprit behind it. No evidence was presented for this assertion, and none has been forthcoming. And yet every news report assumes to this day that this is not only true, but patently obvious. How bad is the lack of evidence against Osama? The FBI's "Wanted" poster of him does

---

[102] "Crafting a new historical genre," http://hnn.us/articles/10256.html
[103] Jim Garrison, *On the Trail of the Assassins* (Warner Books: New York 1991), 98-99.
[104] James Fetzer, ed., *Murder in Dealey Plaza* (Catfeet Press: Peru, Illinois 2000), 75.
[105] Robert Sibley, "The Mysterious, Vanishing Rifle in the JFK Assassination," *The Third Decade,* Volume 6, # 6, September 1990. Obtained at the Poage Legislative Library, Penn Jones Collection, Baylor University.

not include the 9/11 attacks![106] In addition, FBI Director Robert Mueller indicated that the Bureau had "not uncovered a single scrap of paper" leading to evidence of Osama's involvement.[107]

These sorts of incongruities should be immediate red flags.

(2) Our model proposes that the internal structure of conspiratorial events tends to lead up the chain to those with a significant degree of control over the event itself. By identifying players who had definite but limited impact over an event, we are able to trace by steps upward to the prime movers.

Example:

Without becoming unduly complex in the space of this essay, these sorts of associations can be seen quite clearly in the Kennedy assassination. Obviously the placement of Allan Dulles on the Warren Commission set off alarm bells, given that Kennedy had fired him as head of the CIA. There are many more, and valuable work has been done examining people who are only peripherally connected to the assassination, such as Gary Underhill. Our model also proposes that we follow figures who may well have been deeply connected, such as E. Howard Hunt, without *stopping* at Hunt or those who may given him orders. At all times we must let logic dictate what the span of control is for any given individual – and if certain actions are taken that go beyond say, for example, what Lyndon Johnson was capable of doing, then we cannot place the assassination at the feet of LBJ.

(3) Since theoretical models can only achieve – in general – approximations, we keep in mind that we can only make initial assumptions and then bolster them by additional evidence. Our first tentative hypotheses with respect to a given event can then later be confirmed or disconfirmed as evidence continues to accrue. We must also be cognizant that further evidence may counter our whole approach and reveal that the event in question is not a conspiratorial event but represents a truly random accident.

Example:

The 9/11 event has been a billowing mushroom cloud of hypotheses, including the absence of planes entirely, the detonation of the buildings, and so on. When building a structural model of the event, the chain of reasoning is only as strong as its weakest link.

(4) The model proposes that conspiratorial events are

---

[106] See for yourself: http://www.fbi.gov/wanted/terrorists/terbinladen.htm.
[107] http://www.commonwealthclub.org/archive/02/02-04mueller-speech.html.

fundamentally *analogous* to one another and this leads us to compare and find links between them. Often the people themselves are relevant.

A REAL-WORLD EXAMPLE

There were many people who knew on the date of September 11, 2001, that something was wrong. Some people even described themselves having feelings that took them back to the Kennedy assassination, as they realized the official story had major problems. In the course of their researches, probably without ever making it explicit, they had internalized the set of circumstances that leads one to understand conspiratorial events. Like a good investigator who learns what to look for in a murder case, these people had developed solid intuitions that worked as a kind of shorthand and sped up their investigation of the event.

This happened to me, and no doubt many other researchers, with the alleged bust of the New York terrorist plot. The facts that came about were so immediately problematic (and reminiscent of other events) that one couldn't help but draw the obvious conclusion.

Like the Miami terrorists, they appeared to be thoroughly confused, possibly mind-controlled, or even retarded.[108] Even *The Economist* magazine pointed out what a mess the Miami terrorists are. This is extraordinary since this outlet has been the voice of the British financier class ever since it was launched in 1843 to sell an earlier version of globalist economics (and, incidentally, led directly to the Irish potato famine). When even *The Economist* won't buy a story like this, it has to be for embarrassment at the crudity of the propaganda.

We might also think of the shoe bomber, Richard Reid, who attended the notorious Finsbury Park mosque and recruited into an MI6-infiltrated "terrorist" group before boarding that fateful plane with his idiotic plan, thus forcing us all to take our shoes off prior to flying.[109]

---

[108] "Those alleged terrorists arrested in Miami," *The Economist Magazine* 29 June 2006, http://www.economist.com/research/Backgrounders/displaystory.cfm?story_id=7117914.
[109] Chris Marsden, "Britain: Why did it take so long to bring Abu Hamza to

As soon as the New York terrorists were arrested, problems began to crop up.

The men planted fake bombs:

"The suspects were arrested Wednesday night, shortly after planting a 37-pound mock explosive device in the trunk of a car outside the Riverdale Temple and two mock bombs in the backseat of a car outside the Riverdale Jewish Center..."[110]

In a strange detail mentioned by every news report, they bought a digital camera at Wal-Mart.

"The defendants bought a digital camera at Wal-Mart to take pictures of targets, they spoke in code, and they expressed their hatred of Jews on several occasions, according to a criminal complaint."[111]

This makes sense, I suppose, since in this terrible economy terrorists might want to take advantage of Wal-Mart's low prices and 24-hour service.

Although they had converted to Islam, they had trouble grasping the religion:

"Payen, who officials said is of Haitian descent, occasionally attended a Newburgh mosque. His statements on Islam often had to be corrected, according to Assistant Imam Hamin Rashada, who met Payen through a program that helps prisoners re-enter society."[112]

Despite their apparent adherence to the Islamic religion, they do like to smoke:

"During the hearing Cromitie told the judge he had used marijuana on Wednesday but was clear-headed enough to understand the proceedings."[113]

They had been infiltrated from the very beginning by the FBI:

"Even at that early stage the police was aware of his intentions. An informant posing as a member of an extreme Pakistani group was in contact with Cromitie at the mosque and remained closely

trial?" 20 February 2006,
http://www.globalresearch.ca/index.php?context=va&aid=2014.
[110] Robin Schulman, "At N.Y. Mosque, Many Suspected an Informant Before 4 Were Arrested in Plot," 22 May 2009, http://www.washingtonpost.com/wp-dyn/content/article/2009/05/21/AR2009052100424_pf.html.
[111] Ibid.
[112] "FBI: New York terror suspects sought 'to bring death to Jews'," 22 May 2009, http://www.haaretz.com/hasen/spages/1087134.html.
[113] Ibid.

associated with him, using hidden audio and video equipment to record conversations over the next 11 months."[114]

They were, by all accounts, idiots:

""The group was relatively unsophisticated, penetrated early and not connected to any outside group," said Charles Schumer, one of New York state's two US senators."

"Despite the apparently naive nature of the conspiracy, Michael Bloomberg, mayor of New York, said it showed that threats against the city were "sadly all too real.""[115]

"Relatives said the defendants were down-on-their-luck men who worked at places like Wal-Mart, a landscaping company and a warehouse when they weren't behind bars. Payen's lawyer said he was "intellectually challenged" and on medication for schizophrenia. Marilyn Reader said he has "a very low borderline" IQ."[116]

The government improved upon the staged Miami incident in that the group had been infiltrated for over a year before being set up into a harebrained scheme which the government can then take credit for foiling. In fact, it was the FBI agent who got them their weapons. As some know, this same thing happened during the 1993 attack on the WTC, except in that case the FBI refused to substitute fake bombs, leading directly to the attack.[117]

Although this particular incident is too small-scale to really be worth a full cover-up, as is the case for the various assassinations of the 1960's and 1970's, it does show how the same skeptical reasoning can be employed to take issue with such events as they are reported in the major media.

And it doesn't have to stop with government events. Conspiratorial events happen all the time, and most of them get reported. For example, it turns out that "every psychiatric expert involved in writing the standard diagnostic criteria for disorders such

---

[114] Ed Pilkington, "Police: Men planned terror attack in New York to avenge deaths of Muslims," 21 May 2009, http://www.guardian.co.uk/world/2009/may/21/new-york-terrorism-plot-synagogues.
[115] Ibid.
[116] "NYC terror case latest of many homegrown plots," Associated Press, http://news.yahoo.com/s/ap/20090521/ap_on_re_us/us_temple_plot.
[117] Ralph Blumenthal, 'Tapes Depict Refusal to Thwart Bomb," *The New York Times,* 28 October 1993, http://www.nytimes.com/1993/10/28/nyregion/tapes-depict-proposal-to-thwart-bomb-used-in-trade-center-blast.html.

as depression and schizophrenia has had financial ties to drug companies that sell medications for those illnesses, a new analysis has found."[118] In other words, the drug companies benefit via sales, so they pay experts to claim that the drugs are necessary, even if they aren't. A conspiracy theory? No, merely self-interested capitalism in action.

All of us have to make assumptions. We assume there is an external world. We assume we are not brains in vats. The key thing is to have, insofar as it is possible, justified assumptions within a conceptual framework allowing us to reference past events and interpret future incidents. The media gives you one option: Listen to us. The model outlined in this essay, it seems to me, is another. Armed with a framework, we are better equipped to understand the unfolding saga of corruption.

As Carl Sagan wrote:

> The business of skepticism is to be dangerous. Skepticism challenges established institutions. If we teach everybody, including, say, high school students, habits of skeptical thought, they will probably not restrict their skepticism to UFOs, aspirin commercials, and 35,000-year-old channelees. Maybe they'll start asking awkward questions about economic, or social, or political, or religious institutions. Perhaps they'll challenge the opinions of those in power. Then where would we be?[119]

I can't say it any better than that.

---

[118] Shankar Vedantam, Experts Defining Mental Disorders Are Linked to Drug Firms, 20 April 2006, http://www.washingtonpost.com/wp-dyn/content/article/2006/04/19/AR2006041902560_pf.html.
[119] Carl Sagan, *The Demon-Haunted World* (Ballantine Books: New York 1996), 416.

MANNING MARABLE'S MALCOLM X

"What I tried to say then, and will try to repeat now, is whatever hand pulled the trigger did not buy the bullet. That bullet was forged in the crucible of the West, that death was dictated by the most successful conspiracy in the history of the world, and its name is white supremacy."
- James Baldwin, "No Name in the Street" [120]

"In our time, Malcolm X stood on the threshold with the oppressor and the endorsed spokesmen in a bag that they could not get out of. Malcolm, implacable to the ultimate degree, held out to the Black masses the historical, stupendous victory of Black collective salvation and liberation from the chains of the oppressor and the treacherous embrace of the endorsed spokesmen. Only with the gun were the Black masses denied their victory."
-Huey Newton, "In Defense of Self-Defense."[121]

"Such a man as Malcolm is worthy of death."
-Louis Farrakhan, in *Muhammad Speaks*, Dec. 4, 1964

"Do something about Malcolm X enough of this black violence in New York."
-J. Edgar Hoover, telegram to the FBI New York office, June 5, 1964

WHO WAS MALCOLM X?

[120] Baldwin, James. *The Price of the Ticket: Collected Nonfiction 1948-1985* (St. Martin's Press: New York 1985), 510.
[121] Newton, Huey. *To Die For the People* (88)

As permanent a fixture in American history as George Washington, brother Malcolm was a gangster, a thief, an inmate, a scholar, an orator, a demagogue, a revolutionary, a messenger of peace and a hero. He lacked formal education beyond the 9th grade but crossed swords with Arthur Schlesinger and William F. Buckley, knew and inspired Maya Angelou, Muhammad Ali, James Baldwin, Ossie Davis and Ruby Dee, met with countless foreign dignitaries, and grew into a man whose words carried massive international historical impact. In our own time he is a powerful influence on popular culture, perhaps even moreso than Martin Luther King, often considered his counterpart although they only met once. He is forever associated with the Civil Rights movement, although unlike many of his contemporaries he was not, for most of his life, congenial to its aims. And he had a genius for communication, both in terms of his ability to select a phrase for maximum effect and in deploying his gifts of diction and inflection; he was the Mozart of the spoken word.

In his new book, the eminent founder of the African-American studies program at Columbia University, Manning Marable, attempts to decipher the contradictions and complexities of Malcolm X's life and death. In a sad turn of events, Professor Marable died just as his book was released to the general public, meaning that this is truly his last word on the subject. It was a project that took him ten years to complete, with access to FBI files that have only been released during that period, and the resulting book has been worth the wait.

The author points out that Malcolm's life has always been understood as being made up of discrete, ascending chapters. The legend begins with little Malcolm Little, son of a Garveyite father murdered by the Klan. Then comes his gangster phase, wearing a conk inspired by Latino 'Zoot Suit' gangs and adopting the name Detroit Red. Then his prison education – ("I'm proving to you that Jesus is black," he tells the chaplain) – and conversion to the Nation of Islam. Afterward follows his career as the chief spokesperson of that organization ("the white race is the devil.") Then, finally, his expulsion from the NOI and pilgrimage to Mecca, at which time he becomes an ambassador for a much broader revolution. Marable finds this all too facile, too comfortable, too shaped by the man himself in collaboration with Alex Haley. What results us a mass of detail as self-contradictory and complex as any of our own lives would be.

FATHER TO THE MAN

Of all the key events that "created" Malcolm X in the early years, the one that may have played the largest role is his own father's death. The inherent lesson in the disparity of justice for black and white could not have been plainer. Of Earl Little's death at a set of railroad tracks, there were two versions: one, the accepted story of the authorities, and two, the one transmitted by their victims. "The Lansing coroner ruled Earl's death accidental, and the Lansing newspaper account presented the story that way as well. Yet the memories of Lansing blacks as set down in oral histories tell a different story, one that suggested foul play and the involvement of the Black Legion."[122] The Black Legion were a Klan offshoot that wore black robes instead of white ones.

Another event that stained itself on Malcolm's memory occurred once he had moved to New York. Struggling, but enchanted with the city, he found himself staying at the famous YMCA on west 135th in New York and washed dishes at Jimmy's Chicken Shack, where Charlie Parker had done the same a decade earlier.[123] It was during this period that a singular event took place in Harlem.

In 1943, the Metropolitan Life Insurance Company, known today for its association with "Peanuts" characters in friendly television commercials, brokered a deal to build a housing complex where the famous Savoy had stood in Harlem. The Savoy had been closed by a bogus campaign that blamed an explosion of venereal disease on prostitutes in the area. Met Life, with the agreement of Mayor LaGuardia, came forward with a plan to build a whites-only tenement. After much public outcry, it was determined that similar tenements in the future could not be segregated, but the Met Life tenement went on as planned. [124] Young Malcolm thus understood that racism in the North was every bit a structural component of everyday society as in the South. In some ways, things have not

---

[122] Marable, Manning. *Malcolm X: A Life of Reinvention* (Viking: New York 2011), 31.
[123] Ibid, 49-51.
[124] Ibid, 57-58.

changed much to this day. One thinks of the Katrina situation, in which the Wall Street Journal immediately crowed how, after the terrible Katrina storm passed through Louisiana, natural disaster could provide an impetus for white businesses to move in.

Malcolm determined it made little sense to fight in a white war. He was designated 4-F, in one of the humorous anecdotes of his life, after he told military recruiters he couldn't wait to join the army in order to "steal us some guns and kill crackers."[125]

The final key event of his early life was, of course, being sent to prison. Under the tutelage of the Nation of Islam (NOI), writing letters directly to the Honorable Elijah Muhammad, he educated himself and began to effectively channel his gifts. It should be noted that the Nation of Islam had the respect even of revolutionaries who did not share their religious views at the time. The most important influence on Huey Newton, Robert Williams, wrote positively of Elijah Muhammad in his seminal work *Negroes with Guns*.[126] For its part, there is no doubt that the NOI gave a tremendous focus to Malcolm and helped him understand the nature of American propaganda. In one of the most famous passages in modern American literature, the former Detroit Red looks up definitions of the words "white" and "black," finding their connotations anything but neutral. "I could spend the rest of my life reading," he reflected. "I don't think anybody ever got more out of going to prison than I did."[127]

Marable points out that Malcolm does not say that he ever perpetrated crime in Harlem, but the author finds this illogical. He feels that there is some revisionist history in Malcolm's account. It's not clear why Marable thinks this, except that Malcolm would have been struggling to make ends meet during this time and presumably it would have been easier to steal closer to home. Perhaps, but it's unclear what his evidence would be.[128]

Marable also calls attention to the odd passage in the *Autobiography* detailing Malcolm's friend Rudy, who tells a story about putting talcum powder on an old rich man for money, which causes

---

[125] Ibid, 59.
[126] Williams, Robert. *Negroes with Guns* (Wayne State University Press: Detroit 1998), 74.
[127] Marable, 91.
[128] Ibid, 61.

the old man to reach climax. [129] From this, the author concludes: "Based on circumstantial but strong evidence, Malcolm was probably describing his own homosexual encounters with [his white friend] Paul Lennon."[130] One looks in vain, however, for Marable's source for this conclusion, although presumably it comes from some of the interviews he undertook that inform the rest of the chapter. For myself, it would not matter at all whether he was gay or not; but for Marable to throw this comment into his book without further elucidation or sourcing is both bizarre and unfortunately reminiscent of JFK books that have sex as their main theme.

NOI DAYS

Malcolm wrote a letter to President Truman that arrived on June 29, 1950 in which he asserted that he was a Communist. Not coincidentally, the FBI began its monitoring of Malcolm X on that day. [131] Seven years later, Malcolm's position had grown to the point that the FBI realized that if they could insert a split between him and Elijah Muhammad, they had a chance at driving a stake into the Nation.[132]

Marable's key insight into the ultimately regressive nature of the Nation of Islam is in its position of separation: "The Nation found it difficult to make headway, largely because its appeal was apolitical; Elijah Muhammad's resistance to involvement in political issues affecting blacks, and his opposition to NOI members registering to vote and become civically engaged, would have struck most Harlemites as self-defeating."[133] Indeed, the NOI's position is civically self-defeating by definition; non-involvement in political affairs is a means of draining one's political power, not increasing it. There was always a tension between the NOI's apolitical stance and Malcolm's desire for change. His well-known August 10, 1957 speech, for example, is very early and yet sounds a bit like (a more militarized, to be sure) Martin Luther King in his alluding to "a full

---

[129] Haley, Alex, and Malcolm X. *The Autobiography of Malcolm X* (Ballantine Books: New York 1989), 143.
[130] Marable, 66.
[131] Ibid, 95.
[132] Ibid, 140.
[133] Ibid, 109.

voting voice" and "equal rights struggle."[134]

> The FBI never understood that the NOI did not seek the destruction of America's legal and socioeconomic institutions; the Black Muslims were not radicals, but profound conservatives under Muhammad. They praised capitalism, so long as it served what they deemed blacks' interests. Their fundamental mistake was their unshakable belief that whites as a group would never transcend their hatred of blacks.[135]

Malcolm preached misogynistic attitudes frequently as a member of the Nation of Islam.[136] This continued to be a problem throughout his life, as he does not appear – at least in Marable's account – to have been entirely successful as a husband and father. And with a little thought, one finds this plausible. Malcolm was on the road all the time, and serving in an institutional framework that sets powerful boundaries on women's activities. It should not be surprising that Betty Shabazz, as Marable reports more than once, was often unhappy. However, Marable also reports that Shabazz was unfaithful to Malcolm, although the principal instigator of these stories is Louis Farrakhan, who has his own agenda(s) to promote. Farrakhan (then known as Louis Walcott) was a young man at the time and a Nation of Islam recruit. He claims to have modeled himself after Malcolm and refers to him as "the father I never had."[137]

Nevertheless, it was never in the cards for Malcolm to have been a follower rather than a leader. One should remember that Elijah Muhammad was not merely the spiritual leader of the organization; he was also God. And, bearing this in mind, the Nation of Islam behaved like any similar monarchy in its obsession with bloodlines. This therefore made Malcolm not a candidate to take over the NOI, as many outsiders felt would be a natural progression. Marable notes: "…most members of the patriarch's family rejected him as a potential heir apparent because he was not related by blood."[138] This,

---

[134] Ibid, 133.
[135] Ibid, 154.
[136] Ibid, 116.
[137] Ibid, 114.
[138] Ibid, 118.

of course, made Malcolm a rival – and, later a hated one – in Muhammad's mini-fiefdom. Ironic that in an organization devoted to rising up against white power, that in large part it should duplicate some of the worst aspects of that power. This was certainly one factor playing into Malcolm's eventual separation from the NOI. However, the main issue at hand was his incredible natural leadership.

Most people are familiar with the Reese Poe incident, vividly dramatized in the Spike Lee biopic on Malcolm. On April 26, 1957, a pair of police officers nearly beat Poe to death, before they were stopped by several hundred Harlemites, which by the time of Malcolm's arrival had grown to several thousand. After marching to the police station, Malcolm signaled his power to the police by using hand signals to direct the crowd away in lockstep unison. In the film, Peter Boyle delivers the line (drawn from life): "No one man should have that much power." Marable correctly notes that this is the Origin Story, the beginning of Malcolm X as a public figure on the national, and later world, stage.

The NOI, and indeed Malcolm himself, made overtures to white racists. It came about, as Malcolm himself stated, that unlike dealing with Northern whites, there were "no illusions." (138) They also, ironically, had the same goal: total segregation. As Marable points out, if you come from a framework in which racism will never be conquered and separation is the only means by which peace can be maintained, then there is a kind of devastating logic to the collusion. Marcus Garvey himself had made the same mistake – and Malcolm's own father had been a Garveyite. The grouping of Nazis and NOI members never made practical sense, however, and the flirtation was short-lived. In 1961, the NOI did meet with George Lincoln Rockwell, who had been a mainstream conservative for a while, even working for William F. Buckley, but later turned into a deeply committed Nazi. Rockwell spoke of his admiration for the Elijah Muhammad in having, in effect, "cleaned up" the black population.[139]

THE SEPARATION INCREASES

Mike Wallace owes his career to the Nation of Islam; in 1956, he produced a short film called The Hate that Hate Produced, a tabloid,

---

[139] Ibid, 199.

Bill O'Reilly-style piece about NOI racism against whites. Jack Gould of the New York Times dismissed it as journalism without a conscience, referring to the "...periodic tendency of Mike Wallace to pursue sensationalism." This flies in the face of his later image as the Steadfast Seeker of Truths on *60 Minutes*, the bastion of anti-sensationalism. "It gave him the break he needed," writes Marable.[140] One thinks of Dan Rather, who became "the most trusted man in America" by breaking out as a cub reporter and lying about what he saw in the Zapruder film. However, as a practical matter, the film fueled white fear against black "extremists" and increased Malcolm's public profile. He became a staple of television programs and did extraordinarily well on them.

Malcolm tended to destroy all comers; his unflappable presence, speaking voice, intelligence and command of the facts caused him, in debates, to crush the talking heads on television. However, he did meet his match in a debate against Bayard Rustin. Rustin simply pointed out that for all Malcolm's rhetoric about changing political conditions for blacks, this could not happen as long as the NOI remained a political nonentity. The author feels (with good cause) that this resonated with Malcolm and was one of the propositions that caused him to doubt the NOI's ultimate efficacy, contributing to the break..[141] Indeed, in later speeches comparing the police to an occupying force in black ghettoes, he unconsciously echoed Frantz Fanon's *The Wretched of the Earth*.[142]

Publically, he continued to maintain disregard for the efforts of the Civil Rights movement, denouncing "the Farce on Washington" as having been co-opted by white liberals.[143] Marable calls his view on the events "a gross distortion of the facts" but this was a natural outgrowth of Malcolm's perspective at the time. He could not accept that there was any level of sincerity on the part of Kennedy or other white liberals, nor could he appreciate the public relations coup it represented. The fact that white faces were interspersed with black faces on television during the March on Washington arguably did a great deal to get across the idea of the permanence of assimilation. For many, racial segregation would no longer be respectable or

---

[140] Ibid, 161-162.
[141] Ibid, 177.
[142] Ibid, 187.
[143] Ibid, 256.

acceptable – a small victory, perhaps, but global change is measured in such small victories.

As with his later remarks about the Kennedy assassination, that "the chickens had come home to roost"[144], Malcolm made an error of judgment. In his defense, however, his position (given the historical background) made some sense in terms of realpolitik. And in both cases he may not have been 100% wrong. In the last analysis, however, Malcolm failed to recognize that in the first case (the March), it actually did provide a benefit to his people, and in the second case (JFK), his death truly was a blow to the people's struggle. This time change, as Sam Cooke sang, really was coming.

Following the infamous "chickens" remark, Malcolm, as most people know, angered Elijah Muhammad for causing media trouble for the NOI. Muhammad silenced him indefinitely. Beyond this, of course, it also provided a ready excuse to rein in a powerful underling who had made himself potentially dangerous (in his mind, at least) to his power. "As the weeks lurched forward, the Nation boiled over with enmity toward Malcolm, spurred on by John Ali and Raymond Sharrief, who used their positions at the top of the NOI hierarchy to trigger a cascade of invective down through the ranks. Gross rumors of Malcolm's disloyalty to Muhammad swept through the Nation…"[145] Malcolm's imposed silence thus had the additional advantage of not allowing himself to respond to these rumors. There were several reasons for the NOI's treatment of him: (1) Malcolm had discovered that Elijah Muhammad had been busy impregnating several of the Nation's secretaries, including one of his old girlfriends; (2) as noted, many within the family monarchy, including Muhammad himself, grew concerned about the protégé's massive public profile, and (3) the FBI had paying members of the NOI itself to stir up trouble.
MECCA

There were several reasons for Malcolm's eventual separation from the Nation of Islam and Marable goes through them in some detail. It seems clear that, for someone as intelligent as Malcolm, it must have begun to seem obvious that those beliefs which he held above all others could not be correct. Elijah Muhammad had committed moral wrongs, and now the Nation folded itself on him to protect his secrets, including firebombing his home. Malcolm had an

---

[144] Ibid, 256.
[145] Ibid, 279.

extremely difficult and no doubt painful correction during this period, in which he was forced to renounce some of his prior public statements and make a public declaration of a change of heart and mind. Malcolm wrote in a letter to Alex Haley, on April 25, 1964: "I began to perceive that 'white man,' as commonly used, means complexion only secondarily; primarily it describes attitudes and actions."[146]

> For the first time, he publicly made the connection
> between racial oppression and capitalism, saying 'It's
> impossible for a white person to believe in capitalism
> and not believe in racism.' Conversely, he noted,
> those who had a strong personal commitment to
> racial equality were usually 'socialist or their political
> philosophy is socialist.' What Malcolm seemed to be
> saying was that the Black Freedom Movement, which
> up to that point had focused on legal rights and
> legislative reforms, would ultimately have to take aim
> at America's private enterprise system.[147]

It was at this point that Malcolm X became one of the most dangerous men in America. His removal from the NOI, although it brought many hardships, freed him; he became a general ambassador to the oppressed world. He embodied resistance to the Genghis Khan morality of mass capitalism.

Malcolm decided to bring evidence of America's racial crimes before a United Nations tribunal. FBI wiretaps recorded his plans and, recognizing their potential global impact, the FBI shared the information with the Department of Defense, military intelligence, and the CIA.[148] As Malcolm had embarked on a world tour of sorts, traveling to meet Castro in Cuba and with Saudi Arabian royalty, among others, the FBI followed him along every stop. Attorney General Nicholas Katzenbach sent a memo to J. Edgar Hoover suggesting at one point that Malcolm might be prosecuted under the "...Logan Act, which made it illegal for citizens to enter into unauthorized agreements with foreign governments."[149] In a sense

---

[146] Ibid, 310.
[147] Ibid, 336.
[148] Ibid, 343.

this underscores the incredible nature of Malcolm's personal stature – greeted as a foreign dignitary at every spot, and tracked by a U.S. government that recognizes his extreme level of threat, despite his lack of resources. This in spite of the fact that, as the author points out, they were well aware that he had come to a "…spiritual epiphany in Mecca, [broken] with the Nation, and even [made] overtures to the Civil Rights movement."[150]

His movement away from his former views even distressed his new followers in the newly created MMI (Muslim Mosque, Inc.) and OAAU (Organization of Afro-American Unity). When Malcolm, after returning from Mecca, talked about equality for women, members of his own group grew confused and even angry.[151] "Yet in other ways Malcolm had become more tolerant. He announced his new views about interracial romance and marriage: 'How can anyone be against love? Whoever a person wants to love, that's their business."[152] A remarkable statement for someone who had declined association with anyone white, in principle, just a few years before.

Unfortunately, without the organizational structure of the NOI, Malcolm found himself surrounded by volunteers, friends of friends, and loose associates. This was a ripe opportunity for infiltration, and the government made the most of it.

> The most important police operative inside the MMI and OAAU was Gene Roberts. A four-year veteran of the U.S. Navy, Roberts was admitted to the NYPD academy…By late 1964 Roberts had become an integral member of the MMI security team, standing guard at public events as one of Malcolm's bodyguards…Through Roberts, all of MMI's and OAAU's major decisions and plans would be promptly revealed to the NYPD.[153]

THE ASSASSINATION

---

[149] Ibid, 366.
[150] Ibid, 373.
[151] Ibid, 374.
[152] Ibid, 386.
[153] Ibid, 422.

Like John Kennedy, Malcolm eventually found himself surrounded by powerful enemies capable of guaranteeing his death.

> Finally , the convergence of interests between law enforcement, national security institutions, and the Nation of Islam undoubtedly made Malcolm's murder easy to carry out. Both the FBI and BOSS placed informants inside the OAAU, MMI, and the NOI, making all three organizations virtual rats' nests of conflicting loyalties. John Ali was named by several parties as an FBI informant, and there is good reason to believe that both [Malcolm associates] James Shabazz of Newark and Captain Joseph fed information to their local police departments as well as the FBI…the CIA had kept up surveillance of Malcolm throughout his Middle Eastern and African travels.[154]

Although Marable does not definitively point the finger at government agency, he does point out that the FBI continues to refuse to reveal "thousands of pages of evidence connected with the crime." What national security object would be threatened by revealing such evidence, from 1965, is unknown.

Marable goes further than most academics in the direction of conspiracy, but we might be able to go still further. To the well-traversed political researcher, the assassination of Malcolm X has the morphology of a government hit. That is to say, the duck both walks and quacks.

SECURITY STRIPPING

Researchers are familiar with the details in other assassinations. Let's run through them briefly:

JFK – The car rode without a bubble top, and the secret service men (who had been out drinking all night) were ordered off riding on the car's running boards. (There is video evidence showing this.) As Fletcher Prouty pointed out, the hairpin turn and open windows would never have normally been allowed for a presidential

---

[154] Ibid, 422.

motorcade.

RFK – Kennedy was led away from his security team at the main door due to a last-minute change of plans which caused him to go through the kitchen pantry in a huge crowd of people.

Fred Hampton – Hampton's friend and treasurer is an FBI informant who puts drugs in his coffee to ensure that Hampton is asleep when is murdered by Chicago police.

9/11 – 9/11? Yes, 9/11:

"Captain Charles Leidig, the Deputy for Command Center Operations at the NMCC, takes over temporarily from Brigadier General Montague Winfield and is effectively in charge of the NMCC during the 9/11 crisis. Winfield had requested the previous day that Leidig stand in for him on September 11. Leidig had started his role as Deputy for Command Center Operations two months earlier and had qualified to stand in for Winfield just the previous month. Leidig remains in charge from a few minutes before the 9/11 crisis begins until about 10:30 A.M., after the last hijacked plane crashes. He presides over an important crisis response teleconference that has a very slow start, not even beginning until 9:39 A.M."[155]

Now, having said all this, can we guess what happened at the Audubon the day Malcolm was murdered? Marable tells us: "The principal rostrum guards that afternoon were Charles X Blackwell and Robert 35X Smith, unusual choices as they did not usually serve in this role and had little experience guarding Malcolm."[156] His normal, more experienced security people were out of the area.

On the day Malcolm gave his talk, just as he was getting started, a commotion broke out in the audience. The commotion had been staged to draw the attention of security, which it did. FBI man Gene Roberts was also in the room, toward the rear, and approached after the argument broke out. After this diverted the security guards, another distraction occurred in the form of a smoke bomb near the entrance to the building. Taking this as his cue, Willie Bradley stood up and shot Malcolm in the chest with a hand-held shotgun. Once this happened, two other men – Talmadge Hayer and Leon X Davis – came forward with pistols and emptied them into him as well. Bradley took off down a side door to make his escape, while the latter two instead tried to run out the main entrance, which meant

---

[155] Thompson, Paul. *The Terror Timeline* (Regan Books: New York 2004), 364.
[156] Marable, 436.

they had to run all the way back from the stage through the people, smoke, and confusion. Hayer was shot, and then beaten up by several followers as the other men escaped.

Both police and emergency services behaved appallingly on the day.

Although one of the city's major medical centers was only several blocks away, no ambulance arrived from the Audubon, which is why Malcolm's own men had to run to the emergency room to pick up a gurney...MMI and OAAU members were outraged when the police finally showed up. 'Their appearance was so ridiculously late,' Mitchell recalled, 'that one tearful woman yelled and waved them aside, saying, 'Don't hurry; come tomorrow!'"[157]

The police conducted a leisurely investigation, with some officers literally with "their hands in their pockets." For the rank and file, this was simply a case of a black man who had overstepped his bounds and had been asking to be killed, and brought to bear all the seriousness to which they normally investigated a gang shooting in a black neighborhood. For those in positions of authority within the police structure, more sinister activity had taken place. James 67X, an associate of Malcolm, had left the scene after the shooting and returned soon after. He found himself being asked why he left by the police. "...'How do they know that I left?...They must have photographed the whole thing.' Days later the police showed him 'a seating plan...where everybody was seated in the Audubon Ballroom."[158]

> For the detectives working the case, too many facts didn't make sense. The request from Malcolm's team that the usual police detail be pulled back several blocks from the Audubon seemed strange, as did the police's agreement to do so in light of the recent firebombing. The detectives were also suspicious when they learned that nearly all the MMI and OAAU security had been unarmed and that none of the audience had been checked for weapons.(445)

---

[157] Ibid, 444.
[158] Ibid, 443-444.

However, none of this is as unbelievable as what happened that evening. Malcolm was killed at approximately three in the afternoon. Police arrived late, but nevertheless did eventually show up at the scene. However, no forensic examination was ever performed. The Audubon was a recital hall, after all, and there was a dance scheduled for seven that evening. In one of the more astonishing turn of events from all of the terrible history of the assassinations of the 1960s, the police agreed to leave the scene and allow cleaning people to take over by six. The George Washington Birthday Party went off as planned.[159] Four hours after Malcolm X was murdered, people were dancing in the very same hall.

AFTERMATH

The FBI had "at least five undercover informants [in the ballroom] at the time of the shooting." We will never how many really were in there, of course, but based on the released documents and interviews this was the number Marable came up with. These included Charles Kenyatta, who "cashed in one his political kinship with Malcolm for decades" and Benjamin 2X Goodman[160]. He notes: The NYPD had two priorities in conducting its investigation: first, to protect the identities of its undercover police officers and informants, like Gene Roberts; and second, to make successful cases against NOI members with histories of violence. Its hasty and haphazard treatment of forensic evidence at the crime scene suggested that it had little interest in solving the actual homicide.[161]

The media also had little interest in pursuing the facts. As with other high-profile assassinations in the 1960s, the major media immediately began a propaganda campaign in support of the state-approved version of events. Marable quotes several national publications on their reactions. The New York Times editorial characterized Malcolm as having used his "many true gifts to evil purpose" and blamed his own "exaltation of fanaticism" as leading to his own death. Henry Luce's CIA-endorsing TIME Magazine went further, taking a similar line in blaming Malcolm for causing his own

---

[159] Ibid, 445.
[160] Ibid, 467-468.
[161] Ibid, 451.

death, but then also invented a story in which "characteristically [Malcolm] had kept his followers waiting for nearly an hour while he lingered over tea and a banana split at a nearby Harlem restaurant." Malcolm, a fastidious and militarily precise man, is thus made ridiculous in playing on the stereotype of the "lazy Negro" to its white, comfortably racist audience.[162] For his part, the Honorable Elijah Muhammad made a public statement: "Malcolm was a hypocrite who got what he was preaching."[163] White America seemed to agree.

As noted, one of the assassins had been captured and beaten by the crowd. He eventually faced trial along with two other former Nation of Islam members, selected seemingly at random by police.

> The prosecution's star witness was Cary 2X Thomas (also known as Abdul Malik). Born in New York City in 1930, by his mid-twenties he had become a heroin addict and narcotics dealer. For years he was in and out of jail on drug charges, and in early 1963 was assigned to Bellevue Hospital after a nervous breakdown. In December of that year he joined Mosque No. 7, but soon left, siding with Malcolm in the split. Thomas's extremely short tenure in the Nation meant that he knew relatively little about the organization, or the reasons for Malcolm's separation. After detectives interviewed him, the district attorney's office decided to arrest him as a material witness. For almost a year he was held in protective custody. On one occasion, highly disturbed, he set fire to his jail mattress."[164]

Shades of the state retaining Marina Oswald for months, or the embarrassing key witness in the James Earl Ray assassination, a man so drunk he was unconscious at the time of the assassination.

Unfortunately, Cary 2X Thomas misidentified the shooter, and claimed to have seen the other two people (Johnson and Butler) at the scene of the murder, despite the fact we know they were not

---

[162] Ibid, 454-455.
[163] Ibid, 461.
[164] Ibid, 466.

involved. During the court proceedings, Talmadge Hayer himself announced that Johnson and Butler were definitively not involved. Unfazed, the judge continued with the trial. Then Betty Shabazz took the stand. As she was leaving, she pointed at all three men and screamed, "They killed him!" Defense requested a mistrial, which was denied. The three men were convicted. (465)

Perhaps the most incredible part of this story concerns Willie Bradley, the man who actually fired the first, killing shot against Malcolm X. He continued his life as a petty criminal afterward, but was arrested for bank robbery in 1968. Marable tells the story:

"On April 11, 1968, the Livingston National Bank of Livingston, New Jersey, was robbed by three masked men brandishing three handguns and one sawed-off shotgun. They escaped with over $12,500. The following year Bradley and a second man, James Moore, were charged with the bank robbery and were brought to trial. Bradley, however, received privileged treatment, and he retained his own attorney separate from Moore. The charges against him were ultimately dismissed; meanwhile, after a first trial ending in a hung jury, Moore was convicted in a second trial.

Bradley's special treatment by the criminal justice system in 1969-1970 raises the question of whether he was an FBI informant, either after the assassination of Malcolm X or very possibly even before. It would perhaps explain why Bradley took a different exit from the murder scene than the two other shooters, shielding him from the crowd's retaliation. It suggests that Bradley and possibly other Newark mosque members may have actively collaborated on the shooting with local law enforcement and/or the FBI."[165]

It most certainly does, and it is very good of Dr. Marable to address the issue in his otherwise highly academically respectable book.

There are many fascinating details and side stories to follow in the tangle of Malcolm's life and murder. The weblike structure of personalities and events will also be familiar to those who have done research into the other major assassinations, and I am unable to chase them all in the course of this review. The reader is directed to Marable himself, whose book, for all its flaws, is a major entry into the field to be sourced and argued with for years. It's a shame that Marable himself will not be around for those discussions. One thing,

---

[165] Ibid, 475.

beyond everything, seems clear: The existing power structure had no use for post-Mecca Malcolm X. A dismissible ideologue, dangerous but containable, became a genuine threat to capitalism itself, which deals with such people as white blood cells do a virus.

Malcolm had been in an almost constant state of transformation – indeed, his rise from Detroit Red to unofficial ambassador to the revolutionary is as outsized as myth. Marable calls its 'reinvention' and asserts that some of this myth was self-created. Perhaps, in the sense that all of us, consciously or unconsciously, might invent or assemble a persona for ourselves. And yet the major events of his life all unquestionably happened; his public statements provide a record of his evolution.

The real tension exists in one simple fact: Malcolm's story is one of the great human stories, but it is not one of the great American stories. This is not Horatio Alger, Benjamin Franklin, or even John Galt. His success as a human being is not measured in terms of wealth or prestige. It is measured in moral terms. His was not a life to be evaluated within the basic assumptions of mass capitalism. He cannot be reduced to a postage stamp or a children's book. In his final days, Malcolm recognized that this is a worldwide struggle of the people versus mass capitalism, which was out of control in 1965 and now out-Orwells Orwell. This marked him for death in our society. It also made him one of the great figures of world history. If we ever figure out why this is true, we might have a chance at social transformation – a reinvention, as Manning Marable puts it.

RAT'S NEST: TWO BOOKS ON THE CIA-NAZI-DRUGS NEXUS

The Essential Mae Brussell: Investigations of Fascism in America
edited by Alex Constantine
Feral House, 359 pp, $18.95

Drugs as Weapons Against Us
by John Potash
Trine Day, 420 pp, $18.60

It was a masterstroke of Quentin Tarantino's film *Inglorious Basterds* to make a point of Nazi flight in the wake of a losing war. Lt. Aldo Raine (Brad Pitt), after learning that a Nazi captive is going to burn his uniform and never wear it again, informs him: "Yeah, we don't like that. We like our Nazis out in the open," right before carving a swastika into his forehead. Then, in the immensely satisfying end of the film, Aldo does the same to Colonel Hans Landa (Christoph Waltz), an officer who has made a deal to ensconce himself into the loving arms of the U.S. military. In the opening scene, Landa describes the Jewish people as rats; but in the end, it is Landa who is the rat, scrambling to desert the sinking Reich.

In watching the film, I recognized that the ending might be more satisfying for me than for some others, because many people do not know that Nazi officers and scientists flooded into the U.S. after World War II or how much influence they had over our history. Following the "good war," the Pentagon and the CIA seemed hell-bent on giving cover to as many Nazis as possible. Some of them went into the U.S. Army historical division (the person who wrote the official Pentagon history of World War II was an official historian of the Reich) and others were scientists who would hold the chief positions at NASA and elsewhere for decades yet to come.

One character who did escape to America after the war was Reinhard Gehlen, where he became a willing instrument of the military establishment's desire for a Cold War. CIA Director Allen Dulles funneled over $200 million to Gehlen. The idea was that Gehlen would use his old contacts to set up lines of information against the Soviets, while also training mercenary forces to fuel revolutionary movements within Russia. (Does this sound familiar?) Indeed, the CIA itself, created in 1947, was largely a combination of the old OSS (Office of Strategic Services) and Gehlen organization members. (Brussell 61) Additionally, as Mae Brussell notes in a new collection of her work put out by Feral House, "Some of [Gehlen's] spies were schooled at the CIA's clandestine base in Atsugi, Japan, where, in 1957, a young Marine named Lee Harvey Oswald was posted to the U-2 spy plane operation there." (Brussell 23)

Mae Brussell has been described as the Queen of Conspiracy numerous times, which is a belittling nickname even if not expressed with such intent. She was, instead, one of the most brilliant intuitive thinkers who ever lived, and legendary at analysis. I never met her, alas, but heard many stories about her from my friend John Judge, as she and Penn Jones were his mentors. And while recordings of Mae are easy to find (the best collection can be accessed at www.worldwatchers.info, along with other Mae-related material), print has been rare. This new collection, edited by Alex Constantine, contains her most well-known pieces and examples of her prodigious facility. Having the book in print is also nice for those who wish to slowly digest the material, as listening to her radio shows can be challenging for the uninitiated as she zips from topic to topic.

What Brussell specialized in was milieu. She figured out who the players were in any situation she investigated, then who was related to whom, and who was connected to whom, and eventually she revealed the dark tunnels underneath the American dream. As she discovered, the fascists rule in secret while our Punch and Judy "democracy" keeps people distracted. Her ability to analyze events this way made her prescient, as when she warned Mary Jo Kopechne's family that she was about to be killed shortly before Chappaquidick, or even writing a warning letter to Richard Nixon.

There are other observations sprinkled throughout the book with deep consequences. For instance, she mentions in passing that Clay Shaw, the subject of the Garrison trial and the later Oliver Stone film *JFK*, happened to die a few weeks after being publicly outed as a CIA asset in Victor Marchetti's *The CIA and the Cult of Intelligence*. (B 115) Like Penn Jones, Brussell did a great deal of work on suspicious deaths, and the timing of such deaths. She also observed that Hale Boggs, a Warren Commission member who expressed doubts about the final report's conclusions, died one month after the Watergate arrests were made, in a plane crash. According to a Los Angeles Star story, she points out, Boggs was planning to make public links between the Kennedy assassination and Watergate. (B 113)

Brussell also wrote astonishing exposes of CIA operations such as the Symbionese Liberation Army's kidnapping of Patty Hearst, which occupies a large section of the second half of the book, and even the deaths of West Coast rock and roll stars. As she points out, the two biggest bands of the era became associated with murder and hate – the Beatles via Vincent Bugliosi's ridiculous conspiracy theory regarding Charles Manson, and the Rolling Stones via the Hell's Angels murder of an unstable fan during the Altamont concert. (B 277)

What is the purpose of all these intrigues? She relates it to the underlying white power structure. As she puts it:

> Competition for jobs between Indians, Blacks, and Chicanos is caused by a racist power structure in this country that refuses to allow jobs in the first place…IQ tests have been proven to be racist, thereby dropping off otherwise qualified students. By keeping minorities out of the professions except entertainment and athletics, the white community can keep their residential areas white, their schools white, their churches white, perpetuate the racism. (B 133)

Despite the articles in this book being decades old, none feel out of date. They feel more relevant than ever. Indeed, what has happened is that the power structure has gotten *better* at it. They've turned pro, both in a raw political sense but also in a cultural sense. The list of musicians that Brussell talks about is sobering: Hendrix, Joplin, Morrison, Phil Ochs, Gram Parsons, John Lennon, and Otis Redding, among others. Is there anyone on the current cultural scene of that quality and impact? The obvious answer is no. When Lennon looked like he was getting ready to re-enter the mainstream, he was gunned down by another lone nut, which America seemingly specializes in producing. In response to this, Brussell has the single best advice I have ever read about such murders:

> When someone is gunned down who is controversial, has political enemies, is hated by the wealthy and well-organized religious movements, and is an open opponent of government policies at home and abroad, that kind of murder requires much more inquiry into the background of the assassin. (B 284)

Exactly.

As if to prove the timeliness of Brussell's observations, a new book – *Drugs as Weapons Against Us* by John Potash – will be coming out next February on Trine Day. Potash, who previously authored *The FBI War Against Tupac Shakur*, states in his book that he is building on the work of other researchers such as Peter Dale Scott, Brussell, and Constantine, the aforementioned editor of *The Essential Mae Brussell*. There is a slight difference in focus as explained by the title Potash gave to his work, but it fits snugly alongside in terms of the research and point of view.

Potash tackles a broad spectrum of topics that converge on the topic of drugs, with an emphasis on the 1960s to the present. He first sets out some of the historical background of the opium wars and then quickly gets into government experimentation and abuse of mind-altering chemicals. And it's here that Potash may create some controversy with readers of his book: he doesn't support marijuana use or LSD use for mind expansion. As he points out, the CIA used the latter for purposes such as disorientation and truth extraction, but not for achieving higher levels of consciousness (Potash 32). He even quotes William S. Burroughs, famed author and heroin addict, as saying "LSD makes people less competent." (P 37)

The book also suggests that Ken Kesey and Tim Leary may have been (unknowingly?) doing the government's bidding in promoting drug use. Kesey himself actually participated in an MK-ULTRA (mind control) experiment in 1960. In describing the Magic Bus, Potash notes with interest several people connected to it who had military and/or blueblood backgrounds, and whose primary function seemed to be financing and encouraging figures such as Neal Cassady and Kesey. Further, what would somebody like the CIA's John Gittinger be doing at Acid Test parties featuring the Grateful Dead? How did the Grateful Dead break out of the San Francisco scene to become a national success? The answers are both convoluted and fascinating, and in the book.

Drugs as Weapons Against Us gradually throws up a pattern constituting a street-level cultural war. COINTELPRO went after movements like the Black Panthers and targeted individuals like Dr. King and Malcolm X; at the same time, the CIA infiltrated the music scene. Many people find this difficult to believe – why would government forces be interested in someone like Jimi Hendrix, for example?

> Scotland Yard claimed to quote Hendrix's attending doctor, Dr. John Banister, saying Hendrix was 'dead on arrival…[dying] in the ambulance or at home.' The ambulance workers denied this. The hospital's official report had Hendrix's hospital arrival time as 11:45 and pronounced dead at 12:45. [Monika] Danneman claimed Hendrix was alive when the ambulance workers took Hendrix from their apartment. If Hendrix was dead on arrival, what happened during that hour? Scotland Yard couldn't give Danneman an answer. When she asked what Dr. Bannister had to say about it, Scotland Yard told her that he had been struck off England's official medical register of all doctors in the country, without any further explanation. (P 145)

At the same time, Hendrix's manager, Mike Jeffery, had connections with the Mafia and FBI and had formerly worked for MI6, Britain's intelligence agency. (P 146) There is more, a great deal more, and the devil is most certainly in the details. It's an incredible story, but just one of a hundred in *Drugs as Weapons Against Us.*

Potash also takes us through the attacks on hip-hop artists, Panther leaders, Bob Marley, and in a startling set of chapters, the murder of Nirvana frontman Kurt Cobain. He also brings us up to date by describing how an unknown party dosed people with acid at Burning Man events and comparing it to the Grateful Dead's long association with LSD. It is literally true that the year after Jerry Garcia died and touring stopped, LSD use dropped considerably in the U.S. "Slate magazine writer Ryan Grim wrote, 'For 30 years, Dead tours were essential in keeping many LSD users and dealers connected, a correlation confirmed by the DEA in a divisional field assessment from the mid-1990s.'" Fortunately for LSD dealers, the band Phish entered the gap to help keep their business rolling. (P 281-283)

The extraordinary scope and detail in *Drugs as Weapons Against Us* makes it difficult to summarize. Readable, compelling, and packed with stunning information, Potash's book works both as a terrific introduction for the beginner and an excellent resource for the veteran researcher. It serves as a kind of textbook to modern American history, covering all the aspects history books typically ignore. Taken together with the Brussell volume, these are vital and necessary defenses of the mind against the idiotic, and sinister, propaganda fed to us daily by major media.

SHORT TAKES & MEMORIALS

Here I collect memorials I've written, all for the Examiner, in the wake of the passing of three men over the last few years: Daniel Schorr, Carlos Fuentes, and Chinua Achebe. The first was of historical importance; the others were too, but also personally important in terms of influence. In addition, here are a few of the observational pieces I've done to address specific topics in the areas of 9/11, civil rights, and other matters.

DANIEL SCHORR, 1917-2010

Daniel Schorr was a key figure in the Congressional investigation into CIA abuses that began in 1975. It began when Gerald Ford was engaged in an off-the-record discussion with Arthur Sulzberger and other big shots at the New York Times and let it slip that the U.S. had been involved in conspiracies to assassinate heads of state. One of the reporters immediately asked "Domestically?" to which Ford replied, "Foreign!" This was supposed to be an off-the-record talk, as noted, but the story was leaked to Schorr, who was at CBS News at that time. (Schorr had been recruited by the great Edward R. Murrow in 1953.)

> Ever since the investigation of C.I.A. plots began,
> there has been a growing question of whether United
> States activities might in some way be connection
> with the shooting of President Kennedy.[166]

Schorr's report led directly to the Pike Report and the Church Committee, whose documents showed that the CIA had been implicated in the assassination of such figures as Patrice Lumumba and others. When Frank Church started getting too hot to handle, Ford intervened and appointed his Vice President, Nelson Rockefeller, to head up an "independent" investigation. The Rockefeller Commission included such luminaries as Operation Northwoods author Lyman Lemnitzer and former Joe McCarthy supporter Ronald Reagan, and it produced a report that naturally whitewashed a great deal of this activity. (Besides the obvious, journalist Seymour Hersh had already shown during Rocky's confirmation hearings that he had made large "donations" to people

---

[166] "Ford Seeks Curb on Data on Plots," *New York Times*, 3 November 1975

in the government's sphere of influence, such as Henry Kissinger.) However, the report was forced to disclose that the CIA had forced LSD trials on U.S. citizens, done aerial spraying over San Francisco, run a private bordello (the receipts are in the public record, and they are hilarious), and started the MK-ULTRA project to attempt mind control for the purpose of creating agents for targeted assassination.

A good example of the conflict created by this tug of war is this telephone call between Senator Inouye (who would become the first head of the Senate Intelligence Committee, a post created by the Church Committee) and Henry Kissinger:

Henry Kissinger and Senator Inouye:
12 November 1975

I: Sorry I didn't return your call earlier. I just found out about it.

K: That is alright. I am sorry this has turned into a test of manhood. I am not trying to keep anything from you. I am not going to let you have these documents. We are not trying to maintain that our aid is based on the Sinai agreement. I trust you and your associates but the way our classified information is being handled is getting to be a dangerous thing for the country. I can cope with it but my successors will suffer. I have the highest regard for your committee, but my worry is how will I handle the other Committees. My Committee leaks more than yours. Some day come over for a drink and I will explain what worries me. I want you to know it has nothing to do with you and I will send you these documents as official documents.

I: OK. And I accept your invitation.

K: Any documents we give to the Senate Foreign Relations Committee appear in the newspapers. We have a problem on how to conduct diplomacy when this happens and how to conduct matters with the

Congress.

I: That is a problem.

K: We will talk about this but not on the telephone.
You won this one and I will send the documents.

I: It is not a matter of winning.

K: OK.

(Oh, incidentally, while all this was going on, the head of the CIA was
William Colby. Colby had been criticized internally for being too
cooperative with the various committees and confirming too much of
what the CIA had been doing. Colby was let go and replaced
by...drumroll...George H.W. Bush. The same George H.W. Bush
who allegedly had zero experience with the CIA, despite the fact that
he *now has a building named after him*. Bush ended all cooperation.)

> From the outset I had been, of course, aware that
> many in the administration did not approve of my
> cooperative approach to the investigations, and I had
> felt myself increasingly isolated from the White
> House team as the year progressed. I had been
> criticized for not categorically denying Hersh's story
> at the very beginning; I had been criticized for turning
> material on Helms over to the Department of Justice;
> I had been chided for being too forthcoming to the
> Rockefeller Commission; I had been scolded for not
> stonewalling at every Congressional hearing.[167]

> But I would not and could not change my basic
> approach. I believed in the Constitution; I believed in
> the Congress' constitutional right to investigate the
> intelligence community; and I believed that, as head
> of that community, I was required by the Constitution
> to cooperate with the Congress.[168]

---

[167] William Colby, *Honorable Men* (Simon & Schuster: NY 1978), 443-444.
[168] Ibid, 444.

Note the difference in attitude. DCI Richard Helms had lied to Congress about CIA involvement in the Chilean coup of Salvador Allende and was proud of it. His CIA friends paid his ridiculous $2000 fine.

Although this has been disputed, it hardly seems possible to argue that Bush did not replace Colby in order to carry out a coverup.

> Then, on November 3, Church was approached by reporters outside of his Senate hearing room and asked by Daniel Schorr about the firing of Colby and his likely replacement by Bush. Church responded with a voice that was trembling with anger. "There is no question in my mind but that concealment is the new order of the day," he said. "Hiding evil is the trademark of a totalitarian government." Schorr said that he had never seen Church so upset.

Church's former speechwriter Loch Johnson is quoted as saying:

> 'The nomination of George Bush to succeed Colby disturbed him and he wanted to wind up the speech by opposing the nomination...Church wanted me to stress how Bush 'might compromise the independence of the CIA – the agency could be politicized.'[169]

The Times noted Bush's background in the article describing the so-called "Halloween Massacre."

> Mr. Bush is an Eastern elitist who has prospered in a Republican Party that has largely turned its back on such persons. The son of Prescott Bush,a Republican Senator from Connecticut, he was educated at the Andover School and at Yale before heading for Texas to make his fortune in the oil business.

---

[169] Webster G. Tarpley & Anton Chaitkin, *George Bush: The Unauthorized Biography* (ProgressivePress: 2004), 292.

He was twice defeated in attempts to win a seat in the
United States Senate, but that did not prevent his
appointment as chief American representative at the
United Nations, chairman of the Republican National
Committee and United States representative in China.[170]

In February of 1976, a month after Bush was appointed, the House
voted to suppress the report. Schorr obtained an advance copy and
leaked it to the Village Voice, which published it. Schorr was
suspended from CBS. (Paley had already tried to censor Schorr's
reporting on Watergate, which had landed the latter on the White
House Enemies List.) He was also investigated by a House ethics
committee, who eventually cleared him in a split vote.

Needless to say, Schorr left CBS.

One footnote: William Colby was found dead in May of 1996,
after deciding to go on a canoeing trip, by himself, without a life
jacket. It was apparently a sudden decision, as he also left the lights
on in his weekend home, his dinner uneaten on the table, his radio
on, and the front door unlocked.

Nominated as Director of Central Intelligence by
President Richard M. Nixon in May 1973, Mr. Colby
led the nation's espionage services through two of
their most turbulent years. On his watch, the Central
Intelligence Agency came under fire as never before,
accused by Congress and the press of a range of
misbehavior that included spying on Americans and
plotting to assassinate foreign leaders.

In many cases Mr. Colby chose, in effect, to plead
guilty with an explanation. Much of what is now
known of the C.I.A.'s history became public because
he disclosed it. For his candor and cooperation with
Congress, he was dismissed by President Gerald R.
Ford in November 1975. A future President, George

---

[170] "Ford Discharges Schlesinger and Colby and Asks Kissinger to Give Up His
Security Post," *New York Times,* 3 November 1975

Bush, succeeded him in January 1976.[171]

---

[171] "Body of William Colby Is Found on Riverbank," Tim Weiner, *New York Times*, 7 May 1996

CARLOS FUENTES: 1928-2012

(Note: There will be other obituaries, eulogies, attempts to get at the whole of Carlos Fuentes, but this is merely my personal remembrance: subjective, incomplete, and with unstable emphases.)

I was always going to be a writer; as a child, my favorite Christmas gift from my parents was a typewriter. I sold my comics to the other kids beginning in the first grade, started writing short stories as a boy, completed a hilariously bad science fiction novella when I was about 11 (and which only a handful of people have seen – you know who you are.) However, it was not until my late teens that I began to think about becoming a novelist, and more specifically a Latin American novelist, in that sacred tradition.

On the surface, this seems unlikely. Growing up in Laredo, my experience with Mexico had more to do with the local nightclubs across the river than anything literary. It is impossible, however, to grow up in that town without certain influences being cast upon you; a culture that includes La Zona, Taco Palenque, Catholic school, and the sing-song cadence of the demented Spanglish we speak in that region. I am not sure how I first got the idea of being a Latin American novelist, but in retrospect it seems almost inevitable to flirt with the notion.

Eventually I would find Jorge Amado, and Gabriel Garcia-Marquez, and Mario Vargas Llosa, and Julio Cortazar, and the almighty Jorge Luis Borges. But before any of those arrived I found Carlos Fuentes. Mexico's greatest novelist. An international "man of letters," a concept that hardly exists anymore. Fuentes was probably not the greatest influence on my younger self at that time, but he was midwife to all the others.

Thinking of Fuentes now makes me recall the Laredo Public Library, which was not a place I spent a lot of time in, having grown up near the local university library. I can see the bum sleeping on the bench outside, hear the twitter of birds on the thin trees, smell that unmistakable odor of unwashed clothes and bad ventilation. But mostly I remember exactly where the aisle was where they kept the books by Carlos Fuentes. It's been more than 20 years, but in my mind's representation I know just where they are.

I am pretty sure I began with a book called *Cambio de Piel (A Change of Skin)*. It was a baffling exercise of a book to me then, and remains terribly flawed now, but it still remains a favorite. There is, as in all of his writing, power there. Fuerza.

When the four of you entered today all you saw was the narrow filthy streets and the packed houses that are all alike, all of one story, all a blind wall with a too wide door of cracked wood, all daubed yellow and blue.

And I was off.

When I first embarked on this adventure (and adventure it seemed), I had a certain trepidation that the culture of the novel was too different, that I would be literally lost in translation. That fear evaporated. Certainly *A Change of Skin* was not like any previous novel I had ever read, being metaphysical, self-conscious, political, and utterly alien and strange. The novel is aware of novelistic construction and deliberately subverts it. The characters give long diatribes about their chosen subjects, at times in the voice of Fuentes, at times not. Then, at the end, we find the author of this book signs his name, "Your ever lovin' Freddy Lambert." The author signs his work with a fictitious name? Or another character, this narrator distinct from Fuentes? (Hint: the 'Freddy' invoked is from Friedrich Nietzsche, although it's hard to imagine anyone calling him Freddy.)

> So here we go, Dragoness. That's called taking the sword in your mouth and swallowing it up to the hilt, and sure enough, the Fair-Haired one told us, "There are eunuchs who have become eunuchs only to win the kingdom of heaven." So, you see, the Gnostics put their balls on the table so that Baudelaire and Breton could be born, and Genet and Miller, so that we could dream the American Dream that enacts the crimes of Monk Ambrose in the feudal castles of Beverly Hills with the bleeding nun, la Belle Dame Sans Merci, Pollyanna Equanil of our masturbating dreams; you can hear his steps on the carpets of the

glass prisons. And in regard to Marcion, when
Polycarp saw him, he shouted, "I know you, First-
Born of Satan!" simply because Marcion, a hipster if
there ever was one, had been the first to understand
that God is the Alien, the entirely Other...

You see what I mean by midwife. He actually mentions *Hopscotch*
(Rayuela) by name in the book, leading me by the nose directly to
Cortazar.

A Change of Skin was written in 1967 and has the hallmarks, as
you can see. But in my teenage self, desiring to know All That There
Is, and being presented with a succession of names, some familiar,
some unknown, I was driven to find out what Fuentes was going on
about. In those pre-Internet days, that meant much time spent in
libraries, for whom (yes, whom) I retain a lasting affection. I can see
now that this altered my taste in important ways, giving me an
unshakable ardor for the Continent, its ideas and customs, its cinema
represented by Herzog and Antonioni watched on poor VHS copies
on television, its languages manifested in my dabbling with French
and German.

This was also during the period in which I became aware of
Freytag's Triangle – the arc of drama – and so there were certain
technical innovations that struck me. In *The Death of Artemio Cruz*, he
distinguishes passages from one another by using first, second, and
third-person narration. In *Distant Relations* the tense changes
continually (but logically). However, beyond technique and the
Continental obsessions, Fuentes did have a flair for gorgeous
observation. In *Distant Relations* (a book that may have been one of
the inspirations for *My Dinner with Andre*; in any case it is in the same
métier) the storyteller remarks:

> The elderly sleep very little, Branly repeats now. They
> feel besieged by the need for vigilance, and in this, old
> age is wise. Adjustments are made so that it is not
> psychologically necessary to sleep as much as before,
> as in the days when one came home worn out after
> poking into every corner of one's grandfather's castle,
> or after playing in the Parc Monceau, after making
> love with Myrtho in a nest of rose-colored

eiderdowns, or after nights beneath the sulphurous lightning flashes of the trenches.

***

There were once Gods, and the Gods were defeated, or taken, or razed without mercy, but now and again they may flex their divinity among us moderns.

As in H. P. Lovecraft, there is a sense of historical foreboding in all of Fuentes' work. Underneath the surface of things there is a past which has been trampled on by those same Europeans whose art we so admire. Sometimes it happens directly, as in the short story "Chac-Mool," from his collection *Burnt Water* (and it is interesting, perhaps, to cross-reference the direct apparition in this story with "The Idol of the Cyclades" from *Blowup and Other Stories* by Cortazar, which features possession), but most often it is inherent in the structures, the people, the social world without direct manifestation. Sometimes this is handled with humor, as in *Christopher Unborn*, in which Mexico decides that a child born on October 12 with the appropriate surname will be "proclaimed PRODIGAL SON OF THE NATION, with practically unlimited powers of election, succession, and selection…MEXICAN MACHOS, IMPREGNATE YOUR WIVES – RIGHT AWAY!
TOMORROW MAY BE TOO LATE
WHEN THE FROST IS ON THE PUNKIN
THAT'S THE TIME FOR DICKIE DUNKIN"

However, in most cases, the historical reality of this living past, which achieved perhaps its most definitive expression in Octavio Paz, is a subject for philosophical reflection, whether in the remembrances of Artemio Cruz or the adventures of Baltasar Bustos in the struggle for Mexican independence in *The Campaign*. The Mexican story of invasion and manipulation from outside countries, conquest and control, is a constant theme of Fuentes's work. It appeared to some extent in his most famous novel – one of his worst – called *Old Gringo*, which has a fascinating subject (what happened to Ambrose Bierce, who disappeared in Mexico?) but a certain laziness in execution.

We're always being remembered for all the wrong things.

126

That probably makes sense in this case, however. It sets the paradigm, fits in with the theme. The past viewed without nostalgia, the old gods respected, the cycles of generative pain acknowledged.

In his story "Constancia," Fuentes describes the feelings of an El Salvadoran refugee couple forced to part with their daughter:

> Stay here, be reborn here, let us die, but you must go
> on living, Constancia, in our name, don't let yourself
> be vanquished, don't let yourself be destroyed by the
> violence of history, you must live, Constancia, you
> musn't yield to exile, you must stem the tide of
> fugitives, at least save yourself, dear daughter, mother,
> sister, don't let yourself be pulled under the current of
> exile, you at least remain, grow, be a sign: they
> survived here. Protect us with your memory, seal us
> with your eyes…

I imagine, I can only imagine; I do not *know* anything, even though I have felt the pain of separation, being far from the one I love, have felt it deeply, to the point of tears. But now I can only imagine them – Constancia, Plotnikov, the dead child – because I finally see them as part of something greater, something I had not understood before. How long, Constancia, did you give life – my life – to your dead?

I understand that better now than I ever have.

I turned out not to be a novelist. Wrote some novels, none I deemed publishable, found a niche as an essayist and film critic, eventually put out some short stories and now am primarily a playwright I've stayed with the written word even when it didn't seem to care for me too much.

We're all more indebted to others, near and far, for the collage that constitutes ourselves. Carlos – hopefully I can call you Carlos – I never met you but I owe you a lot. See you soon, I'm sure.

And don't forget your ever lovin',

Joe Green

CHINUA ACHEBE: 1930-2013

I can't even pretend to understand the complexity and fullness of the life lived by the Nigerian novelist Chinua Achebe, but the failing is mine, not his. I read *Things Fall Apart* when I was perhaps nineteen years old and going through a kind of cultural revolution in my mind. The book found fertile ground to take root in me, as it did with so many others; and in that same year I discovered *Invisible Man* and the *Autobiography of Malcolm X* and, a little later, the writings of Huey Newton and Bobby Seale.

Achebe is gone now. He was one of the unquestioned literary giants of the age, in an age where that is a damnably rare thing, although he remained controversial in the best way possible. Okonkwo, the hero of *Things Fall Apart*, becomes incensed with British colonial rule and winds up killing a fellow African – tainted with British employment – before committing suicide. Achebe is not promoting this, of course. It is a record of frustration rather than a call to action, but it is instructive to note that Achebe's protagonist is, from the perspective of the state, a terrorist.

In reading the book, we come to identify with Okonkwo. We empathize with his position without necessarily agreeing with his choice. And for someone with only the most tenuous understanding of the day to day existence of an African in Nigeria, it is an eye- and soul-opening experience.

There is nothing simple in Achebe's analysis – he was as critical of the internal failures of African rule as of the British colonial mentality – but there is little question of who the right side is in the argument. The same kind of thinking that created Rhodesia from Zimbabwe, birthed from Cecil Rhodes and the Round Table's desire to conquer the world for the benefit of the Union Jack, is the engine of destruction for the peoples of the exploited continents. Should we analyze the perspective that immediately thinks well of a person who has achieved a "Rhodes Scholarship" instead of regarding such an individual with fear and loathing? A Rhodes Scholarship, in the view of most people, represents intellectual achievement rather than a desire for conquest, but failure to understand the origins of things may lead to misunderstanding the key questions of humanity.

On a more literary scale, in his essay "An Image of Africa," he went after Joseph Conrad particularly in *Heart of Darkness*, arguing that Conrad was a racist because Africa became a metaphor used to show the breakdown of one individual, rather than having African characters taken as individual entities in themselves. In a strange way, Achebe was using a decidedly Western idea, adopted from the philosopher Immanuel Kant, that we should maintain respect for human beings and never see them as means rather than ends. I have always agreed with this principle and tried, in my own stumbling way, to adhere to it. His perspective broadened my own, and his work informed my argument in a review I wrote of the film *The Legend of Bagger Vance*, in which a reductionist African-American character is meant to be tolerable because he is represented as good. It isn't the good or evil in representation that matters – as W.E.B. DuBois observed, there can be white Othellos and black Iagos – but rather the empathy inherent in the presentation. We have trained ourselves to ignore this in films, as the hero's friend often dies near the end to fulfill the life goals of the hero, and in life too, by treating people as stepping stones rather than the reason for existing in the first place.

I hate to tag the writer Chinua Achebe with the terrible appellation a "moral teacher," but for me he has been, as well as being a fantastically gifted writer. He opened my horizons and helped me form some of my ideas at a young age, and for that I will be forever grateful. And to the extent to which I have failed to live up to those ideas, the failing is mine, not his.

PORTRAIT OF A NEOCON: FAREED ZAKARIA

I noticed a photo of Barack Obama reading a book. It is still a bit charming to have a President who actually reads books, so I am inclined to view this as a positive. However, the book turned out to be *The Post-American Future* by Fareed Zakaria.

So is this sinister? Probably not, since Zakaria is a big shot (he is the editor of TIME Magazine international, among other things) and the book was a bestseller and one doesn't simply read what one agrees with. Still, this is a bit troubling, since we've been told more than once that the neocons are dead but the suckers keep coming back to life.

So who is Fareed Zakaria? His B.A. is from Yale (he was Scroll and Key – probably too "ethnic" for Skull and Bones) and his Ph.D. is from Harvard. His mentor at Harvard was Samuel Huntington. Huntington is a famous neocon and the author of a number of books, including *Who are We?* and *The Clash of Civilizations*.

By neocon we mean of of course "neoconservative," which is to say a descendant in the intellectual lineage of Leo Strauss, which is to say an opponent of democracy, or if we want to get serious, a fascist. Strauss proposes there are two levels of truth, the exoteric and the esoteric, one set of doctrines he publishes for the outside (which are lunacy by themselves) and then, another, more radical doctrine which is spoken only to his chosen few. It is an attitude that also pervade the religious organization "The Family" which has been much in the news over the last year or so, a group which believes that Jesus held back his real doctrine for the elected few and contradicted the "exoteric" Jesus who seemed to believe in healing the sick, helping the poor, etc.

Allan Bloom was another of these neocons, the author of *The Closing of the American Mind* and whose self was immortalized in his friend Saul Bellow's book *Ravelstein,* highly recommended for anyone wanting to gain further insight into the Ethan Brand-charcoal heart of a neocon. Francis Fukuyama was another, the author of *Our Posthuman Future,* but his ascendancy to become the new Henry Kissinger appears to have stalled despite his own attempts to distance himself from the neocon disasters and also because Kissinger, of course, does not die but lives on like Nosferatu.

Zakaria seems to be the new neocon golden boy. Like so many of these people, he benefited in the public eye from 9/11; in his case, due to an essay he wrote called "Why They Hate Us" which was published in TIME. In this article, he placed the blame for Arabic problem squarely on the Arabs:

> If there is one great cause of the rise of Islamic fundamentalism, it is the total failure of political institutions in the Arab world. Muslim elites have averted their eyes from this reality. Conferences at Islamic centers would still rather discuss "Islam and the Environment" than examine the dysfunctions of the current regimes. But as the moderate majority looks the other way, Islam is being taken over by a small poisonous element, people who advocate cruel attitudes toward women, education, the economy and modern life in general. I have seen this happen in India, where I grew up. The rich, colorful, pluralistic and easygoing Islam of my youth has turned into a dour, puritanical faith, policed by petty theocrats and religious commissars. The next section deals with what the United States can do to help the Islamic world. But if Muslims do not take it upon themselves to stop their religion from falling prey to medievalists, nothing any outsider can do will save them.[172]

Pay no attention to the long history of intervention by Great Britain and the United States in the region, but instead point the finger of blame directly at the Arab world. Of course. We're only here to help.

---

[172] http://www.newsweek.com/2001/10/14/the-politics-of-rage-why-do-they-hate-us.html

Zakaria is the author of two other books besides the one Obama was seen reading. One is called *The Future of Freedom*. I could summarize it here, but the summary provided on Amazon.com is so succinctly astonishing that I just want to quote it in full here:

> Democracy is not inherently good, Zakaria (*From Wealth to Power*) tells us in his thought-provoking and timely second book. It works in some situations and not others, and needs strong limits to function properly. The editor of Newsweek International and former managing editor of Foreign Affairs takes us on a tour of democracy's deficiencies, beginning with the reminder that in 1933 Germans elected the Nazis. While most Western governments are both democratic and liberal-i.e., characterized by the rule of law, a separation of powers, and the protection of basic rights-the two don't necessarily go hand in hand. Zakaria praises countries like Singapore, Chile and Mexico for liberalizing their economies first and then their political systems, and compares them to other Third World countries "that proclaimed themselves democracies immediately after their independence, while they were poor and unstable, [but] became dictatorships within a decade." But Zakaria contends that something has also gone wrong with democracy in America, which has descended into "a simple-minded populism that values popularity and openness." The solution, Zakaria says, is more appointed bodies, like the World Trade Organization and the U.S. Supreme Court, which are effective precisely because they are insulated from political pressures. Zakaria provides a much-needed intellectual framework for many current foreign policy dilemmas, arguing that the United States should support a liberalizing dictator like Pakistan's Pervez Musharraf, be wary of an elected "thug" like Venezuela's Hugo Chavez and take care to remake Afghanistan and Iraq into societies that are not merely democratic but free.

Amazing. Democracies require "strong limits," the Germans "elected" the Nazis (this is a radical oversimplification of what happened – the Nazis never held a popular majority of any kind), Singapore, Chile, and Mexico represent "good" governments and Hugo Chavez is "bad," and the World Trade Organization is "effective" because it is "insulated." This is jaw-dropping stuff, as unsubtle as a propaganda cartoon during wartime.

So what is *The Post-American World* about? It is globalist cheerleading, a book that in its own words describes a world in which America has not declined but it is rather the rest of the world which is rising up to meet us. (Indeed, the Amazon.com page for this book features a fawning interview between Zakaria and propagandist Thomas Friedman.) How glorious! It is part and parcel of the worldview that somehow if all the countries of the world participate in monopoly capitalism's future, that we all can benefit (or, more likely) perish equally. The neocon's idea of democracy is that everybody gets equally reamed. The good news, one supposes, is that great profits can be made by those in the know.

JAMES HOLMES: MK-ULTRA?

This article was written and appeared the day after James Holmes shot dozens of people at the screen of a Batman film. It noted some of the unusual aspects of the case and drew some comparisons. It was the most popular article I ever wrote for the Examiner, and I have not updated it, leaving it to serve as the instant snapshot that it was.

Another lone nut gunman has struck, this time in Aurora, Colorado. The grandson of a U.S. Naval veteran, the 24-year-old neuroscience student James Holmes murdered 12 people and injured dozens of others on July 20, 2012, at a screening of the Batman film *The Dark Knight Rises.*

Many questions surround the shooting (for one, where did he get the money to pay for all his paramilitary equipment?) and some of the answers will no doubt emerge over the next few days. However, for the moment, this article will touch on some of the historical coincidences and other side-aspects of this terrible incident. These things may turn out to be related or not, but for the moment we will be scanning the possibilities.

First is the location: Aurora, Colorado, is less than 20 miles from Littleton, Colorado, where another famous shooting took place on April 20, 1999. There were a number of odd factors in that incident, mostly surrounding the witness statements (identifying several other shooters) and the murders that took place in the ensuing weeks after the initial crime. April 20 is, of course, Hitler's birthday.

July 20 is the anniversary of the failed plot to assassinate Hitler, in which a bomb killed members of his staff but left him virtually untouched. The story was told in a recent film, *Valkyrie.* It also happens to be the 30-year anniversary of an IRA bombing incident in

England that killed 11 people. Otherwise seemingly unconnected, it is interesting to note that the person arrested for this crime turned out to be a 27-year-old graduate in physics.

Although it is too early to tell, it is also remarkable to note the behavior of Holmes, who calmly shot dozens of people in a theater and then calmly surrendered himself to police. This calm echoes the behavior of some other past "lone nut" shooters. Mark David Chapman, who shot John Lennon, is a classic example. After killing him, he sat down and began to read a paperback he'd brought with him, *The Catcher in the Rye*, written by J.D. Salinger, who served in U.S. Army Counterintelligence during World War II in the same unit as Henry Kissinger. This unit, incidentally, was where the Nazi Klaus Barbie was recruited and aided in his escape after the war into South America.

Chapman remained reading at the scene despite being exhorted to leave by the doorman, Jose Perdomo, who coincidentally turned out to be an anti-Castro Cuban involved in Operation 40 after the Bay of Pigs.

The University of Colorado, Denver is mentioned as one of the institutions involved in the MK-ULTRA project of the CIA, which focused on controlling the minds of ordinary citizens so as to induce them into performing assassinations. An account of one such experiment, from all the way back in 1954, showed that it was possible to get individuals to fire a gun and then forget about it. (Incidentally, this is precisely the pattern evinced in the Sirhan Sirhan shooting. Sirhan fired a pistol in the general direction of Robert Kennedy, but then after being apprehended was never able to remember anything about the case.) The New York Times reported on the MK-ULTRA mind control program in 1978, following the wake of the Church Committee Hearings.

Many universities and hospitals were involved in the program and took money to perform the experimentation. The doctors involved in hypnoprogramming American citizens were at the top of their fields – such figures as, for example, Ewen Cameron and Jolyon West.

Related to these incidents is a very interesting book written by Emile Franchel in 1957 called *254 Questions and Answers on Practical Hypnotism*. Franchel was perhaps the most famous hypnotist of his time and his book has some quite interesting information in it. For example one of the questions is "I have heard you say many times during your television programs that a subject under hypnosis 'Cannot be made to do anything that is against his moral or religious beliefs.' How can you say that now?" His answer:

> I am afraid you have not been listening too closely to what I was saying. The only similar remark I have made is, 'IT IS SAID that a person under hypnosis cannot be made to do anything that is against their religious or moral beliefs.' I trust the implication is clear. (77)

He is also asked this broader question: "Has hypnotism ever been used on masses of people, far larger than any auditorium can hold?" His answer:

> From what I can see at this time, hypnotism is being practiced on millions of people at this moment, both inside and outside this country. The hypnotic techniques being employed at present make the hypnotic technicians of the ex-Nazi regime look like well-meaning psychiatrists…One of the great dangers of hypnotism is its simplicity of operation and how easily it can be disguised. (63)

My heart goes out to the victims of this tragedy. It remains to be seen what the final answers will be, but this background may help knowing what to look for.

30 FACTS ABOUT OSAMA BIN LADEN

All of this information is culled from a variety of mainstream sources and is easily verifiable.

1. The CIA, together with the British Special Air Service, trained 100,000 mujaheddin to fight against the Soviets in Afghanistan from 1980-1989, as well as providing weaponry to do so. Osama bin Laden therefore received training and weapons from the U.S. and British governments. Bin Laden supported the mujahideen at the behest of Saudi Arabian royalty.

2. Zbigniew Brzezinski has stated in *Le Nouvel Observateur* that the U.S. began supplying the mujahideen rebels with weapons six months prior to the invasion.

3. One of Osama's brothers, Salem bin Laden, stated in 1985 that Osama was serving as a liaison between the US government, the Saudis, and the mujahideen.

4. Al-Qaeda, which means "the base," is formed in 1991, shortly after the US invasion of Kuwait.

5. Bin Laden traveled back and forth to London many times in the early nineties, and in fact was interviewed in 1996 in London.

6. Both bin Laden and his friend Khalid bin Mafhouz (who lived in London) were heavily invested in the Bank of Commerce and Credit International (BCCI). The BCCI is a notorious criminal enterprise which funded dictators and drug and arms trafficking all over the world, a key element of the Iran-Contra scandal. Oliver North had multiple accounts at BCCI.

7. In 1993, 18 US soldiers were killed in Somalia (the famous

Black Hawk Down incident). Bin Laden is implicated by the US for training some of the individuals involved.

8. In 1994, the Advice and Reform Committee (ARC), based in London, set up a secure communications system for bin Laden to contact London from Saudi Arabia. The phone calls are all routed through Denver, Colorado, using military lines abandoned after being used during the first Gulf war.

9. Also in 1994, during the civil war in Yemen, the Al-Qaeda fighters help the US-backed North Yemen forces defeat Communist south Yemen. This is not the only instance of the US and Al-Qaeda being on the same side of a conflict.

10. Bin Laden was kicked out of Sudan in May of 1996, when he took a C-130 to establish operations back in Afghanistan.

11. The Pakistani ISI (their CIA-equivalent agency) convinced the Taliban in 1996 to give back to bin Laden all the old camps that he ran during the Soviet war. The Pakistani ISI was trained in covert operations by the American CIA.

12. In 1998, ABC News refers to bin Laden as "the most dangerous man in the world." Bin Laden allegedly participates or organizes two US embassy bombings in August and issues a general fatwa encouraging attacks against the West.

13. The Taliban actually put bin Laden on trial in 1998, and formally request evidence from the United States in order to continue with the trial. When the US fails to respond, he is released.

14. A Deutsche Bank joint account of bin Laden and a Pakistani businessman sent $250 million to Pakistan in the year 2000.

15. In March of 2000, Osama bin Laden develops renal failure and is forced onto a dialysis machine.

16. As widely reported in numerous international sources, bin Laden met with CIA officials in a hospital in Dubai where his kidney problems forced lifesaving medical care. This is in July of 2001.

17. On September 11, 2001, America is attacked. US media, fed in part by Richard Clarke's identification, begin stating that bin Laden is behind the attacks.

18. September 11, 12, and 16 & 28 (formal statements): bin Laden denies a role in the attacks. This is confusing because terrorists generally take credit for their successful attacks; otherwise, what is the point?

19. On October 10, 2001, the FBI issued a list of the most

wanted terrorists in the world, with bin Laden at #1. However, the FBI wanted poster does not include the 9/11 attacks in his list of crimes, and is never updated to include these crimes.

20. On November 28, 2001, US forces have bin Laden trapped in Tora Bora, but he mysteriously escapes, according to a US special forces soldier in Fayetteville, North Carolina. Following this incident, several bizarre murder/suicides take place at the Fayetteville military base over the next six months.

21. Over the next few months after 9/11, several bin Laden videotapes surface, all of which depict wildly different-looking bin Ladens. According to numerous published reports all over the international press, bin Laden dies in December 2001. This allegedly is due to pulmonary problems but one must also remember bin Laden was on dialysis whilst hiding in the caves of Afghanistan.

22. FBI Director Robert Mueller notes that they have not found a single piece of hard evidence linking bin Laden or Al-Qaeda to 9/11.

23. In 2003, the CIA went on record admitting they produced a fake bin Laden tape. They allege that the tape was never actually used publicly.

24. October 2004: Right before the 2004 US elections, bin Laden suddenly appears in a videotape taking credit for the 9/11 attacks. He has never done so before.

25. In 2005, the Executive Director of the CIA, Buzzy Krongard, states that it is better for the world that bin Laden remains free. Krongard is a former executive of Deutsche Bank, a bank well-known after 9/11 because numerous "put options" – bets that airline stock would go down – were placed through the bank on 9/11.

26. April 2005 – bin Laden is once again reported to be dead.

27. March 2006 – bin Laden is reported to have died in Iran.

28. September 2006 – bin Laden reported dead by the French press.

29. November 2, 2007 – Benazhir Bhutto remarks in passing that bin Laden is dead. She says that her own security forces may assassinate her. She thinks they want her dead because, among other things, she wants to stop terrorism in Pakistan. She is in fact assassinated that December.

30. May 1, 2011 – US forces allegedly assassinate Osama bin Laden. He is buried at sea. No dialysis machine is found at his home.

It is first reported that one of his wives attempted to help him, then that report is later denied. It is reported that bin Laden had a gun, then that report is denied. NPR claims that although he did not have a gun, he "resisted." How he resisted is not explained. No physical evidence is produced to show that he is dead. Major news organizations all over the US run a photoshopped image of Osama with a bullet hole in his head. Americans across the country celebrate the assassination.

VIOLA LIUZZO & GARY ROWE

These two names may be unfamiliar, but they are connected to an incident which occurred in 1965. It's a grim story and very reminiscent in some ways of the 9/11 story, in particular with respect to the Able Danger revelations.

Viola Liuzzo was a civil rights activist in Alabama who was shot and killed while driving another activist, Leroy Morton, home from a protest. The shots were fired from a passing car with four men in it.

Gary Rowe was one of these four men, and he would testify later that although all four of them had guns, he had only pretended to shoot. He did admit to participating in the planning and, of course, put himself at the scene. He did nothing to stop the incident, and we only have his word that he did not actually fire the gun he held in his hand – although even if true, this hardly seems exculpatory.

Gary Rowe was working for the FBI. He had been working for them since 1960, allegedly as an informant undercover in the Ku Klux Klan.

> In 1975, wearing a bizarre cotton hood that resembled a Klan headpiece without the point, he told a Senate committee that the F.B.I. had known of and condoned his participation in violence against black people and had ordered him to sow dissent within the Klan by having sexual relations members' wives.

> He admitted to taking part in a baseball bat assault on Freedom Riders in Birmingham in 1961 and told the Alabama police that he had fatally shot a black man, never named, in a riot in 1963 and that Federal authorities knew about these incidents. As late as 1983, Mrs. Liuzzo's children brought an unsuccessful

$2 million suit against the F.B.I., charging that through its negligence in recruiting, training and controlling Mr. Rowe, it bore responsibility for the killing.[173]

So Gary Rowe says that the government knew about the fact that he had murdered a black man in 1963, and he nevertheless continued working for them and receiving paychecks from them. He then participated in the murder of an activist who happened to be white, which is why this particular case received national attention. Once this happened, somebody must have told LBJ that Rowe was important:

> The US President, Lyndon B Johnson, had intervened in the case from the very beginning.
>
> The day after Mrs Liuzzo's murder he announced on television that four members of the KKK had been arrested, including Gary Rowe – later revealed as an undercover FBI agent and who testified against the other three.[174]

He must have done a terrific job of informing. The FBI probably gained a whole lot of intelligence from this guy, which they used to destroy the KKK forever, right? After all, if they are paying a guy to beat and kill people, one would hope that it's for a damned good reason.

Unfortunately, the answer is no. The FBI has a long history, under J. Edgar Hoover and through COINTELPRO, of being a racist organization willing to try and induce Dr. Martin Luther King into committing suicide (at minimum), and murder Fred Hampton and Mark Clark, among other Black Panther leaders.

As I mentioned in my first book, *Dissenting Views*, across from the U.S. Justice Department to this day there is a statue of Albert

---

[173] "Gary T. Rowe Jr., 64, Who Informed on Klan In Civil Rights Killing, Is Dead," *New York Times*, 4 October 1998.
[174]
http://news.bbc.co.uk/onthisday/hi/dates/stories/december/3/newsid_4119000/4119070.stm

Pike – the only Confederate soldier to have a statue in Washington, DC. Pike was many things, but one of them was a top leader in the Ku Klux Klan. Gives us some idea about what kind of justice the DOJ is talking about.

MY PLATFORM

It's fair to say that no one is electing me to run any kind of high office. I inhaled, among other things. But these would be positions I would support if I were elected, in the twenty minutes I lived before I died of a sudden heart attack, crashed a plane, or "decided" to send a .22 bullet bouncing around inside my skull.

Assuming I were to run for public office – let's say President since we're being ambitious – these would be 12 of my major tenets. (Needless to say, I am not running for any kind of public office.) Some of these may seem rather extreme, but it's just a function of our present societal situation in which poor people face heavy penalties for crimes they commit and rich and powerful people face virtually no penalties whatsoever, despite the fact that rich and powerful people have far more scope and leeway to do widespread damage.

1. Legalize all drugs under the present California model; i.e., licenses and federal oversight. All drug offenders will receive immediate release. All non-drug offenders shall be moved to federal prisons. All private prisons shall be closed. No person or corporate entity shall ever be granted the power to make profit from the imprisonment of others. Addicts will be hospitalized, of course.

2. Ban all drug advertisements, to include alcohol, in all media. No drug companies (which includes alcohol) can sponsor sports stadiums or anything of the like. They can stay in business – I like a Long Island myself from time to time – but the playing field is completely equal and we want to reduce the all-encompassing nature of alcohol in our society a bit.

3. All presidential candidates must pass a basic skills test,

including general knowledge questions in economics and geography. There will be essays and an oral exam. It need not be excessively difficult – we could perhaps use a general knowledge exam designed for English public school students, for example. We just want to make sure anyone who runs for office isn't a complete fucking toolbag. They need to know the Earth goes 'round the Sun. The question of whether a magical snake talked to Adam and Eve should not be something that requires heavy thought.

4. The death penalty will be federally mandated, with several important provisions and limitations:

All people of color must be convicted by a jury of their peers; that is, the jury must be composed of at least 50% people of color as well. In certain areas in the South, this is raised to 75%. All current death penalty cases will be re-examined by independent investigators to determine the evidence used to obtain their conviction, and will be stayed until approval to move forward is received. The manpower to do these independent investigations shall be found in the local communities and there will also be more people available because all drug cases are going away.

The death penalty will be greatly expanded to include white-collar criminals. For example, attempted bribery of a public official, whether by direct or indirect means, will be punishable by death. The CEO of any company whose products result in even one person's death as a result of malfeasance or disregard shall be charged with murder and put to death. Any executive who can be demonstrated to be knowledgeable of any hazardous material being placed in an area such that it directly or indirectly causes the death of a single individual shall be charged with murder and put to death. Any CEO or executive who knowingly participates in a scheme wherein funds are mismanaged to a degree that 1,000 or more people are put out of work shall be put to death. Any less than that number is merely life in prison with no possibility of parole. All higher-ups shall be responsible for every accountant, so that they are held accountable for their employee's actions; the "I was unaware" defense is invalid.

With regard to war-making, any member of any government body, whether in the legislative, executive, or judiciary branch, who agrees to commit troops to any war under false pretenses shall be put to death. The "I was unaware" defense will also be invalid in this case. It is their responsibility to be aware.

Any police officer convicted of using excessive force which results in the death of a person, accidental or not, shall face the death penalty. Police officers will receive no special protections in prison and will be among the general population; however, it will be made known to the other prisoners who among them was formerly an officer. Any police officer who is found to have committed perjury in the trial of any person, under any circumstances, will face the death penalty. Any police officer who is found to have planted evidence or otherwise aided the false prosecution of any person will face the death penalty.

5. All anti-sodomy laws are hereby repealed. All private sexual activities are legalized as long as they are between consulting adults.

6. Any public relations firm who is found to have knowingly provided disinformation or lied on the behalf of any individual or corporation shall be broken up and the funds used to rebuild infrastructure in the communities of the affected persons.

7. Corporations are no longer persons and have no person-specific protections. Executives must be responsible for their own actions under penalty of law.

8. The "three strikes" law is hereby dissolved.

9. Prostitution is legalized. Federal case centers are set up so that prostitutes can get health care, regular medical checkups, work standard shifts, and obtain their licenses.

10. All medical patents last for 5 years maximum. Minor changes in "medicines" which do not alter their constituent elements do not count for purposes of re-patenting. Anything naturally occurring shall not be patentable; i.e., animals, plants, and people are not patentable, and neither are their cell structures or DNA. Viruses are considered "living" for purposes of non-patentability. Terminator seeds are hereby banned and all patents to that effect are revoked. Any further experimentation along those lines will be punishable by death.

11. Investments can only be in tangible entities and for a tangible productive purpose. All derivatives-based gambling is hereby banned. Any funds invested in that manner and lost cannot be re-collected and all such debts are considered null and void. All companies who solely trade such entities shall be broken up and the monies gained used to rebuild infrastructure in the communities most affected.

12. Companies whose businesses are in the United States but whose primary holdings are in banks other than the United States

shall be subject to increased taxation. Those tax burdens are lessened to the extent that the monies stay in U.S. banks. Those tax burdens are eliminated if those same monies are used to rebuild infrastructure in the communities they serve or fund programs that serve the inner cities. Small profits will be allowed in the operation of these programs for businesses who use this money in such a productive capacity. Businesses would also be allowed to discuss their funding of these programs in their advertising, so there would be an incentive to have the best and most productive assistance programs so as to engender people to buy their products generally.

Anyway, these are just a few of the ideas. It's a start...

CINEMA

I've always loved movies. I worked as a film critic for the San Antonio Current for a few years, and still occasionally work freelance in this area since then. I just finished working as a writer and coproducer on a documentary about the 50th anniversary of the Kennedy assassination called KING KILL 63. I've also been attached to a film called DALLAS IN WONDERLAND as a research and script consultant since 2012 that is still in pre-production. That's a good story too, but will have to wait for a different book…in the meantime, here are two essays on film: one called REALITY AND THE MOVING IMAGE that first appeared in the Political Film Blog, and RFK AND THE PARALLAX VIEW, which is published here for the first time.

REALITY AND THE MOVING IMAGE

It is important that films be hypnotizing, or trance-inducing, or mesmerizing. Why would anyone want to make a film that did not cast a spell on spectators and sweep them away from the tedium of everyday life?[175]

Small groups of people can, and do, make the rest of us think what they please about a given subject.[176]

The most important cultural currency for the United States in the world today is the Hollywood film. In a country without an industrial base, films are our last export. People all over the world imitate and adopt styles derived from entertainment stars. Movies have been chiefly responsible for the remaining vestiges of goodwill still present in our relations with the citizens of other countries. Even when Venezuelan President Hugo Chavez made a speech comparing George W. Bush to the devil, he did so in the context of a Hollywood metaphor: "As the spokesman of imperialism, he came to share his nostrums to try to preserve the current pattern of domination, exploitation and pillage of the peoples of the world. An Alfred Hitchcock movie could use it as a scenario. I would even propose a title: *The Devil's Recipe.*"[177] For his part, British comedian Eddie Izzard proposes two methods for dealing with anti-American sentiments while traveling abroad. "Say you're Canadian," is one.

---

[175] Sharon Packer, *Movies and the Modern Psyche* (Praeger Publishers: Westport, CT 2007), 51.
[176] Edward Bernays, *Propaganda,* (Horace Liveright: New York 1928), 57.
[177] "Chavez: Bush 'devil'; U.S. 'on the way down'", CNN, 21 September 2006, http://www.cnn.com/2006/WORLD/americas/09/20/chavez.un/index.html.

The other is to invoke universally admired heroes: "Just say Shaggy and Scooby!"[178]

For better and worse, a good percentage of the world makes judgments about the United States based on what they see in such films. This was brought home to me in a jarring way with the advent of the DVD. I was house-sitting for my girlfriend's parents one weekend and they had purchased one of the first DVD players. Anxious to see the new technology in action, I put in their copy of *Armageddon*. Having always been interested in languages, I decided to watch the film in French with English subtitles. However, halfway through the movie a sinking feeling overcame me. The film was a bleating hodgepodge of sound and image, as expected – but the sudden revelation that *people all over the world* were consuming this product and making judgments about the United States on the basis of its merits was depressing. It reinforced all the stereotypical notions that one imagines they already believe about us anyway – that we are stupid, sentimental, egocentric, lacking in subtlety: The Ugly American as cultural export.

Fortunately, not all Hollywood films bear the same implied characteristics as *Armageddon,* although most of the popular ones do. There is in fact a strain of American film that attempts to delve into the issues of real life in a real way, some in the level of observational detail in a microscopic sense, and others in the macroscopic perspective of social and structural analysis. Real insights can be gained from such "small films" that concern themselves with individuals above all, as in the work of John Cassavetes, Jim Jarmusch, or the early films of Richard Linklater. Other filmmakers work on a broader canvas, attempting to summarize keystone historical events, such as Oliver Stone in *JFK* and Spike Lee in *Malcolm X*.

It is this latter genre of film that will be the concern of this series. I am going to attempt to make the case that certain American films have been able to get away with a type of historical analysis that often cannot make its way into print – especially newsprint. The peculiarities of the cinematic discourse make such enterprises difficult, but when done well, they are able to create images that intensify the experience and (in the best circumstances) generate

---

[178] Eddie Izzard, from his standup performance in the film *Eddie Izzard: Dress to Kill* (1999).

further interest in the topics at hand.

RADICAL SKEPTICISM

Audiences tend to want characters that always behave in a straightforward manner, even when their own experiences should tell them that human actions can often appear random. They believe, and thereby become involved with at varying degrees, one film or another, one character or another. Often, since movies – more than any other art form – depend on audience identification with the protagonist, their favorite films will be those which correspond most deeply to their own set of experiences. They seem "real," or truthful, in some way. This imprinting is what causes people to think, "Don't open the door," about an onscreen heroine or experience a little thrill when James Bond leaps from an airplane without a parachute. It affects one's perspective to such a degree that deeply individual reactions to films are not uncommon. Although one can get large-scale agreement from the populace occasionally – *Casablanca* or, say, *Gone With the Wind* come to mind – idiosyncratic or seemingly absurd choices are bound to crop up, because of this identification process. Pauline Kael, perhaps the most influential film critic of all time, took everything personally – and wrote some wildly eccentric reviews as a result. James Agee preferred *Key Largo* over *Double Indemnity*. Gene Siskel's favorite movie was *Saturday Night Fever*. Roger Ebert once wrote a film, the amusing if sexually chaotic *Beyond the Valley of the Dolls*. I think there is some evidence to believe that films provide a unique experience which demarcates them from other forms of artistic expression; they seem to supply a kind of mainline into the unconscious, a yellow brick road for the id.

Because of the demonstrably subjective nature of the film experience, there are those who disbelieve in any Hollywood version of anything. At a more primitive level, there can be a knee-jerk response of "It's only a movie." A more sophisticated viewer might observe that all filmmaking is lying, in that one must make subjective choices at every instance when trying to recreate the truth. Why those words? Why that angle? Why that image juxtaposed with the next? Indeed, these arguments are practically as old as film itself. Robert Flaherty never stopped arguing that his 1922 "documentary" *Nanook of the* North was anything but the truth, despite its obvious staging.[179] All the techniques of film, it could be argued, can be used to create any effect that the director wants, thus making any cinematic communication insidiously unreliable. Indeed, in commercial advertising, these methods are used in just such a pernicious manner.

> A McDonald's commercial, for example, is not a series of testable, logically ordered assertions. It is a drama – a mythology, if you will – of handsome people selling, buying, and eating hamburgers, and being driven to near ecstasy by their good fortune…The television commercial has oriented business away from making products of value and toward making consumers feel valuable, which means that the business of business has now become pseudo-therapy. The consumer is a patient assured by psycho-dramas.[180]

What is the difference, one asks, between the director who wishes to instill in his or her audience a desire to eat hamburgers and one who wishes to generate adherents to his personal vision of a particular historical event? Aren't all films propaganda of one kind or another? The author Richard Biskind makes a related observation in the way that modern filmmakers may use such elements once designed for a political purpose: "[George] Lucas's genius was to strip away the Marxist ideology of a master of editing like Eisenstein, or the critical irony of an avant-garde filmmaker like Bruce Conner, and wed their montage technique to American pulp."[181] Of course, to say that Lucas was not using montage in the manner of Eisenstein is not to say Lucas removed *all* meaning from his own work. *Star Wars* has a message and a purpose, on a semiotic level, just as much as *Battleship Potemkin.* And all films, regardless of their intent, employ manipulation at some level, whether for pernicious purposes or not.

---

[179] Richard Barsam, *Looking at Movies* (W.W. Norton & Company: New York 2004), 41.

[180] Neil Postman, *Amusing Ourselves to Death* (Penguin Books USA: New York 1985), 128.

[181] Peter Biskind, *Easy Riders, Raging Bulls* (Simon & Schuster: New York 1998), 343.

A study done by professors at New York University reviewed MRI-readings of people who watched different types of films and measured the extent of their brain activity. Highly manipulative works produced high levels of attention as measured by brain function, while static shots produced low levels. Alfred Hitchcock, as one might imagine, produced the highest results in their study.[182]

We can perhaps begin by acknowledging that there is a sense in which every speech act is a kind of propaganda. There is also a sense in which all forms of radical skepticism have a point, albeit one of limited utility in the real world. All points of view are subjective; I can never be you, and vice versa; and one's beliefs inform one's perspectives and one's susceptibility to ideas at all times. And yet to take the position of radical skepticism seriously, one is led by a short trail to solipsism; for it isn't just *movies* that exhibit this subjective character, but *every institutional fact in the known world*. As the American philosopher John Searle has pointed out, all of our lives are in fact interconnected webs of metaphysical symbols which we utilize with unconscious ease. We accept a world in which certain objects can be paid for with *money;* or, at another level of abstraction, with a *credit card*. We accept the very fact of a mercantile system. We get married, an enterprise which is wholly institutional and metaphysical in nature.

> In the philosophical tradition there is a pervasive further ambiguity in the notion of realism that I need to expose and remove. Typically philosophers who discuss these issues treat them as if they concerned how the world is in fact. They think the issues between, say, realism and idealism are about the existence of matter or about objects in space and time. This is a very deep mistake. Properly understood, realism is not a thesis about how the world is in fact. We could be totally mistaken about how the world is in every detail and realism could still be true. *Realism is the view that there is a way that things are that is logically independent of all human representations. Realism does not say how things are but only that they are.*

---

[182] "Film Content, Editing, And Directing Style Affect Brain Activity, Neuroscientists Show," *Science Daily,* 9 June 2008, http://www.sciencedaily.com/releases/2008/06/080606105432.htm

And "things" in the previous two sentences does not
mean material objects or even objects. It is, like the
"it" in "It is raining," not a referring expression.[183]

There is also a certain sense in which we ourselves are fictional
entities, walking narratives of ourselves. Do we remember every
single instance which occurs to us? No. And yet we never think of
ourselves as anything other than a particular self, and experience an
unbroken chain of selfhood moving through time. The illusion of
particularity (which the philosopher Daniel Dennett refers to as the
illusion of the "central meaner"; i.e., the "I" who appears to be
making the decision to, among other things, write this very sentence)
is a profound existential fact which every one of us takes utterly for
granted.

> Think of Ishmael, in *Moby Dick*. "Call me Ishmael" is
> the way the text opens, and we oblige. We don't call
> the text Ishmael, and we don't call Melville Ishmael.
> Who or what do we call Ishmael? We call Ishmael
> Ishmael, the wonderful fictional character to be found
> in the pages of *Moby Dick*. "Call me Dan," you hear
> from my lips, and you oblige, not by calling my lips
> Dan, or my body Dan, but by calling *me* Dan, the
> theorists' fiction created by…well, not by me but my
> brain, acting in concert over the years with my parents
> and siblings and friends.[184]

Dennett's ultimate conclusions about the nature of
consciousness are rather involved and I wish to do no disservice to
them here by trying to summarize. The larger point, for the purposes
of my discussion, is that the argument about how film is perceived
and correlated is irretrievably connected with the argument about *all*
forms of human perception. Our very humanness is one such limit, as
Kant observed in his twelve categories of perception from the
Critique of Pure Reason. Thomas Nagel, in his well-known essay "What

---

[183] John Searle, *The Construction of Social Reality* (The Free Press: New York
1995), 155.
[184] Daniel C. Dennett, *Consciousness Explained* (Little, Brown, and Company:
Boston 1991), 429.

is Like to Be a Bat?" observes this same limitation need not apply solely to events outside the known world. It may be impossible for us to get inside the skin of a humble bat, for instance. "Certainly it is possible for a human being to believe that there are facts which humans never *will* possess the requisite concepts to represent or comprehend...Reflection on what it is like to be a bat seems to lead us, therefore, to the conclusion that there are facts that do not consist in the truth of propositions expressible in human language."[185] What these facts are, we can't know; but it points to an inescapable subjectivity in the nature of our everyday experience.

We don't have to resolve all of these issues in interpreting film, of course. However, by keeping such ideas in mind, we are in effect arming ourselves for the battles of interpretation to come, the analysis of representation that is itself further representation. I simply wish to stress that movies are not unique in the respect that they are artifacts of representation to the senses.

Now, as a matter of course, the only people who do not believe in an actual, physical external world (leaving aside certain Eastern religions) are a few philosophers and perhaps some physicists. All that we experience is accepted by our minds at face value, which is why we can be terrified of a rubber shark in *Jaws* or moved by the fate of lovers in *Dr. Zhivago*. There are very good evolutionary reasons why this so, most importantly that it is better to mistake a shadow for a tiger, thus expending some unnecessary adrenaline, than risk missing a real tiger and becoming lunch. When watching a movie, we are thus in a vulnerable position. We can be manipulated; indeed, the goal of a filmmaker is precisely to manipulate our reactions. We can be disappointed or even fooled, if in the hands of an incompetent or corrupt filmmaker. We have to be on our guard at all times.

> Without the human bias toward belief, the media
> could not exist. What's more, because the bias is so
> automatic and unnoticed, the media, *all* media, are in
> a position to exploit the belief, to encourage you to
> believe in their questionable sensory
> information...The media, all media but particularly

---

[185] Douglas R. Hofstadter, ed., *The Mind's I* (Basic Books: New York 1981), 396.

the moving-image media, which present data so nearly
natural, effectively convert our naïve and automatic
trust in the reliability of images into their own
authority.[186]

    So with films, as with all our experiences, we must be wary. We
must *think*. We must think *individually,* an even more difficult task
because movies are typically a shared experience, in which we both
generate and receive cues from the social gathering. Such activity can
reinterpret data for us – after all, how often has it been that you've
seen a comedy that worked in a theater and died on a TV screen?
Howard Bloom describes an experiment done at MIT in which
students were given contrasting biographies of a given speaker – half
of which described the speaker as cold, the other as approachable.
The students reacted to the speaker just as they had been prescribed.[187]
The social element of film-watching is yet another factor that must be
taken into account when evaluating ours own perceptions.
    This last element is by no means dominant, however. Once
the projector starts and the images begin fluttering in sequence, we
each distill those images at our own level and in comparison with our
own internal narratives. At the beginning of every cinematic
experience, we indulge in a social contract with the filmmaker. The
good filmmaker rewards our trust, while the bad or incompetent
filmmaker betrays it.

POINT OF VIEW

    What point of view is the popular Hollywood film likely to
carry? Well, to begin to answer that question, we should perhaps
look at inherent biases within the medium itself. Movies (and
television dramas) are, first and foremost, *dramatic* mediums: they are
therefore prone to show dramatic visual events that may or may not
capture the complexity of a given situation, but in any event must
privilege *image* over *text*. At its best, film works like poetry, in which
specific associative images are ordered together to create a meaning
beyond the thing-in-itself or in some cases an elegance that can be

---

[186] Jerry Mander, *Four Arguments for the Elimination of Television* (Harper
Collins: New York 2002, 1978), 249-250.
[187] Howard Bloom, *Global Brain* (John Wiley & Sons: New York 2000), 76.

superior to words. One example, much debated, occurs at the end of the M. Night Shyamalan film *Signs*. The film concerns a character, played by Mel Gibson, who has lost his faith and given up preaching due to the death of a loved one. Just after the dramatic climax to the picture, there is a brief pause and we open on Gibson getting dressed in his bedroom. His back is to us at first, but then he turns and walks out, wearing a clerical collar once more. The simple and wordless sequence resolves the arc and tells us that Gibson has regained his faith.

These dramatic biases can also be a severe detriment. It is almost impossible to make intelligent points about the hard sciences, mathematics, and economics within the constraints of the medium. Umberto Eco observes: "The shark in *Jaws* is a hyperrealistic model in plastic, "real" and controllable like the audioanimatronic robots of Disneyland...For their part, the devils that invade films like *The Exorcist* are evil relatives of the healing divinity or Oral Roberts; and they reveal themselves through physical means, such as greenish vomit and hoarse voices."[188] That is to say, films depict action and physicality. Film is very good at providing exciting pictures of events such as protesters at the G8 meetings, and the violence that sometimes results from provocateurs, but has a hard time if asked to quantify the precise nature of the disagreements at hand. It is a true fact that the assets of the three wealthiest people on the planet are equal to the approximate assets of 600 million people in 48 developed nations,[189] but such information is difficult to convey cinematically. Jerry Mander observes that television crews at a nighttime riot often focus on trash can fires, partially because they are dramatic, but also because "they provide adequate light for filming."[190] From such pedestrian necessities are our information channels circumscribed.

Besides these inherent biases, there are also the social conditions that inform and define a medium that – because of the great expense involved in producing a film – must be more aware of popular concerns than other art forms. In 2004, for example, then-MPAA head Jack Valenti stated that an average film costs $103 million to

---

[188] Umberto Eco, *Travels in Hyperreality* (Harvest: San Diego 1986), 57.
[189] David McGowan, *Derailing Democracy* (Common Courage Press: Maine 2000), 39.
[190] Mander, *Four Arguments for the Elimination of Television*, 75.

produce, of which $39 million is used on marketing alone.[191] Also, due to the process of audience preview screenings, many mass-market films tend to be simplified and broadened prior to a general release. And if one looks at the most popular films in terms of worldwide dollars, the list is dominated by big, special-effects dominated pictures made for family audiences – i.e., *The Lord of the Rings,* the *Harry Potter* films, *Star Wars, Jurassic Park,* and cartoons like *The Lion King.*[192] The domestic grosses are slightly different – *Gone With the Wind* is still the most popular movie of all time in adjusted dollars – but since we are more concerned with how films travel around the world, this list works better for our purposes. The most obvious thing that all of these films have in common is that they are all fantasies, all portray stark battles between Good and Evil, and involve magic powers or futuristic technology. But this is a matter of nomenclature – one remembers Arthur C. Clarke's famous remark that any sufficiently advanced technology is indistinguishable from magic.[193] This retreat into fantasy could be identified with the mass-production and export of mental disassociation in the way of generating a global schizophrenia. Certainly the degree to which such films have devotees who make their experience the defining moments of their lives gives one pause. I will say more about this later, but for now I wish to merely invoke the idea that the more definable and simplistic – even within a fantastic milieu – the themes of a film are, the better chance they have of translating to a worldwide audience.

Of the top thirty grossing films on this world list, there are two films which do not really fit the mold. They are *Titanic,* by this measure the most popular movie in the history of the world, and *Forrest Gump.* Much has been written about *Titanic,* both pro and con, and William Goldman even went so far as to say that it deserved the Oscar for its screenplay – despite the banal dialogue – because the structure of the screenplay was such that it carried audiences to (for many) an emotionally devastating conclusion. That is, if structure is screenplay, then no other structure was as successful that year.[194] It

---

[191] Carl DiOrio, "Average cost of a movie: $102.9 million," *Video Business,* 23 March 2004, http://www.videobusiness.com/index.asp?layout=article&articleid=CA614600.
[192] Information from http://www.boxofficemojo.com/alltime/world/.
[193] Arthur C. Clarke, *Profiles of the Future* (Phoenix: New York 2000 [1961]).

may be useful to briefly analyze *Titanic* for a moment, because from the first time I saw it, I was struck by how calculating it was for the audience. The character played by Leonardo DiCaprio is a street-smart young man, struggling with no money, but possessed of roguish charm, good sense, good looks, and a disdain for snobbery. Lead characters in popular movies frequently have such characteristics, and if they can snap off a wisecrack or two so much the better, as with the John McClane character in the *Die Hard* pictures. In addition to all this, there are rich snobs (most notably the one played – in a performance so inane it approaches a kind of surrealism – by Billy Zane) to contrast to DiCaprio's inherent goodness. The Kate Winslet character comes from the upper-class world, and although used to the accoutrements of a comfortable existence she nonetheless falls in love with penniless DiCaprio, thus earning audience empathy.

There are gargantuan fantasy elements here in the treatment of social class. Although somewhat unusual for an American film in that it *recognizes* the existence of social classes (albeit safely in the past rather the present), the presentation is infantile. Indeed, the politics of *Titanic* are no more complicated, nor is the love story substantially different from, the Disney film *Lady and the Tramp*.

In the last half of the picture, the ship meets its fate, crashing and coming apart in as effective and dramatic a fashion as possible for $250 million. There is some more heavy-handed attempt at social commentary, as DiCaprio races to save a group of people locked away at the bottom of the ship. However, this is mostly a backdrop to serve as further evidence of DiCaprio's inherent heroism. Eventually both he and Winslet get off the ship, but he dies saving her life, leaving her with a lifetime of memories that haunt her forever – That Perfect Boy Who Saved Me. Besides being a fantasy vision of a real human relationship, of which there are none in the picture, the film operates in the sort of underlined drama that is easily translatable and therefore marketable to the people of the world: a world united in its desire for uncluttered sentiment in beautiful and dramatic surroundings.

Forrest Gump, the other oddity on the list of thirty, likewise uses big emotions and big symbols to get its points across, and is arguably one of the most insidious films ever made. The movie tells the story

---

[194] William Goldman, *The Big Picture* (Applause Books: New York 2001), 241.

of the idiot Gump, played by the likable Tom Hanks, and his adventures in misunderstanding. Although uncomprehending of any single event that occurs to him, he manages to survive although almost everyone he knows dies or is maimed in some tragic event. At the end of the film, he delivers the signature line of the piece, in which he states that some people think we live in a godless, uncaring world, and some people think that a kindly God looks after us. Gump theorizes: "I...think it's both." Critic Roger Ebert found the film insightful:

> As Forrest's life becomes a guided tour of straight-arrow America, Jenny (played by Robin Wright) goes on a parallel tour of the counterculture… Eventually it becomes clear that between them Forrest and Jenny have covered all the landmarks of our recent cultural history, and the accommodation they arrive at in the end is like a dream of reconciliation for our society. What a magical movie.[195]

The concept that *Forrest Gump* covers "all the landmarks of our recent cultural history" is so ludicrous as to be held in contempt. The film's attempts at historical reference include such notable occurrences as the invention of the 'smiley face' and digitally placing the actor Hanks into existing footage of LBJ, for example. For Ebert to postulate that utopian societal reconciliation is depicted in the relationship between a mental deficient and a suicidal drug addict is lunacy. Nevertheless, audiences agreed with Ebert at some level, as indicated by its massive popularity. The themes of simplicity, happiness, an implied religiosity, and a participation in all of the key institutions of patriotic life are depicted in *Forrest Gump*. Gump is a successful football player, acquits himself well in Vietnam, always behaves in a simple, ostensibly moral fashion and even raises a child on his own. The fact that he learns nothing, is in fact *incapable* of learning, never made a dent in the fantasy-seeking audience. The most telling moment in the film occurs when Gump is enlisted into the army. A drill sergeant asks him what he should do. Gump answers: "Whatever you say, Sergeant." To which the sergeant replies: "That is the most

---

[195] Roger Ebert, *Roger Ebert's Four-Star Reviews, 1967-2007* (Andrews McMeel Publishing LLC: Kansas City 2007), 265.

outstanding goddamn answer I've ever heard, Gump! You must be some kind of goddamn genius!" Of course. Gump is the perfect soldier and the perfect citizen, one who is happy and content in a world of meaningless symbols, following the orders of authorities and reveling in the wisdom of convention.

SCREENWRITING CONVENTIONS

Screenwriters are aware of the conventions of film, and indeed in any Screenwriting 101 book you will find a description of the structure and techniques used to create characters for drama. Some characters can be dramatized and some cannot. If your lead is a shy, book-obsessed librarian, then your story had better be a romantic comedy about how an extroverted character gets the lead out of his or her shell. (E.g., Jim Carrey and Kate Winslet in *Eternal Sunshine of the Spotless Mind*; if Winslet had also been a nebbish, then there's no movie.) A plot involving two bookish characters talking about books is, in the best of circumstances, an independent film made in verité style with no budget.

If you want your movie to appeal to a mass audience, it had better have explosive sequences, and they better be up front, in the first ten pages of script. Screenwriting guru Syd Field describes the ridiculous opening sequence of *The Matrix* (in which a woman dressed in black leaps across tall buildings to elude the Bad Guys) with "Whoa...if that's not a grabber, I don't know what is."[196] A good example of this convention is illustrated in the James Bond films, which typically begin with some bit of excitement unrelated to the main plot.

A standard script has 120 pages, as one page of correctly formatted script corresponds roughly to one minute of screen time. Field goes on to dissect the formula script as one which has three acts. These consist of the Set Up (pages 1-30), followed by what he terms Plot Point I, the Confrontation (pages 30-90), Plot Point II, and then the Resolution (pages 90-120). A plot point, according to Field, is an incident in the story that causes action or changes the direction or flow of the action.[197] Different books have different names for these contrivances, but almost 100% of all film scripts

---

[196] Syd Field, *Screenplay* (Random House: New York 2005), 152.
[197] Ibid, 200-201.

follow this pattern. It is therefore quite easy for someone familiar with the structure to instantly deduce the plot from a trailer, or even a two-sentence description or poster in some cases. The flow of a given picture generally follows an arc in which the lead character is revealed to have a problem or weakness in the first act which is resolved in the final act. For example:

> For *Cliffhanger*, Sylvester Stallone – always a strong
> protector of his popular character – insisted on
> adding the opening scene, in which his high mountain
> ranger fails and a girl falls to her death. This
> destroyed his [i.e., Stallone's character] confidence,
> which he was then able to recover (redeem) his heroic
> actions in the subsequent story.[198]

Redemption is a highly popular dramatic motif. It is present in virtually all sports films: *Remember the Titans, Miracle, Pride, The Natural,* etc. Romantic comedies start with a character that has a certain problem which is resolved by the other person. The ending of such films typically has the male and female leads gazing into one another's eyes before kissing and then fade-out. In bad romantic films, Plot Point II is often the female lead seeing the made lead in some activity that seems morally disreputable but is actually explained by information the audience has and the female lead, by various contrivances, doesn't. (For example, she walks in on him when he seems to be kissing another girl, but in reality he is fending off her advances, or it's a goodbye kiss after he's explains how much he loves the heroine, etc.) In the movie *French Kiss,* Meg Ryan thinks that Kevin Kline has slept with a dynamite French girl but it turns out he couldn't go through with it because he inexplicably preferred Ryan. And so on.

Denny Flinn offers the following advice to budding screenwriters: "Think of a Hollywood movie as a good roller coaster ride,"[199] and "Don't leave anything unresolved."[200] Exactly. The bulk of Hollywood films are meant to be enjoyed as one enjoys ice

---

[198] Denny Martin Flinn, *How Not to Write a Screenplay* (Watson-Guphill Publications: New York 1999), 172-173.
[199] Ibid, 152.
[200] Ibid, 164.

cream. This generally applies even to "social event" films or "Oscar" type films. They employ a different motif, but the structure is just as present, albeit often with better acting (though not always) and slightly altered music cues. A great many Oscar-winning films have the same characteristics noted by Denny Flinn, in that they present a roller coaster ride in which everything is resolved. *A Beautiful Mind, American Beauty, The English Patient, The Departed, Gladiator, Crash,* the aforementioned *Gump,* and numerous others have these qualities.

Another typical screenwriting how-to book was written by Tom Lazarus, author of the screenplay for *Stigmata.* He insists that screenwriters place the lead character at the center of every scene: "We pay the actor who plays the lead the most money and we want to see him front and center."[201] He agrees with Flinn on endings: "Endings should answer all questions, tie up all loose ends."[202] And he proposes a structure for the screenplay that resembles attention-deficit disorder: "You want to present to your reader very different images on the end of one scene and on the beginning of the next scene."[203] This is a very interesting note, and it is reflected in modern films, with their vernacular of the "smash cut" (meaning a "hard" or especially disorienting cut to a different scene) and their emphasis on constant movement. The result of this can sometimes be an entire film that looks like a two-hour commercial, as in *City of Angels,* which from a dramatic standpoint appeared to be selling insurance, and *The Constant Gardener,* which employed techniques learned from television commercials to painful effect in annihilating the otherwise compelling story. It also specifically encourages the constant disorientation of the reader (or viewer) *as a means of maintaining attention.* This extraordinary note reflects the raw speed of the visual world presented to us on a daily basis via television and the internet. With fewer and fewer people able to maintain any level of extended concentration, the focus moves to a constant flow of unrelated invention, a perpetual startling of the viewer. Thus screenplays (and their accompanying films) begin, more and more, to look like someone flipping channels randomly on a television set – as in the *Charlie's Angels* films, for example.

---

[201] Tom Lazarus, *Secrets of Film Writing* (St. Martin's Press: New York 2001), 96.
[202] Ibid, 144.
[203] Ibid, 170.

Most amusingly, in Lazarus's book he takes a firm moral tone with regard to cinematic violence. He castigates *Saving Private Ryan* for the "disgusting" and "unrelenting gore."[204] However, several pages later, he describes a meeting he took with the creators of the television program *Hunter,* a cop show. He earned this meeting due to his yeoman work on the David Hasselhoff series *Knight Rider.* He describes himself pitching an idea for a story for Hunter, about "pornography and snuff films" to be called – no kidding – *Rape and Revenge.* The idea is accepted with enthusiasm.[205]

PERSPECTIVES

There is a war of perspectives going on, with attendant attempts to bury the past in iconography. Even when political considerations are not uppermost, in any adaptation from life, complexity is often the first thing to go due to the nature of films.

Whereas the establishment, with its police, military authority, and impenetrable sense of order had been viewed primarily as working for Good, by the end of the fifties cracks began to show. A few films began to question the premises behind the Cold War, for example, and then following the Kennedy assassination a number of films were made questioning the value of the military industrial complex and whether the "American Way" was American at all. These films still moved ahead against the grain, however, digging their way into the stubborn mainstream, often disobeying the conventions of both the larger society and the cinematic language itself.

Perhaps oddly, I wish to draw upon the work of a Jewish Biblical scholar as a model. In *The Death of Jesus,* Joel Carmichael outlines his approach for reviewing the Gospel material of the Bible. He first notes that all of the Gospels had been heavily edited and altered in the centuries following the time of Christ. Indeed, certain books had been deemed non-canonical, such as the Gospel of Thomas and so on. Now this editing and structuring had the political point of asserting a universalizing Pauline Jesus rather than a Jewish prophet. It is a kind of literary transubstantiation in which an obscure (and historically dubious) figure from a Jewish sect bent on

---

[204] Ibid, 178.
[205] Ibid, 192.

political revolution becomes a worldwide Savior. However, during the process of this editorializing, not all of the original content conflicting with editorial preference could be removed, due to the fact that some stories and events were too well-known. He thus adopts a methodology for reviewing the original texts:

> This theme is basic in any study of Christian origins; it will be reverted to often as our inquiry proceeds.

> We shall examine the multiple, disparate elements woven into the Gospels under the influence of this double shift of perspective – theological and historical.

> This will give us our cardinal criterion: *Anything that conflicts with this transformation of perspective is likely to be true.*

> That is, any fragment we can manage to isolate that runs counter to the prevailing Gospel tendency of exalting Jesus, of preaching his universality, and of emphasizing his originality, will be regarded as *ipso facto* probable (other things, of course, being equal).[206]

Carmichael's readings thus attach importance to incongruity in the text – those odd moments and incidents which seldom are discussed during sermon. He identifies and highlights the events that swim upstream from the general narrative. This is what I have tried to do in the context of film criticism – identify those going in the wrong direction, isolate the reasons why, and identify the truths that lie behind that movement.

I don't think it's a coincidence that the bulk of the films that lend themselves to this kind of treatment were made in the 1970's – besides being a golden age of American film in general, it is also the golden age for realistic adult films of the macroscopic type, the film of social analysis. The adult world was put aside, seemingly forever, with the explosion of *Star Wars* and its imitators, but it seems as

[206] Joel Carmichael, *The Death of Jesus* (Barnes & Noble Books: New York 1995 [1962]), 12.

though such films are making a comeback, with the assistance of George Clooney and a few others. This is perhaps a hopeful sign in a United States which seems to have forgotten its history – even its most recent experiences with Watergate, Iran-Contra and beyond.

RFK & THE PARALLAX VIEW

A President and his brother are assassinated, for what reason and by whose order I'm still not certain.[207]

                                        -Republican Senator George Murphy, 1970

The killing of Robert Kennedy on June 5, 1968, essentially ended the left-wing democratic movements that had been surging throughout the decade. With his brother John dead, as well as Malcolm X and Martin Luther King – in April that same year – there were no other figures of equivalent stature remaining to carry the banner for the left. Meanwhile, the civil rights gains so celebrated now had alienated the Southern Democrats, and as a result the Republicans had been able to flip once-blue states to red.[208] The immediate beneficiary of the shooting, of course, was Richard Nixon, who gained in 1968 what JFK had denied him in the election of 1960.

The emotional impact on the people still associated with the Left was devastating, throwing into chaos the 1968 Democratic convention in Chicago. Congressman Allard Lowenstein, who had aided Bobby Kennedy's election campaign, appraised it as such: "A man was killed on the fifth of June…and our experiment in democracy – in political action – was stopped."[209] Lowenstein himself proved to be far more moderate than the political forces he allegedly represented, and indeed had been compromised by his

---

[207] Bill Boyarsky, "Murphy Hints at Plot in Kennedy Murders," *Los Angeles Times*, 16 September 1970.
[208] Kevin Phillips, *American Theocracy* (Viking: New York 2006), 179-181.
[209] Richard Cummings, *The Pied Piper: Allard K. Lowenstein and the Liberal Dream* (InPrint.com, Inc.: New York 1985), 359.

association with the CIA.[210] It was to these forces that the Democratic Party was ceded.

Warren Beatty had gotten a close-up view of this situation. Taking time out from Hollywood, he had joined the Robert Kennedy campaign in March of 1968. Beatty had been a friend of the Kennedy family for years; John once told him that he would have preferred Beatty for the lead in *PT 109,* the film based on JFK's own experiences in World War II. The role was eventually played by Cliff Robertson.[211] After the assassination, Beatty was understandably shaken. He later described the RFK assassination "as a 'horror' in a handwritten letter to Jean Howard, Charles Feldman's first wife, a week later."[212]

Whether this experience led him to make politically conscious films (eventually devolving into the unfocused cynicism of *Bulworth*) is unknown, as he has never addressed the subject in detail. One might venture that such an event must have had some long-term effect on his political views. In any case, in 1973 he teamed with the director Alan J. Pakula to make *The Parallax View,* one of the most incisive, political, and indeed radical Hollywood films ever made. The structure and observations of the film remain trenchant to this day.

Pakula himself had already made *Klute,* which depended on a feeling of paranoia created largely by the claustrophobic beauty of Gordon Willis's cinematography and the motif of a recording device that plays a conversation at irregular intervals during the film. The suspense in *Klute,* however, depended on a single deranged personality; by contrast, *The Parallax View* depicts the system itself as mad. Pakula commented: "We live in a Kafka-like world where you never find the evil. It permeates the society...We live in a world of secrets, a world in which we can't even find out who is trying to destroy our society."[213] These "destroyers" serve the will of

[210] David Harris, *Dreams Die Hard* (St. Martin's Press: New York 1982), 108; also see "Allard Lowenstein: an Exchange," *The New York Review of Books,* Volume 33, Number 1, 30 January 1986, which cites, among other things, an FBI informant who told the agency about Lowenstein's CIA status.

[211] Suzanne Finstad, *Warren Beatty: a Private Man* (Harmony Books: New York, NY 2005), 389.

[212] Ibid, 394.

[213] Jared Brown, *Alan J. Pakula: His Films and His Life* (Backstage Books: New York 2005), 126.

bureaucratic men, as nameless mercenaries operating for a private network outside the government. The film draws as inspiration the details surrounding the assassination of Robert Kennedy, and goes on to explain that murder in the context of these private networks, which presage corporations like Wackenhut and Blackwater. I will be looking at both of these connections at length.

THE OPENING SEQUENCE

Frederick Ives applied for a patent in 1930 on an object he called the "parallax stereogram," a device producing a three-dimensional image for the viewer. The technique used was analogous to stereo, in the sense that separate images were presented to the left and right eyes. It was the combination of the two independent visualizations that connected to form the single three-dimensional illusion. The parallax concept – merging distinct points of reference into a single illustration or measurement – refers to a literal process in calculating the distances of astronomical objects, but also serves as a useful metaphor in our case.

In *The Parallax View*, the concept is applied to vantage points both in a literal sense and a larger epistemological sense. At one level, the key event is an assassination, and the attempt by one reporter to piece together the various points of reference to produce a single image of the real killer. On another level, the investigation leads into an analysis of how one regards reality. Is reality simply the collected observations of the participants, or something beyond that? Pakula suggests this second theme in his use of surreal moments and 'time-stretching' scenes that crop up at odd intervals. The story, credited to screenwriters David Giler and Lorenzo Semple, Jr., is also quite ahead of its time in supposing that hired mercenaries and/or assassins could emerge from a private network with no particular loyalty to anything other than money.

The opening sequence of the film is a beautifully executed set-piece by director Alan J. Pakula and cinematographer Gordon Willis. We first see a totem pole in the foreground as the camera shifts slightly to allow the Seattle Space Needle to emerge in the background. Then we are at the ground floor of the Space Needle, as reporter Lee Carter (Paula Prentiss) narrates events for a television audience: As Senator Carroll pulls up with his wife, she mentions his independent nature, possible presidential aspirations and how good-looking the couple looks in person. As someone who makes her living from visual presentation, she seems unable to discuss anything but the symbolic virtues of the candidate. "He's the perfect husband, the perfect father figure," she says. Carter then interviews Carroll's aide, Austin Tucker (William Daniels) who refuses to second the reporter's suggestion that Carroll will run for President while not seeming displeased at all by the remark. Then, in a characteristic Pakula move, we first see the main protagonist Joe Frady (Beatty) in a group of other people with no effort made to pick him out for the audience. Frady, apparently lacking press credentials, tries to use Lee Carter to get up in the elevator, but she declines in such a way as to indicate a past relationship. Being ever resourceful, he manages to get up to the top anyway.

Pakula doesn't bother to show us how this occurs; as a recurring motif in the film, Pakula often denies us the "how." In trimming the story down to its most efficient elements, Pakula leaves out a great deal of the action – appropriate for a mystery in which much will be unresolved, including the specific identities of the killers. This is just one of the many idiosyncratic elements that give the picture quite a different feel from other thrillers. In place of Point A to Point B choreography, the film relies on the viewer to make intuitive jumps to connect the flow of action – again, highly appropriate given the content of the piece. Instead, the director opts for a sometimes languid surrealism.

The film cuts to a pan inside the Seattle Space Needle. A thin, small-statured waiter goes from the restaurant out to the observation deck. One can't help but notice that he bears a marked physical resemblance to Sirhan Bishara Sirhan, the accused assassin of Robert Kennedy. A series of cuts tells the story: We see another waiter (Bill McKinney) exchange glances with the "Sirhan" waiter and the latter gives his tray to the former. Meanwhile, the "Sirhan" waiter goes back inside the Space Needle restaurant. The Senator takes the microphone and begins his speech by stating that it is July 4th, Independence Day, and that he has been called "too independent for my own good." At that moment two shots strike him in front, go out his back and he slumps to the ground. The "Sirhan" waiter has a gun in his hand and is being wrestled by bystanders. Meanwhile, the Bill McKinney character, whom we now see was also firing, puts his gun away and calmly walks away from the scene. The presumed assailant breaks free, climbs onto the roof, and after a struggle falls to his death.

The montage that tells this story, despite the horrific nature of the sequence, is executed with a great degree of elegance and efficiency. Each cut tells us only what we need to know in as little time as possible. From the shot of McKinney putting away his gun, to the amazing shot of the "Sirhan" patsy rolling off the top of the Space Needle, the sequence is an object lesson in cinematography and editing.

In addition to being an attention-getting opening for the picture, the sequence also contains many parallels to the Robert F. Kennedy assassination, and it seems clear the filmmakers had this in mind. Besides the physical similarities between Sirhan Sirhan and the patsy in the film who fires shots at Senator Carroll, there are numerous other parallels. The most important of these concepts is the notion of a 'second gun,' which we become aware of in the movie by a quick shot of a second man – the real assassin – pocketing his revolver. This shot tells us that the man who fired the shots and falls from the roof is not the real shooter but merely a distraction.

After the fall occurs, the film cuts to the grinning Bill McKinney character, now at street level and several blocks away from the Space Needle. He's escaped. Another cut and the credits begin, as a governmental commission – the most obvious analogue of which is the Warren Commission, although there have been several such entities that produced questionable reports after the fact – declares that the dead man was the lone assassin and there is no conspiracy.

We thus begin the film in a privileged position. We *know* there is a conspiracy because we've seen the second gunman. That places us in a very different position from those who investigate real-life crimes, and it also gives us an advantage over the Joe Frady character. He starts off not believing in conspiracies, only acknowledging their existence because of the evidence. We follow along with him as he uncovers one detail after another, fleshing out the malevolent system behind the assassin that we, as the audience, have already glimpsed.

PARALLELS

What are the true facts in the Robert Kennedy case, and how do they relate to what Pakula and Willis present in *The Parallax View*?

To begin with the most basic facts, the murder occurred at 6:30 in the evening inside the Ambassador Hotel. Kennedy had just given a speech in reference to the California primary. Following the speech, he rode the service elevator down to the kitchen pantry of the Embassy Ballroom inside the hotel. He addressed the crowd there briefly and was escorted out through the pantry by assistant *maître d'* Karl Uecker at approximately 12:15 a.m. Sirhan Sirhan at this point approached Kennedy from the front and began firing.[214] Once Sirhan had been apprehended and the confusion had subsided, Kennedy was transported to Good Samaritan hospital, arriving at 12:50 a.m. He was pronounced dead at 1:44 a.m.[215]

The gun Sirhan used to shoot in the direction of Robert Kennedy was described as a .22 caliber Ivor Johnson. It was an eight shot revolver, and according to the official police report, it expended every shot because eight shell casings were found. Of these shots, one was lodged in the plaster ceiling; four struck other victims; and three struck Kennedy. Kennedy received entrance wounds in the "right rear back," in the "right rear shoulder," and the "head behind the right ear." Each shot struck him at a distance of "one to six inches."[216]

It was later discovered, however, that there were in fact ten bullets recovered from the scene. Two bullets had been found in the center divider panty doors in the kitchen.[217]

The closest person to Senator Kennedy, Karl Uecker, who was in fact holding his wrist at the time Sirhan fired the shots, testified that Sirhan was in front of Kennedy:

> I have told the police and testified during the trial that there was a distance of at least 1½ feet between the

[214] LA County District Attorney's Report, part 1, from the FBI's file on the RFK assassination.

[215] LA 56-156 FBI report on time of death, from the FBI's sub-file Vol. 1 on the RFK assassination.

[216] Officer DeWayne A. Wolfer's official report dated 8 July 1968. Obtained at the Poage Legislative Library, Baylor University, Penn Jones Papers.

[217] "Ten shots from an eight shot revolver," *Los Angeles Free Press*, 6 June 1969. Obtained at the Poage Legislative Library, Baylor University, Penn Jones Papers.

muzzle of Sirhan's gun and Senator Kennedy's head. The revolver was directly in front of my nose. After Sirhan's second shot, I pushed his hand that held the revolver down, and pushed him onto the steam table. There is no way that the shots described in the autopsy could have come from Sirhan's gun. When I told this to the authorities, they told me that I was wrong. But I repeat now what I told them then: Sirhan never got close enough for a point blank shot, never.[218]

Uecker testified to the grand jury that Sirhan fired only two shots before he was able to grab Sirhan and hold him down. According to police, eight shots had been fired. According to the physical evidence, more than eight shots had been fired. This is just the first anomaly – could Uecker, the closest witness, a man who actually wrestled the gun from Sirhan at the scene, have been wrong about his firing two shots instead of eight or more? All of the witnesses agreed on the arrangement of Sirhan in reference to Kennedy, generally within 1½ to five feet away when the shooting began.[219] This showed some slight variation at the furthest end of the observed distance; Pete Hamill, for example, who witnessed the shooting, thought that Sirhan was "seven or eight feet" away.[220] However, there were *zero* witnesses who placed Sirhan behind Kennedy or closer than 1½ feet. In addition, the autopsy report prepared by Chief Los Angeles County Medical Examiner Thomas Naguchi confirmed that the bullets all entered from the rear at an upward angle (e.g., as if the person who shot Kennedy had been behind him and on the floor.)[221]

As it turned out, there was a man standing behind Kennedy: a security guard named Thane Eugene Cesar. He worked for the Ace

---

[218] Statement by Karl Uecker, *Stern* Magazine, February 1995 issue.
[219] Lilian Castellano, "Truth Committee Releases Conspiracy Evidence on RFK," *The Midlothian Mirror*, 22 December 1970. Obtained at the Poage Legislative Library, Baylor University, Penn Jones Papers.
[220] Police interview of Pete Hamill, 6 August 1968, from the FBI's file on the RFK assassination.
[221] Jerry Policoff, "New Evidence That Sirhan Missed Bobby," *The Iconoclast*, Vol. VII, No. 12, 8 June 1973. Obtained at the Poage Legislative Library, Baylor University, Penn Jones Papers.

Guard Service, where he had been working day shifts at Lockheed. He told police that he was standing directly behind RFK, had been knocked to the floor, and even that he had withdrawn his gun. He thus put himself at the scene in an ideal position to create the wounds noted by the Naguchi autopsy report.[222] In an interview in Ted Charach's documentary about the RFK assassination, Cesar even admits that he didn't particularly like Bobby Kennedy and would not have voted for him. In fact, Cesar belonged to the furiously right-wing John Birch Society.[223] Despite these remarkable concessions, Cesar was never more than a witness to the investigation, rather than its focal person of interest.

As anyone can see, the RFK case is quite simple. The eyewitness reports, physical evidence, and coroner's report all agree: Sirhan Sirhan did *not* shoot RFK. It is scientifically impossible. And yet the general public and every media outlet "know" that Sirhan did it and to suggest otherwise is crazy. Contrary to that knowledge, a little research into the true facts of the murder show that suggesting Sirhan did the shooting is crazy.

An enormous amount of information supports the notion of a second gun in the RFK case (indeed, the evidence supports a possible third gun) but much of this came to light after 1973. Additionally, the farcical trial of Sirhan Sirhan (in which his own defense lawyer, Grant Cooper, stipulated to Sirhan's guilt, thus denying the jury the opportunity to hear the evidence regarding the second gun) supports the conspiracy verdict.[224] Relevant to our discussion, however, is what was used in *The Parallax View* to construct the opening sequence. It derives principally from the notion of having a patsy witnessed in full view at the scene, a real assassin at a totally different angle from the patsy, and the concept that an establishment body, within a few months, declares the total absence of a conspiracy based on a lone nut theory.

With regard to the target, Bobby Kennedy had revealed the same streak of independence that Senator Carroll in *The Parallax View* echoes. When his brother was murdered, his first call went to

---

[222] William Turner and John Christian, *The Assassination of Robert F. Kennedy* (Carrol & Graf: New York 1993 [1978]), 166-168.
[223] Interview can be seen in Ted Charach's documentary film *The Second Gun*.
[224] James DiEugenio and Lisa Pease, ed., *The Assassinations* (Feral House: Los Angles 2003), 539.

Langley, where he demanded: "Did your outfit have anything to do with this horror?"[225] That is, *did the CIA kill John Kennedy?* He later met with John McCone who assured him this was not the case, but this apparently did not settle the matter for him. As reported in David Talbot's *Brothers:* "There were others behind Lee Harvey Oswald's gun…the Kennedys made it clear that they did not believe he was acting on foreign orders. They were convinced that JFK was the victim of U.S. opponents."[226] He had therefore made himself a danger to the establishment in that it seems clear, in retrospect, that one of the things Bobby would have done as President was to reopen the case of his brother's death.

There were those who publicly questioned the RFK investigation in the years following the murder. One of them was, ironically, Allard Lowenstein, who drew attention to the disparities between the evidence and the official version, accusing authorities of covering up the crime.[227] In addition, a ballistics expert from Southern California, William Harper, made the same charge, stating that the LAPD had not only suppressed evidence but that microscopic analysis revealed a second gun was used to kill Kennedy.[228]

JOE FRADY'S DISCOVERY

After this opening scene plays out, Frady is told by his friend and former lover Lee Carter that "someone" is killing off the witnesses to the crime. This seems to be a reference to the large number of suspicious deaths following the JFK assassination that Penn Jones, one of the earliest Warren Commission critics, did a great deal to publicize.[229] Frady dismisses her fears, but after she is found dead, he reassesses the situation and begins investigating the murder himself. At this point Pakula sets up a couple of action sequences designed, I think, to seduce the audience into believing that Frady will be able to overcome any obstacle. He first gets into a standard 1970's bar fight with a deputy, replete with broken tables

---

[225] David Talbot, *Brothers* (Free Press: Simon & Schuster: New York 2007), 6.
[226] Ibid, 32.
[227] United Press International (wire), 20 February 1975.
[228] Zodiac News Service (wire), 17-18 February 1975.
[229] John Kelin, *Praise from a Future Generation* (Wings Press: San Antonio TX 2007), 315-317.

and people crashing through walls. Then, after besting an evil sheriff, he shows off his driving skills by navigating a 1970's police chase, complete with air jumps and gaping onlookers. Car chases of this nature were, of course, a standard motif in films of the period, and the one in *Parallax* is more akin to *Live and Let Die* then, say, the more realistic *Two-Lane Blacktop*. The subliminal message is that despite his countercultural attitude and long hair, we are dealing with a two-fisted Hollywood superhero and can relax: Pakula's not going to kill Warren Beatty. Alas, this expectation is subverted in the film's climactic sequence.

All of the action sequences end after the 35-minute mark in the film, when Frady takes a questionnaire he's found to a psychologist. The questionnaire, designed to pull out "potential homicidal qualities," belongs to the Parallax Corporation. Frady's inevitable slide toward destruction begins with his decision to enroll *himself* as an assassin in an attempt to find out the inner workings of the organization. Frady, a newspaper reporter, becomes blinded in chasing the story, because it never seems to occur to him that his behavior is more than dangerous – given what he's already seen, it's suicidal.

It is in this latter section that rather than looking backward (i.e., at the details of the Robert Kennedy assassination) the film instead begins to acquire a prescient quality. We are introduced to the concept of a privatized network of trained assassins. In the film, Frady discovers that the Parallax Corporation is in the business of recruiting assassins on a purely mercenary basis, without regard to political affiliation. In fact, the assassinations which bracket the main action of the story are of two candidates on opposite ends of political ideology.

The film shows us two of their techniques in recruitment once a possible candidate for employment has been found. First, Parallax deploys a handler to meet face to face. In this case that man is Jack Younger, played with relish by Walter McGinn. Younger is urbane, unfailingly polite, and yet sinister, and when he feels he's established a rapport with Frady he exudes a certain grim sexuality. In one notable scene, Frady has deliberately given Parallax a false identity for them to uncover and reveal his second false identity as a flasher. Younger takes his confession with serenity. "I've tried to be a friend to you," he tells him in a slithery Peter Lorre voice as they both sit in darkness. "Isn't that right?" Younger's façade invites both fatherly trust and incestuous affection.

In addition to this direct handling, the second tactic employed is active brain-washing, depicted in what is perhaps the film's most famous sequence. Frady is asked to come to the Parallax offices. He is told to sit down on a chair and place his fingers down carefully on the provided slots. (One may speculate that the direction is both to monitor his physical responses but also to obtain his fingerprints, which are then used on the gun found at the end of the picture.) The lights go out, a screen comes down and Frady watches a drama unfold – a series of images with both Freudian and Jungian overtones. The commencement of violent, sexualized, and patriotic images encourages the subject to identify with both a photo of a weeping child but also, by the end, with the Marvel Comics character Thor as an embodiment of Aryan godlike power. The five-minute film thus depicts brainwashing by way of self-actualization.

The film itself is a striking montage of stark horrors intermixed with Rod McKuen-like fantasies of childhood love that gradually climax in repeated showings of the Thor image to complete the ego-identification of the subject. The subject, assumed to be a social misfit, receives a new and palatable explanation for his prior failures to connect with other human beings. It is not due to any inherent problems within the subject, but rather to his incipient power and greatness. The brilliant sequence was entirely composed in post-production by Pakula himself, who tinkered with the various images for four months before settling on what is shown in the movie.[230] Most previous commentators have noted the intense nature of the film and its potential effects on an actual psychopathic personality. While there is no doubt of its interest in that vein, it could also be seen as a metaphor for the moviemaking experience in general. After all, Frady enters into a dark room, sits down, and then receives a series of images arranged to depict an onscreen fantasy version of *himself*. Isn't this precisely what most films do? In "Trash, Art, and the Movies," Pauline Kael observes that audiences "don't see the movie as a movie but part of the soap opera of their [own] lives."[231] Since most movies depend on an ego identification with the "hero"

---

[230] Brown, 134.
[231] Philip Lopate, ed. *American Movie Critics* (The Library of America: New York 2006), 364.

of the story, and the heroes of most Hollywood films are near immortals (think of James Bond dodging machine gun fire while sniping away with his Walther PPK, or Clint Eastwood killing hundreds in such entertainments as *The Outlaw Josey Wales*), isn't the typical movie creating a Godlike personality for each audience member to experience? William Goldman addresses this same point in talking about the real-life heroic actions of a fireman and whether it would play onscreen. Even a dynamic rescue by a fireman whose heroism makes the morning papers is insufficient to tickle the interest of audiences, however. "This is what Sylvester Stallone does in an action picture before the opening credits start to roll...Stars do not – repeat – *do not play heroes* – stars play *gods.*"[232] Precisely.

Here the epistemological question is raised: What is the relationship between the moving image and reality? And more explicitly, how do we know that our own perceptual cues coincide with the real world? In formal logic, many problems arose from the assumption that the syntax of language formed a one-to-one correspondence with the objects in existence. This creates philosophical confusion when one gives attributes to things that do not exist; for example, one can correctly say that Joker is the enemy of Batman without also insisting that the Joker and Batman exist as anything other than concepts. (If this seems elementary, please note that it did not seem so to Plato. Indeed, a similar confusion underlies Kant's ontological argument for the existence of God, in which "existence" is categorized as "one of the perfections.") Bertrand Russell attempted to get around this with his theory of descriptions.[233] However, the main philosophical point for our purposes is that *The Parallax View* touches upon some of these issues as well as the more overt political references. Just as logic was once thought to bear a correspondent relationship to reality, so it could be argued that our perceptions give us a direct line to it. In the real world, things are more complex than that, and it gets muddier still when one considers the brainwashing aspect of Parallax's operation.

A MANCHURIAN CANDIDATE

---

[232] William Goldman, *Which Lie Did I Tell?* (Random House: New York 2000), 83.
[233] Bertrand Russell, *A History of Western Philosophy* (Simon & Schuster: 2007 [1945]), 830-831.

The cult mentality or "brainwashing" aspects of *The Parallax View* also directly echo the evidence in the RFK shooting. Going back to the opening sequence of the film, we may recall that the assassination required a patsy or, in this case, a literal fall guy – the waiter who tumbled off the Seattle Space Needle. Since we've now seen Parallax's homicidal and sexually frustrated corporate training film, we can now infer that the Space Needle patsy had undergone similar "training." That is to say, he was a "Manchurian Candidate." Sirhan Sirhan himself gave many indications of being such a person. The term, of course, refers to Richard Condon's novel (adapted for two subsequent films) about a hypno-programmed assassin. Could such a thing have any basis in reality? Indeed, it could and does.

This is apt to be a controversial claim for some, so we should perhaps first begin by establishing that there was such a thing as a brainwashing program, and that this was pursued by the United States government. In 1978, *The New York Times* reported on internal documents showing that the government began a program to find out whether a person could be made to unconsciously commit murder upon command. It was part of the original Operation Artichoke, which existed from 1949 to 1974. The story goes on: "Several groups have studied the documents from the standpoint of whether they may provide any evidence in the continuing inquiries into the assassinations to President Kennedy or the Rev. Dr. Martin Luther King Jr."[234] Artichoke had started out under the name "Bluebird," one of the operations that eventually became MKULTRA.

Spymaster Richard Helms had been deeply involved in the MKULTRA project. Having been instrumental in Project Paperclip, under which a number of Nazis – including Klaus Barbie – successfully escaped from Germany after World War II, only to receive financial aid from the CIA and jobs training death squads in Latin American countries, Helms knew his way around a covert operation. Klaus Barbie would later turn up in Bolivia in 1980, leading private mercenaries (wearing black uniforms and Nazi armbands) during the famous 'Cocaine Coup.'[235] The future CIA

[234] Nicholas Horrock, "C.I.A. Documents Tell of 1954 Project to Create Involuntary Assassins," *The New York Times,* 9 February 1978.
[235] Michael Levine & Laura Kavanau-Levine, *The Big White Lie* (Thunder's

Director Helms made all future research into MKULTRA difficult when he personally ordered all of the records from the project destroyed.[236]

MKULTRA activities fell under the auspices of Dr. Sidney Gottlieb, head of the CIA's chemical division of technical services staff beginning in 1951. Gottlieb experimented with dosing patients with LSD and other mind-altering substances for the purpose of perfecting mind control. He also assisted with the funding of Dr. Ewen Cameron, the Canadian psychologist who conducted similar torture experiments at the McGill Clinic in Montreal. The financing was handled partially through the CIA and partially through Rockefeller Foundation grants.[237]

One of the locations where MKULTRA mind control experiments took place was at Vacaville Prison in California, while a certain Charles Manson was serving time there. (Later, a certain Donald DeFreeze of the Symbionese Liberation Army, which kidnapped Patty Hearst, would also spend time there.) Over the years, Manson has made several cryptic remarks about that period, including making a reference to a rash of suicides among the doctors performing the testing. "The last wave...the last wave of *these guys* who sent me to Vacaville, are all gone now," Manson says. "Dr. Morgan blew his brains out."[238] It is unclear to what Manson refers, but the implications are interesting. Dr. Louis "Jolly" Jolyon West, one of the most prominent figures in the mind control atrocities committed in this country, worked at Vacaville during the period of Manson's incarceration there. Even more intriguing, his studies focused on behavior modification with an emphasis on *controlling disaffected youth.*[239] Whether there is a connection there I cannot say, but as noted it is interesting – particularly in light of another famous U.S. criminal, Ted Kaczyinski, the 'Unabomber.' As a Harvard college student, Kaczyinski had agreed to be the subject in experiments conducted by another MKULTRA specialist, Dr. Henry

---

Mouth Press: New York 1993), 55-58.

[236] Alexander Cockburn & Jeffrey St. Clair, *Whiteout* (Verso: New York 1998), 198.

[237] Alexander Cockburn & Jeffrey St. Clair, ed., "CIA's Sidney Gottlieb: Pusher, Assassin, & Pimp," *Counterpunch*, http://www.counterpunch.org/gottlieb.html.

[238] Television interview of Charles Manson, 1997.

[239] Cockburn & St. Clair, *Whiteout*, 201.

Murray. Dr. Murray was also well-known for conducting a personality profile on Adolph Hitler at the behest of Wild Bill Donovan, then-head of the Office of Strategic Services, forerunner of the CIA. The experiments Dr. Murray performed on the young Kaczyinski involved brutal psychological torture, and friends reported that he was a changed person after the experiments.[240]

And no wonder. A CIA memo written in 1955 provides a list of the "materials and methods" that the project will be dedicated to finding. Among the items listed are "Substances which will promote illogical thinking and impulsiveness to the point where the recipient would be discredited in public... Physical methods of producing shock and confusion over extended periods of time and capable of surreptitious use," and "Substances which alter personality structure in such a way that the tendency of the recipient to become dependent upon another person is enhanced."[241] Could such experimentation have any effect on subjects like Manson or the future Unabomber?

This experimentation with drugs extended to its own employees, such as in the case of Dr. Frank Olson, who had been employed at Fort Detrick, Maryland, in the biological weapons laboratory. Gottlieb gave him a drink spiked with large quantities of LSD on November 18, 1953. That same evening Olson jumped out of hotel room window and fell to his death. Although some might argue for murder, this was considered a suicide, even during then-DCI Stansfield Turner's testimony at the 1977 MKULTRA Senate hearings:

> **Senator INOUYE.** In February 1954, and this was in the very early stages of MKULTRA, the Director of Central Intelligence wrote to the technical services staff officials criticizing their judgment because they had participated in an experiment involving the administration of LSD on an unwitting basis to Dr. Frank Olson, who later committed suicide. Now, the individuals criticized were the same individuals who were responsible for subproject 3, involving exactly

[240] Alton Chase, "Harvard and the Making of the Unabomber," *The Atlantic Monthly,* June 2000, http://www.theatlantic.com/issues/2000/06/chase.htm.
[241] "MKULTRA Materials and Methods," declassified government document, 5 May 1955.

the same practices. Even though these individuals were clearly aware of the dangers of surreptitious administration and had been criticized by the Director of Central Intelligence, subproject 3 was not terminated immediately after Dr. Olson's death.

In fact, according to documents, it continued for a number of years. Can you provide this committee with any explanation of how such testing could have continued under these circumstances?

Admiral TURNER. No, sir, I really can't.[242]

There are specific reasons why Sirhan appears to be a controlled, Manchurian Candidate-style patsy. Psychologists who spent time with Sirhan realized that he was an eminently hypnotizable subject who, in fact, showed himself to be adept at self-hypnosis. He remembered nothing of the events concerning the shooting of Robert Kennedy and harbored no personal ill-will toward the man.[243] During the shooting, witnesses described the "tranquil" expression on Sirhan's face, and George Plimpton stated that his eyes were "peaceful."[244] Sirhan's lawyer, Lawrence Teeter, described an incident in which a psychologist informed Sirhan, under hypnosis, that he was a monkey. According to Teeter, as soon as he was signaled to do so, Sirhan scrambled up the bars of his cell and hung upside down while making 'monkey' noises.[245]

The passive mental state and readily hypnotizable attitude of Sirhan made him an ideal patsy. To this day, he has never been able to remember nor give a coherent account of the assassination.

The Parallax View dispenses with the two patsies in the film by having them killed at the scene – the ideal situation for a political murder. There is therefore no trial. Even a trial as farcical as the one

---

[242] CIA Director Stansfield Turner's testimony, 1977 Senate Hearings on MKULTRA, 35-36.
[243] Turner and Christian, 194.
[244] Ibid, 197.
[245] "CIA Interventions: The Role of the CIA and the LAPD in the RFK Assassination," lecture by Lawrence Teeter, 14 November 2000, from the DVD *The Life and Work of a Genuine Working Class Hero,* obtained through JusticeVision, http://justicevision.blogspot.com/.

Sirhan received nevertheless provided a written record of numerous anomalies in the case, such as the aforementioned test firings of two different weapons by the LAPD. Even in a controlled investigation, such a record provides evidence for researchers to plumb.

IS FRADY THE ASSASSIN?

In the final sequence of the film, a second assassination takes place. Frady is in the rafters of a high school gymnasium, where Senator John Hammond is having a fundraising dinner. A high school band performs patriotic tunes in rehearsal, and Senator Hammond shows up to go through the motions. We see that the tuba player in the band arrives late, appears to be older than the other students, and seems unable to play. Soon a shot rings out and the Senator is struck.

The somewhat surreal nature of the cutting in this scene may lead to a possible confusion with regard to whether Frady himself actually fires the fatal shot or not. Frady notices that a rifle is up in the rafters with him, but no shot shows him firing the weapon himself, nor anyone else. However, the tuba player from below fingers Frady by pointing up at him and shouting, "There he is!" He attempts to escape, but is gunned down by an unknown assailant – possibly the real Parallax-contracted assassin or perhaps the local authorities. Although Frady never handles the weapon so far as we are shown, as noted it is possible that had his fingerprints been obtained during the earlier brainwashing session, they could have been planted on the rifle here. In any case, the frame-up is now complete, and in the scene following Frady's death we see a new independent commission releasing its verdict that he was a "lone nut" who had "acted alone" in shooting Senator Hammond. By the end, of course, we know the truth: Hammond was a contract killing performed by a highly efficient and professional private company.

BLACKWATER AND BEYOND

Whenever people think of contract killings, it's very often in the context of the Mafia, of mobsters bumping one another off. And the CIA has contracted at least one assassination through the Mob: Fidel Castro. Both entities wanted Castro dead for different reasons.

For the CIA's part, Cuba was of course seen as part of the overall cold war strategy against the Soviet Union, and its proximity to the United States made it a widely discussed threat in Pentagon circles. Santos Trafficante, who had run the Havana operations for underworld boss Carlos Marcello, was also very interested in killing Castro because the latter had ruined all his businesses. Whereas the Mob had enjoyed free reign under the Baustista regime, with the coming of the revolution Trafficante found himself forced to leave the island under threat of imprisonment. The CIA-Mob connection was fostered by Howard Hughes confidant, Watergate figure, and government operative Robert Maheu:

> An alliance with the Mafia was one of the eight
> conspiracies hatched by the CIA from 1960 to 1965
> to eliminate Castro and topple his leftist government.
> In the summer of 1960, the CIA asked Robert
> Maheu, a former FBI agent with Mob contacts, to
> find Mafiosi who could pull off a hit on the Cuban
> dictator. Maheu enlisted John Roselli, a Los Angeles
> hood, who brought in Chicago's Sam Giancana and
> Tampa's Santos Trafficante Jr. Of the trio, only
> Trafficante had intimate knowledge of Cuba and close
> ties to anti-Castro exiles.[246]

However, none of the various plots against Castro ever worked, and most of them were quite absurd. This shouldn't be surprising, since although mobsters may kill each other all the time, this is not the same thing as planning an assassination. A good example could be found in the names provided. Both "Handsome Johnny" Roselli and Sam Giancana were called to testify to the Church Committee in 1976. However, Roselli went missing, only to be found chopped up inside a 55 gallon oil drum. Five days before Roselli's body was found, Giancana had been shot seven times in the head at his home.[247] This is messy work, characteristic of the Mafia.

---

[246] Selwyn Raab, *Five Families: The Rise, Decline, and Resurgence of America's Most Powerful Mafia Empires* (St. Martin's Press: New York 2006), 144.
[247] "Deep Six for Johnny," TIME Magazine, 23 August 1976, http://www.time.com/time/magazine/article/0,9171,945646,00.html.

Assassins, as Kevin Costner observes playing the role of Jim Garrison in *JFK,* are generally military.

We've entered a whole new era of contracted murders here in the United States, in which the relationships are out in the open and justified by the "War on Terror." The contracts, however, go to military-grade professionals, not streetwise petty criminals. And one of the most interesting things about *The Parallax View* is its intimation of this corporatized mercenary industry. It's a quite logical extension of Eisenhower's military-industrial complex, in that Lockheed Martin develops weapons to confer mass casualties on foreign populaces, so why not individual personnel for individual targets? Without civilian oversight, red tape, or any annoying need to make occasional reports to Congress, such an approach makes perfect sense.

In September of 2007, for example, Blackwater employees slaughtered a number of Iraqi civilians. Unfortunately, the firm exists without controls. "CPA [Coalition Provisional Authority] Order 17 says private contractors working for the U.S. or coalition governments in Iraq are not subject to Iraqi law. Should any attempt be made to prosecute Blackwater in the United States, meanwhile, it's not clear what, if any, law applies."[248] Faceless men, trained for war, given full impunity to act as they please on a civilian population without fear of consequences? Would any reasonable person expect anything *other* than atrocities to arise from such a situation? One of the milder effects is the creation of a black market which these mercenaries fill for profit, and indeed Blackwater employees are accused of smuggling weapons into Iraq by the Iraqi government itself.[249]

There are more paramilitary and civilian contractors in Iraq at present (over 180,000) than actual troops.[250] Because of the enormous commitment in the Middle East, the Louisiana National Guard was unable to deploy in New Orleans after Hurricane Katrina struck. In their place marched storm troopers wielding automatic

---

[248] Alex Koppelman & Mark Benjamin, "What happens to private contractors who kill Iraqis? Maybe nothing," (Salon.com, 18 September 2007), http://www.salon.com/news/feature/2007/09/18/blackwater/print.html.

[249] BBC News, "Blackwater 'arms smuggling probe,'" 22 September 2007, http://news.bbc.co.uk/go/pr/fr/-/1/hi/world/americas/7008058.stm.

[250] Koppleman & Benjamin, "What happens to private contractors who kill Iraqis? Maybe nothing"

weapons on the ground, or else driving Sport Utility Vehicles with windows tinted black. "Within two weeks of the hurricane, the number of private security companies registered in Louisiana jumped from 185 to 235." The firms included such corporations as DynCorp, Intercon, American Security Group, Blackhawk, and Instinctive Shooting International.[251] *Instinctive Shooting International?!?* Yes, that's what it's really called – an Israeli company specializing in defending the propertied from the unpropertied like Plato's dogs. The lesson of our times is that there is not one Parallax but many, as the driving engine of mass capitalism breeds imitation; a thousand Parallaxes paid to do the bidding of the powerful.

These Blackwater thugs and Wackenhut security installations have become the new centurions. Indeed, we cannot rule out the involvement of private industries being at the root of numerous assassinations of political figures, mostly of the left, throughout the last 40 years. Many of these killings also bear the earmarks outlined in *The Parallax View*: a seemingly brainwashed, mentally defective patsy, and the possible involvement – in either funding or training – of private institutions. This has happened time and again, with Bobby Kennedy's murder being but one example.

Private industries have been able to perform duties that would normally be handled by federal employees, which not only increases profit but decreases liability. When John Negroponte (himself infamous for studiously failing to notice the presence of CIA-trained Contra death squads in Nicaragua beginning in 1981) became the Ambassador to Iraq, he traveled everywhere with a contingent of Blackwater guards.[252] As previously noted, these guards were above Iraqi, American, and International law, undoubtedly convenient for a man like Negroponte. However, at the same time, Blackwater argued in court that its dead mercenaries were ineligible for anything except government-funded insurance.[253] This slippery mindset – floating between federal and private – should perhaps be unsurprising given that these firms are generally started by people who were once in the federal government. The concept is to get all of the advantages of state power and private means without any of the limitations. Blackwater itself, for example, was started by

---

[251] Jeremy Scahill, "Blackwater Down," *The Nation,* 10 October 2005.
[252] Jeremy Scahill, *Blackwater* (Nation Books: New York 2007), 282-283.
[253] Ibid, 232.

Erik Prince, a former Navy SEAL.[254] Similarly, Wackenhut began as a detective agency in 1954 created by former FBI employee George Wackenhut. With the aid of his influence, the agency lived off government contracts, but the company really took off in the late 1980s with the prison industry. They are now the third largest prison contractor in the United States.[255] Their prisons have a remarkable reputation for poorly trained guards and violent incidents. A report, for example, created for the Scottish government when contemplating expansion of Wackenhut prisons in that country collects numerous violent incidents across six states, notes their terrible reputation, close ties to the CIA, and lack of controls. It also points out that Ronald Reagan's notorious CIA director William Casey, before he was placed in that position, was Wackenhut's lead counsel.[256] Given Casey's involvement in the Iran-Contra operation, among other crimes, this does not inspire confidence in the organization.

This leads perhaps to another pressing issue in the explosion of the privatization of violence. As noted in *The Parallax View*, such companies obey nothing but money and power. It makes no difference to them whether they kill a leftist or a right-winger, a criminal or a great statesman; their loyalties are not to an ideology but their stockholders. Is it an accident that the huge increase in the numbers of private prisons over the last twenty years has been accompanied by an equivalent increase in the number of people incarcerated? Is it an accident that the profit margins of private mercenary firms mirror the increase of instability across the globe? The motivation to pursue profit is not the same thing as the motivation to pursue justice.

Accompanying this change has been a change in how criminality itself is perceived. Whereas criminal behavior had been seen as deviant from prescribed norms or the result of poor socialization, current models show crime as an inevitable byproduct of group activity in a mercantile system. The theoretical position is

---

[254] Ibid, 28.
[255] Kenn Thomas & Jim Keith, *The Octopus* (Feral House: Los Angeles CA 2004), 32.
[256] Phil Taylor & Christine Cooper, *Privatised Prisons and Detention Centres in Scotland: An Independent Report,* http://visar.csustan.edu/aaba/Cooper&Taylor.pdf.

that theft is an outgrowth of the desires capitalist societies instill in their citizens to maintain themselves. Or, as George Carlin puts it: "Thou shalt not covet thy neighbor's goods – now this [Commandment] is just plain fucking stupid. Coveting our neighbors' goods is what keeps the economy going."[257] This attitude, of great utility to those who would profit off crime, means certain changes in the way crime is viewed:

> A thousand small adjustments are required. Replace cash with credit cards. Build locks into the steering columns of automobiles. Employ attendants in parking lots and use close circuit TV cameras to monitor city centre streets…Encourage local authorities to co-ordinate the various agencies that deal with crime.[258]

That is, the movement is to create a surveillance society permeated by new business interests that fill the various social requirements. Close circuit television cameras are made by a manufacturer who has the same goal that every business in a capitalist society has: to expand. This is precisely what has happened at the Pentagon, as contracts are handed out to such entities as Halliburton to take over aspects of war that used to be handled by the government. In 2003 this resulted in a $1.7 billion windfall for the company.[259] This creates a situation in which huge corporations such as Halliburton, Lockheed Martin, McDonnell-Douglas, Blackwater, Wackenhut, DynCorp and Booz Allen Hamilton, among many others, have a vested interest in increasing the relative amount of chaos in this world.

ESTABLISHMENT VIEW

Critical response to *The Parallax View* was generally harsh. In the case of Vincent Canby, he asserted both that the picture was not

---

[257] George Carlin, from his standup performance *Complaints and Grievances* (2001).

[258] David Garland, *The Culture of Control* (University of Chicago Press: Chicago 2001), 129.

[259] Michael Dobbs, "Halliburton's Iraq Contracts Exceed $1.7 Billion," *The Washington Post*, 28 August 2003.

successful entertainment, complaining that the screenplay did not have the "wit [of] Alfred Hitchcock," but also that to "treat a political assassination conspiracy merely as a subject for fun is frivolous." He thereby in the same breath desires that the film be *less* realistic and sober, but also not treat its given subject lightly. At bottom, he doesn't take it seriously:

> According to this film, the Parallax Corporation has a recruiting program as thorough as that of General Motors, and much more paternal. Parallax seems to be vaguely right-wing, but the movie is fuzzy on this. It's also fuzzy on logistics. If, as is shown, Parallax insists on eliminating not only contracted targets but also all possible witnesses, as well as witnesses of witnesses, it would seem the population could, theoretically, be reduced by half in eighteen months.[260]

Richard Schickel, writing for TIME, seems to be offended by the very conception of the film, relying on his amateur psychoanalysis to assess the entire enterprise: "It is apparently comforting for many people to believe that the course of the world is changed more by rational planning, however evil, than it is by irrational individual actions." He actually praises the action genre elements of the film, calling the fistfight and car chase "smartly handled," while failing to understand their placement within the overall context. He then dismisses everything that happens after these routine elements. He goes on:

> But there is no way to build an overparanoid thriller or to provide a satisfactory ending. If the hero can break the conspiracy unaided, it cannot be much of a conspiracy. If, on the other hand, the conspiracy is all powerful, then the audience is robbed of the basic pleasure of identifying with the protagonist's triumph over the odds. Pakula opts for the latter resolution in *Parallax* and it is a downer. Though a touch of paranoid fantasizing can energize an entertainment,

[260] Vincent Canby, "The Parallax View [film review]," *The New York Times,* 20 June 1974.

too much of it is just plain crazy—neither truthful nor useful. And certainly nothing for responsible men to try to make a buck with in the movies.[261]

Schickel thus invokes two highly typical responses to conspiracy films and also conspiracies in general: on the one hand, he states that they are essentially *psychological* constructs rather than evidential ones, while also implying that "paranoid fantasy" is somehow too serious of a subject for commercial exploitation. Like Canby, he seems unable to resolve the internal confusion here. Either the subject is too serious for entertainment purposes, or it is not entertaining enough, but surely it cannot be *both*. And yet Canby and Schickel, both well-respected critics, share this quandary.

For both critics, it seems that in any case a film like *The Parallax View* must be pure fantasy, and a distasteful one at that. It could not be the case that the film could have a kernel of truth at its core. At a more fundamental level, the thought process depicted here in these critiques is that all conspiracy-thinking is not to be taken seriously; indeed, it may even be dangerous. But all of this *a priori* rejection of such thought takes place without reference to any facts, and neither review takes any time to place the film within any meaningful historical context. This deliberately ahistorical approach makes it impossible to understand the deep structures that underlie the drama.

We see this approach taken by establishment writers time and again when facing films like *The Parallax View* in dealing with subjects anathema to national pride. The most extreme example, of course, is with *JFK*, in which TIME Magazine ran a critical story of the picture before it was even released, based on a stolen draft of the script. However, there is this continual methodology of distancing the subject from the real world, and then expressing disapprobation at any overlap, with a hint that the filmmakers have a strong financial motivation to "make a buck" exploiting real-life scenarios. These are, however, the techniques of the propagandist; in applying invented motivations for both the creators and the intended audience of the film, they fail to address the subject head-on. Evidence is dismissed in favor of broad general assessments – a characteristic of thought that Tocqueville, I might observe, felt was instinctual and habitual

---

[261] Richard Schickel, "Paranoid Thriller," *Time Magazine,* 8 July 1974.

with Americans.

Nevertheless, the evaluation of *The Parallax View's* credibility depends entirely on one's familiarity with the evidence that its method of representation has some relationship to reality. For most people, entering into the theater under the veil of ignorance, it represents a yarn, perhaps even a disturbing one. But one cannot appreciate the depth of its critique without having gone through some of the real-world incidents that it observes and reflects. I have tried to dig out and present some of this information, in the interest of changing paradigms blinded by an inability to accept unpleasant truths. Unlike what occurs in the parallax stereogram, alas, the two images – one presented by orthodox wisdom, the other presented by the dirty details – can never be reconciled.

INTERVIEWS

Over the years, I've done a number of interviews with people both in the film world and in the research world (and some like Joe McBride who have a foot in both) and reproduce some of the more interesting ones here.

BOBBY SEALE

Welcome to the modern world. How did it happen that I got a chance to interview Black Panthers co-founder? He friended me on Facebook. That's how it works sometimes. He is still looking for funding for his adaptation of SEIZE THE TIME, which seems like a very worthy project to me.

GREEN: I understand you have a film that you're working called *Seize the Time: The Eighth Defendant*. How far along is the project?

BOBBY SEALE: We are moving along. Over the next few months we are taking the project around the world and collecting email addresses. We need 100,000 email addresses. We're asking for contributions – I called it a "power to the people" cause – because that was our slogan – and there are perks with each contribution. The lowest basic level is $25 to help with contribution. Now that's another thing, we're not trying to raise all the funds this way. We're trying to get development funds because this is an independent film. You see what I'm getting at? There are different levels of funds and once we get that, we go back to the major houses in Hollywood, where we've already been and there is a lot of interest already. We're doing this as an independent production in order to control the artistic value and the real story. High drama. Now there are different levels - $50, $100, $200, all the way up to $10,000 for contribution. The perk for a person who gives $10,000 is that I will come and speak anywhere they want me to – hopefully a college or university or something like that – plus I will supply autographed copies of my books, DVDs, posters, *Barbecue'n With Bobby*, which I did 5 or 6 years ago as a TV show which includes a book where I explain how I do not separate my politics from my cooking. *(laughs)*

They're connected.

The idea behind *Barbecue'n With Bobby* was to raise funds in the 1980s for what I called the Environmental Renovation Youth Jobs Project. If you know anything about me and the history of the Black Panther Party – even before – when I quit my engineering job, I went to work in the grassroots community. So I used to put together real youth jobs programs. That was my shtick back then. I created – my God – 22 community survival programs. Scattered all across the country. I organized 5,000 people while Huey [BPP co-founder Huey Newton] was sitting in jail. How to set up the Free Breakfast program. How to set up the Preventive Care clinics. How to set up and operate the Free Sickle-Cell Anemia Testing program. These were very successful programs in demonstrating the problem – the issues in our community. Hungry children before school. Medical health care clinics. This stuff is going to be dramatized and synopsized in our film.

And also how you yourself started out.

That part of the story really starts out with me in the engineering department at Kaiser Aerospace and Electronics. I was doing electromagnetic field black light non-destructive testing for all engine frames for the Gemini missile program. I put myself in the high tech world. I had already done four years in the United State Air Force repairing high performance aircraft. I had skills. I was also an architect, which I evolved before joining the military. My father was a master carpenter and builder. Architectural design, engineering design, mechanical design, three-dimensional views, that was my shtick, my forte. But I quit that engineering job to work with grassroots communities, and the first one I worked on was North Richmond Tutorial program, which was for youth jobs. Now the city government of Richmond, California, gave me a proclamation for setting up the first-ever youth jobs program in the city. They gave this to me about four years ago. I then worked for the department of Human Resources in the city government of Oakland later and I ran the youth jobs program there and these were all programs that preceded the Black Panther Party. I was still employed by the city of Oakland when I created the Black Panther Party. I knew the Mayor. I knew the chief of police. There's drama there. I used to have to take some of the youth on tours down there and the police detectives would try to make them become fake snitches, and I used to say, "Don't tell them a damn thing."

What year would this have been?

1965.

So let's go back a little – you're an engineer. What causes you to suddenly get involved with social movements?

Dr. Martin Luther King, in 1962, came to Oakland Auditorium and there I was with 10,000 people in the auditorium. I was one of the young students then. He spoke so profoundly. There was one particular thing he said that I never forgot. He was talking about how we have to break down institutional racism and get them to hire people of color – all people of color. Bread companies. He said, (adopting King's voice and cadence) "We're gonna boycott these bread companies. We're gonna boycott Wonder Bread. We're gonna boycott them so consistently and so profoundly we wanna make Wonder Bread wonder where the money went." (laughs) I tell you – when he said that, the whole auditorium stood up. It was a thing – a standing ovation. I was first inspired. The first African-American leader was Dr. Martin Luther King. Later I heard Malcolm. But the point is, that was where I was coming from.

And your emphasis was on programs.

Programmatic organizing. One thing about the history of the Party is I created all these programs. When Dr. King was murdered, I only had 400 members in the Party all along the West Coast.

In '68? Really?

Seattle chapter was pretty good – small group in Portland, Oregon – about 100, I was shocked to find out, mostly female in Sacramento – and the headquarters was in Oakland of course. One little office in Palo Alto, one little one in Vallejo. And a small group in Fresno and L.A. But add them up and it was 400 among all the chapters. Now back then, Dr. Abernathy called me – everybody knew I was the main spokesman of the Party. Huey was in jail. The question was, "Mr. Seale, you've become a prominent organizational group, and would you like to have a representative in a round table and also to help further along the upcoming Poor People's March we're going to have." And my answer was, "Yes, we will participate." They wanted to hammer out greater economic rights. Civil rights is economic rights. And I said, "Yes, sir." We agreed with that. And this was just a few weeks before Dr. King was killed.

Had you known Ralph Abernathy before that?

No, not before the day he called my office phone.

Six or seven weeks *before* Dr. Martin Luther King was killed? When had they scheduled the first group meeting?

They called back, and said – they might possibly have a meeting in the next month or two. Something like that.

Wow. That's really interesting. I did not expect you to say that you got involved in this partly because of Dr. King. Now King had become more radicalized. He started to talk about the Vietnam War. He gave the famous speech on April 4, 1967, exactly one year before his murder. Do you think that he was ever responding to or influenced by the Panthers?

No. Dr. King had said at one point, if this war continues in Vietnam, there may come a time when I may not be able to tell the young militants that we need to continue our nonviolent protest. Something to that effect. Kwame Ture and others had wanted him to come out against the war, and he did come out against the war before he was killed. Now in the research for our film, and this comes from a Senate investigation into the FBI – I have some researchers from UCLA – and the documents show that J. Edgar Hoover had declared Dr. Martin Luther King a violent agitator! *(laughs)* Of all people!

He was worried about a new Black Messiah.

Yeah, he said he was worried about that. Take Malcolm X. He left the Nation of Islam, which I was always happy about.

You were in favor.

There were some aspects of the Nation that were okay, but all the separatism and stuff, I didn't have no time for that. I didn't see the world as they saw it. When I studied Africa, I didn't study it for the aesthetics. I studied it for the mineral resources buried in the bowels of Africa. I was in the high tech world. Metallurgy crosses over into what I'm coming from. So when I'm studying Western Africa, Togoland, Ghana, I find out that there was a smelting plant for bauxite. I knew what bauxite was about – all aluminum products in the world come from bauxite and it is plentiful in Western Africa.

You have a practical edge to your work – programs for the people, and a very practical analysis of how the world works. Huey Newton is more theoretical – he's coming from Frantz Fanon and so on. How did you come together?

I was Huey's supervisor. Remember I was 6 or 7 years older than him. Well Huey was stealing. He'd ask me for a ride – and I'd drop him off at Grove and this happened three days in a row. And finally I asked him, "Where are you going?" He didn't want to tell me but finally I got it out of him. He would go and wait in the bushes in the emergency area at Herrick Hospital and – he wrote it in his own book – he would wait in the bushes for sometimes an hour and somebody would always come up with an emergency situation and they would leave their purses, jewelry, he would rob people. I said, "Man, you can't be doing that, we're trying to start an organization." And he said, "Man, I need the money." I said, "Huey, you can't do no crap like that. You're a common thief." I had heard something – I asked Mr. Lowe with the board "Didn't you mention something about an assistant that could work with me?" [It turned out] there was ten months left [of salary in the budget]. It was about 40% of my salary. My salary was $620 a month, a lot of money in those days. So I called up Huey and said, "Come down here man, I got a job for you."

Wow.

I told him, "You know why I hired you, right?" And he said, "What?" I said, "You can't go down to the hospital and ransack people's cars! Shit, we're talking about starting a new organization, we can't do that kind of shit. You're gonna have near $280 a month in your goddamn pocket. Do you get $280 a month out of people's purses and shit?" And he said, "No." So you see, there's all kinds of drama in my little movie. A prelude to the shootouts.

The Black Panthers are often connect in the public mind with guns. I've always thought the thing that really got Hoover agitated and COINTELPRO going was feeding and educating the children. How do you feel about that?

Well, we have documents on that. You have to understand COINTELPRO. The Black Panther Party was on their list. When they really started to focus on us was right after Nixon got elected. He gets elected in November 1968. One of the first people Nixon meets with – before the inauguration, before January 1969 – is J. Edgar Hoover. Now, right in the middle of December 1968, Hoover is on television saying that the Black Panthers are a threat to the internal security of America. Four months later, he is back on television saying that the Free Breakfast for Children Program is a threat to the internal security of America. He goes on to say it is Communist inspired. *(laughs)*

In our film, we are showing real documents subpoenaed by a Senate committee that our research assistants have gotten ahold of that show Hoover sent out one communique as a directive to 43 district offices of the FBI. In this thing, he is directing them to do – in any creative way you can – to disrupt, discredit, and destroy the breakfast program. You must further try to make sure that moderate blacks and liberal whites do not support this program. In a Gallup poll at the time, something like 90% of the black community approved of the Panthers and the breakfast program. Those programs caused a lot of people to look at us differently from "guns." Hoover didn't like that. And they were on us.

Now when Hoover said that, I sent a directive out to all Black Panther Party offices. I want them fortified. So I took out my drafting pencils and sketched out methods to sandbag, build boxed areas up to the windowsills all the way around, find a joist on the ceiling to install heavy duty hooks so you can install plywood with heavy hinges – synchronized and spaced with the joist to hold them – so when the police come around, everyone can get down behind the sandbags and hit the hooks so these heavy duty covers will fall over the windows. Now, the problem with Fred Hampton is they didn't kill him in the office. It was in his apartment. They just busted in there at five a.m. shooting everybody.

And he had been drugged.

Yes, he had been drugged, that's documented. My film starts out with Fred Hampton.

That's literally and metaphorically the end of the Sixties, I've always thought. He's killed December 1969.

December 4, that's right.

And Little Bobby Hutton getting murdered by the police. It was war. Like Huey's book said, *War Against the Panthers*.

Yeah, it's war, but Huey's book is limited. It's a Ph.D. thesis. There is more than that here. Huey doesn't have the reference points we have – and the point is, he was just knockin' off his thesis. *(laughs)*

Well, he was – a more theoretical sort of guy, right?

He was quite theoretical, but he wasn't an organizer.

That's what I mean.

I gave him a lot of credit in my book *Seize the Time*. I never have forgotten, when he got out of jail, he's sitting in the right hand front seat, I'm in the back next to David Hilliard and my brother, somebody's driving, and Huey says, "Hey, I read *Seize the Time*, you didn't give yourself enough credit." I told him, "I wrote it that way to help you get your butt out of jail." Anyway, my point is, my film here is called *Seize the Time*, but the subtitle is *The Eighth Defendant*. The emphasis is on what I did, how I organized the Panthers, 5,000 strong, while Huey was in jail. The emphasis is on the programs I created. The programs that evolved out of the original 10-point program.

Could this happen today? Could there be programs to do this work now?

Yeah, it could work. The programs would be different. This is what I want to do. Now a certain amount of money I need for my family from the film. But the other money is to initiate the Environmental Renovation Youth Jobs Projects. That's what I would do. Set an example or two, go from city to city and get a whole movement going. Right back to programs. Barack Obama learned his lessons when he ran against Bobby Rush, way before he became a Senator or President. Bobby Rush was a former Panther organizer. He survived the crackdown – when they were out to kill all of us.

Bobby Rush beat him two to one. He still had the Free Health Clinic in his community. So you know what Barack did? He created his own clinic. And it was a great one! Better than anything we ever put together. He was responsible for it. And it's almost like Brother Barack Obama figured out, that is the way to run. And to this day, I love Barack Obama...it's the same stuff I did when I ran for mayor of Oakland. And I was speaking at Santa Clara before the election, talking about these programs and I advised them, Barack Obama is going to give Mitt Romney an electoral ass whoopin'.

That seems like a good place to close. Thanks for speaking with me, sir, it was an honor.

Thank you.

For more information on the film, see
http://www.indiegogo.com/projects/266927.

EUGENE PURYEAR

I first ran across Eugene Puryear in an interview with RT News and felt compelled to get into contact with him. Mr. Puryear is only in his late twenties, and yet he's out doing some amazing work, including his new book Shackled and Chained: Mass Incarceration in Capitalist America. *The book is a concise and often stunning description of both the institutional racism inherent in the American prison system, the inherent corruption in privatizing punishment, and the atrocious conditions of the prisons themselves. As a society we have to ask ourselves: Does it make sense to create prison conditions that force criminals to adopt psychopathy as a survival mechanism? Are we trying to find solutions to the root causes of crime, or are we trying to send people into a living Hell? How demented is a society that incentivizes mass incarceration? Mr. Puryear kindly agreed to an interview to discuss these issues in detail.*

GREEN: Mr. Puryear, if you would, let's begin with what drove the writing of your book, *Shackled and Chained.*

EUEGENE PURYEAR: Primarily I wanted to situate the whole phenomenon of mass incarceration in the broader social context of capitalism in America. What was going on the late 1970s and early 80s when mass incarceration really took off, first ideologically, then progressing into the 1980s materially, through policy. So the question becomes, how do we explain that in the context of that broader social system? Because things do not happen in a vacuum. They happen in relationship not only to things going on in our society, but because we live in a class-based society, they connect to the broader dynamics of the class system. I really wanted to illuminate that.

Related to that, is there an immediate problem with private prisons making the enforcement of law into a commercial enterprise?

I definitely think [that there is]. What it does is turn what should be an issue of law into an avenue for profit-making. And so obviously CCA and Geo Group and these other companies, they are not going to have in their minds questions like, "What is the best way to rebuild communities devastated by mass incarceration?" What is the best way to deal with crimes like possession of drugs – things of that nature. Their only concerns are things like, what is the maximum number of people we can get into a jail?

They will also consistently argue and lobby for anything that will allow them to throw more people in [jail] and to get more contracts. See, right now there is a growing amount of attention being paid to mass incarceration policies. It's interesting, from the point of view of reform, or abolition, or the different perspectives people bring to this issue – there is this element that was not present at the beginning of mass incarceration policies, which is [the existence of] these private prisons. It skews things. They have shifted the arguments from the whole question of imprisoning millions of people and dealing with the underlying social problems that give rise to crime – they know they can't win those arguments – so they've shifted to talking about costs, to being a question of the ability to run a prison more cheaply. It really does skew things away from a focus on people, on humanity and community, to purely focusing on profit.

Now...do you think this is an inevitable outgrowth of monopoly capitalism or is it something more specific? Is it really an extension of imperialism?

I do think it's connected to monopoly capitalism and imperialism, and speaks to the problems that imperialism has always had. Going into the economic crisis of the 1970s, which was a shock because in the post-World War II period, you had these rising standards of living and the expectation – especially after the Civil Rights movements of the 60s – an expectation among black Americans that their lives would improve, but the 1970s really upset the apple cart. The idea of jobs programs, more extensive social problems, all of that went to the chopping block for a variety of reasons, but you also had this other problem – particularly in the black communities, which became the primary targets of mass incarceration – in that they were left outside the social contract, with no prospects for employment or rebuilding the communities that were being devastated. Government policy makers had no desire to help anything other than big business interests and had no desire to deal with these people in a constructive fashion so of course, the issue becomes what do we do with all these people? So that really the mass incarceration "solution" arose out of a surplus population problem. You have a group of people who have been consistently ground down, oppressed, and exploited, and at the same time you need to find a way to deal with them. Just like other forms of what is now called "neoliberalism," mass incarceration came about as a response to a structural crisis within the capitalist system.

Interesting. Now what role does the "drug war" play in our present system?

It plays a huge role. Reagan [becomes President] in 1981. One of the first things he did is set up this Attorney General's task force on crime that was chaired by a number of academics and people high up in the government. That report, in the introduction, says that the biggest issue in crime today is the lack of available prison space. They are already saying this although there is not quite the War on Drugs yet. So the War on Drugs comes along at a fortuitous time when a number of people are pushing for these policies. The Democrats in particular – Joe Biden, Ted Kennedy – had been pushing mandatory minimums since the 70s but they hadn't gotten to really establishing mass incarceration as a policy. The drug war gave them that excuse...quote-end quote "drug crimes" and drug use.

And obviously...you know the numbers, I'm sure, much better than I do...but obviously this is disproportionately affecting young, black males.

Yeah, it's interesting. The federal and state prison population is made up of about 39% black and 23% Latino so I believe about 62% of people in prison are black or brown people. This is so far away from the proportional representation of those populations...and we know from different studies, for example, that blacks don't use drugs as much as whites, but if a white person and a black person are convicted of the same drug crime, the black person is more likely to be sent to prison for that crime. The disparities shine through.

That isn't the only thing...now facing prison is a horrifying prospect in itself. But what kind of prospects does a person have once they get out of jail?

It's really terrifying. It's almost like you are in prison for the rest of your life. Here in Washington, D.C., where I'm from, there are about 50% of the people with a criminal record who are unemployed. And even the 50% who are employed are consigned to roughly six low income job categories. So in essence when you come out of prison your job prospects are slim to none and if you do get one, it's most likely to be in the worst-paying, worst-benefits, and in the most precarious section of the economy. It's a stigma on people that makes employers – wrongly – not want to hire these people once they're out of prison. And it results in even more devastation for communities for people who want to come out and just live their life and provide for their families. They're unable to do so because of the opportunities being taken away from them by being incarcerated.

And a lot of these "crimes" are essentially victimless – possession of marijuana and so forth.

It's a huge issue when we talk about crime. The one thing that rarely gets touched on is what we really define as crime. We see, to a large degree, Wall Street bankers have gotten off scot-free when they wrecked the entire world economy. Obviously there's a lot to be said there. There is ample evidence that actual criminal activity has taken place and hasn't been prosecuted – but also, all these terrible terrible things that have been perpetrated – student loans and things that people find so odious coming from Wall Street and other big businesses are absolutely legal.

But we look at something like marijuana possession which is defined to be illegal. And we have to ask ourselves, what do we define as crime? Why do we define it as crime? Why is drug use – even hard drug use – considered a criminal issue rather than a public health issue? So a huge issue in dealing with mass incarceration is to ask the question, what in fact is a crime? Because if we don't really look at that, we're dancing around the issue to a large degree. There are a lot of people locked up for – like you said, marijuana possession and things of that nature – there's really no point. I mean, it's just not criminal behavior. It's no worse than things that are considered broadly legal – alcohol use and so on, which have caused a lot of social problems. I'm not saying people shouldn't drink, I'm not a teetotaler or anything like that. But the point is that these are not crimes in the same category as murder or rape, even the use of hard drugs like crack and heroin. Why are we not talking about these things as public health concerns rather than crimes? I think that's a key issue – how we define crime and how we deal with "classical" criminals.

And – just to broaden that point – if I rob a liquor store and shoot somebody, kill somebody – I might get the death penalty for that. But if I run a company that – let's say – deliberately installs defective artificial hearts in a large number of people and kill them that way – that will never be a consideration. I may never even be criminally prosecuted.

Sure.

So there's an inherent imbalance there. Is white collar crime somehow more acceptable?

I think it is systemic, and I believe it is considered more "acceptable." Crime in the pursuit of profit-making. There is nothing more lionized in America today than profit making – the cult of the entrepreneur. It's almost considered a little more natural that these things will happen in this pursuit and it isn't necessarily bad in the same way that, say, drug dealing is considered to be. Ultimately it shows a bias in the system toward – well, not that drug-dealing isn't a capitalist occupation –

Yeah (laughs).

It certainly shows a bias toward the largest sections of big business that are

211

legalized in capitalism, not only because they get define in large part what is legal and illegal in the system, but because they get to shape perception in their favor. For example, on a consistent basis rap stars [are criticized for] always promoting reckless materialism and it's ruining their communities, and so on – and okay, fine, that's legitimate and we can definitely have a conversation about the content of a lot of rap music – but people aren't talking about Wall Street bankers who have the most extravagant lifestyles, prey upon society, and are lionized for it. The upper crust. Instead it's look at this Vanity Fair spread about their lives in the Hamptons, which often shows the worst sides of this type of behavior, and yet it's never put into the same conversation. I think it's a perfect example of defining perception. It's a double standard that exists.

I read something that you wrote that struck me: "Bourgeois elections have always played a critical role in channeling dissent into acceptable avenues." Could you expand on that a bit?

Sure. Whenever there is a large upset in society, we always see politicians on either side attempt to speak to that. They try to channel that energy. For example, during the Vietnam War time, during the campaign in 1968 and later with McGovern in 1972, we see this in a number of political movements – the two political parties aren't total inertial dinosaurs. They can see the political waves shifting – and the anti-war movement is a great example in 2006 and 2008 – the Democratic dissent about the Bush war regime was a major issue in the elections, but then we see what happened when [the Democrats] took power. They went forward with what's been happening with the NSA and the drone war and continuing to broaden the "national security," War on Terror imperialist drive around the world. So even though the election was able to suck in large amounts of people interested in opposing these terrible policies, [the elections] ultimately played the role of demobilizing the independent movements.

That's what these electoral campaigns do – they take people out of opposition based on principle and funnel them into opposition based on party and it plays a very key role in making sure there is always an outlet. Because if there's no outlet…I mean, imagine if George Bush had just declared himself Emperor in 2006. People who were already radicalized would have continued their opposition. So if there were no Barack Obama, how would American capitalism have continued to move forward? That's what this system does.

Right on. Related to that, how do you feel when people call Obama a socialist?

(Laughs). I can only chuckle a little bit. It's so outlandish. But it speaks to the mentality of the far right that the only way they feel they can mobilize is to set up Barack Obama this way. In fact, similar to how the liberals set up Bush – it was all about Bush, not about the system. So now it's all about Obama trying to destroy Americanism with this new brand of creeping socialism. Not only does it set up Obama as a boogeyman but it also reinforces this notion that somehow socialism is worse than capitalism. In a way it makes me chuckle because it's so absurd, but it is an important device the far right is using to delegitimize, for a large section of the population, the danger of looking to socialism. It also [has worked] to resurrect the idea of a full free-market fundamentalist capitalism.

And doesn't it serve perhaps to define boundaries – to say that Obama is the furthest one could imagine on the left, when in fact he isn't on the left at all?

Totally. And it also associates socialism with Obama rather than an independent opposition. It justifies them. People who might otherwise be interested in what you have to say in terms of socialist politics, attaching it to Obama serves to delegitimize in advance and set up those redlines for people not to accept socialist or more progressive ideas. The messenger compromises the message, as it were.

Yeah. Now just from my perspective, I feel like over the last fifty years, the word "liberal" has ceased to mean anything anymore in terms of actual content. It's been so debased.

I think that's probably true. You see a lot of liberals casting about. People who previously called themselves liberals now want to be called progressive, because of the pejorative connotation…but I think it just speaks to the broader reality of the American social system where the basis for the liberal system in the past was, as I mentioned, following World War II, a dedication to rising living standards and a strong labor movement. The idea of a reformed capitalism has sort of gone by the wayside. It's really cut out the social base of liberalism. These were traditionally based in the rights of unions, the rights of African Americans, so on and so forth, which has been eviscerated in this right wing assault of the last 30 or so years. Liberals have been adrift and trying to re-orient themselves.

Now there is also – and we touched upon this a bit before – but there is a moral dimension to this as well in which, in this country, poverty is automatically equated with low morality while wealth is equated with respect.

I totally agree. People in poverty are consistently derided as being lazy, or having some sort of personal or cultural defect that prevents them from succeeding, whereas wealthy people are highly motivated, genius individuals whose entire existence is what others should copy. This ignores the fact that no one in this country ever makes it on their own. A lot of these people were born into wealthy families but even if they weren't, they benefited from broader social programs such as public universities, all these sorts of things. There is a high morality placed on those achievements that help the system, whereas if you are in a class of people whose existence shows how it doesn't work, the only way to deal with those people is to demonize them as welfare cheats or something similar.

So what we're really talking about is a propaganda state.

There's no doubt that capitalism couldn't exist if every day, the fallout of capitalism were shown. It could not withstand that kind of sustained critique on its own. These are ingrained biases – they don't even have to be conscious most of the time. If you are just the average person writing for the media who goes through school, does an internship, you don't need a censor to show up in your office or cubicle. You will, by and large, (which is not to indict all journalists), but by and large you will reflect the biases of these institutions which only exist to serve privilege and capitalism in the broadest sense. There is – broadly – a selection bias that exists in the media and politics and so on. They only accept a parameter of ideas that are palatable to the larger social system.

Now I mentioned my affiliation with the Coalition on Political Assassinations, so I've got one last question for you. What do you think about assassination as a tool of politics? Is it an accident that Dr. King, the Kennedys, Brother Malcolm, Little Bobby Hutton, Fred Hampton, these are people trying actively to make a change and are assassinated, whereas other people are not?

I think it is a tool of power, and nothing teaches that more clearly than the drone war. They are attempting to legalize the ability to essentially kill anyone they please. I think ultimately you are correct, and the attempts over the years to kill people in this country have been tools, in addition to all other forms of attack and attempts to delegitimize or stop these movements. They feel that without those leaders, they can either scare others away or hurt the internal infrastructure of these movements.

I don't think it's a coincidence that anytime there is a vast uprising against capitalism or imperialism that political assassinations start to increase and take place among those in the camp of opposition. Now certainly, there is no political equation between the heroes of the 1960s and Al-Qaeda, which is an odious force and I don't want to suggest that at all –

Oh, of course not –

But definitely political assassinations can be a tool of power.

So given this is the situation we are in, what are the best avenues for pursuing real change?

I think that lies in independent mass movements. What we need to do is replace the capitalist system with a whole different system, but how do we get from point A to point B? It's been about organizing around basic principles, whether it's free health care, or working against racism, or mass incarceration, but ultimately movements that push these ideas independently of the major political parties. If reforms come, then reforms come; I don't think we should be opposed to reform and demand revolution right away. The most important thing is for people to get active in movements that speak to progressive principles and not compromise those principles vis-à-vis politicians who want to water them down to make them more palatable to their big time donors. And we've seen with these kinds of movements – civil rights, the labor movement – that independent militant action can truly change society. I think that's the route we have to go.

Great. Now if someone wants specifically to help you out, or the organization you belong to, what should they do?

Sure. My book's website is www.shackledandchained.com. You can also go to www.liberationnews.org. It lists some of the things we do, the struggles we're involved in, and it enables people to connect with us.

Right on. Fantastic. Thanks so much for the interview.

Thank you so much, I appreciate it.

JOHN POTASH

June 16 would have been the 41st birthday of the hip hop artist known as Tupac Shakur. His story is not generally well understood even today by the general public, which actually connects back a generation to the height of COINTELPRO operations against the Black Panther Party. Filling the void in this story – and many other political crimes that are not often known even to researchers – comes John Potash with his book The FBI War On Tupac Shakur and Black Leaders.

I first met Mr. Potash when he gave a tremendously detailed and fascinating account of his research at the Coalition on Political Assassinations conference in Dallas, Texas, the week of November 22, 2011. We were both presenting at the conference and found some common ground, as I spoke about Black Panther leader Fred Hampton. He kindly agreed to this interview in order to cover some of basic groundwork for his excellent book.

His new book, due in February 2015, is called Drugs as Weapons Against Us.

GREEN: How did you first get interested in the Shakur story?

JOHN POTASH: I was doing addictions counseling in Baltimore and someone I counseled said my father was a Black Panther killed by the police. I decided to make him a character in a political novel I was writing and researched the Panthers. Then I saw that Tupac was shot in New York. The Washington Post pointed out "another strange twist" in the case was that the same cops showed up [at the murder scene] as had shown up on a sexual assault charge a year earlier. So I called Tupac's lawyer, Michael Tarif Warren, and asked if he believed police intelligence were targeting Tupac like his mother, Afeni Shakur, one-time leader of the Harlem Black Panthers. He said yes and no one's writing about it. I found out Tupac had

217

similar radical leftist views as myself and published locally, then in Covert
Action Quarterly, started by CIA whistleblower Phil Agee. Then Tupac's
business manager and close political mentor, former Black Panther Watani
Tyehimba, said you have to turn this into a book.

**You received your Master's degree in social work from Columbia
University. I would not have thought that the Columbia milieu would
be conducive to the kind of work you eventually took on. Am I
wrong? How did Columbia shape your views?**

I went to Columbia for its name recognition for jobs outside of New York
and for one particular radical professor, the late Richard Cloward. He and
his wife, Frances Fox Piven, wrote radical leftist sociology classics Poor
People's Movement, Regulating the Poor, and Why Americans Don't Vote.
You might have heard about them being attacked for over a week by Glen
Beck, formerly of Fox News, for their work from decades ago. I studied
closely with him, including a one-on-one tutorial.

**However, you're not just an academic, having worked on
acupuncture drug treatment at Lincoln Detox in the Bronx. How did
that change your perspective?**

I worked in addictions counseling in Baltimore City, around Washington
D.C, and New York City. This allowed me to meet people from many
historically oppressed communities and coworkers similarly in touch with
such communities. Some had similar leftist political views as me and shared
books with me. Lincoln Detox was where Tupac's radical activist
stepfather, Mutulu Shakur, was once assistant director and is now a political
prisoner.

**You write that, after a period in the wilderness, so to speak, Tupac
had begun turning political again – citing, among other things,
"White Manz World." Do you feel this was decisive in his death?**

I argue that the "wilderness" was some months of continuing the Penal
Coercion Tupac experienced in jail. Amnesty International discusses how
Penal Coercion manipulates prisoners' minds with solitary confinement and

other means. They did it to Tupac's Aunt Assata and others. I show the evidence that the "dozens and dozens of police officers" at all levels of Death Row Records had the job of trying to continue this Penal Coercion method of manipulating Tupac. A top Los Angeles police detective, Russell Poole, said his superiors told him these Death Row cops could be considered "covert agents," possibly because he was white and they thought he'd be racist and cooperative with their plans.

Tupac signed a 3 CD contract with Death Row. Once he completed that, he fought with Suge Knight saying he owed them nothing more. He had already started his own record label and film company. Death Row encouraged Tupac to write most of "All Eyez on Me" after they got him stoned and drunk, recording much of it within 24 hours of leaving prison. The next CD, under the name Makavelli, did get back to political statements about freeing Mumia, Geronimo Pratt, Sekou Odinga and all political prisoners. He also had an excerpt from Malcolm X on that song, amongst other political statements.

The East-West rap feud was set up. What is the best piece of hard evidence suggesting this? Was Suge Knight a kind of "inside man"?

I can't say there is one piece of "hard" evidence. It has to be examined in several ways. First, with the amount of evidence around the New York recording studio shooting scene that started it. Secondly, we have to look at the many parallels with the East versus West Panther rivalry the FBI's Counterintelligence Program manufactured between Huey Newton's Oakland National office and the New York Panther 21, in which Tupac's mother, Afeni Shakur, was one of the leaders at the time. And finally, within the context of this New York shooting as, arguably, the fifth attempt by U.S. Intelligence on Tupac Shakur's life.

The New York shooting happened when a man named James Rosemond, an associate of (later West coast-based) Tupac's former friend, Jacques Agnant, offered Tupac $7,000 to rap a line or two on someone else's CD. Tupac needed the money at that time. East coast-based top rapper Biggie Smalls was in the studio upstairs. Tupac was awaiting a verdict on a sex abuse trial at that time where Agnant had set up the whole scene. Tupac's

New York trial lawyer, Michael Warren, who was Mumia Abu-Jamal's European spokesman, said Agnant's huge rap sheet with all the cases dismissed showed him to be an FBI agent.

Tupac was shot twice in the skull at that scene and miraculously survived. Government documents support that Agnant's associate, Rosemond, was collaborating with the government around that time, and Dexter Isaac said Rosemond offered him huge money to kill Tupac.

Police malfeasance at the scene included the same cop showing up at that incident as had shown up first at the alleged sex abuse scene a year earlier. Also, a guard at the New York recording studio had the incident on security camera videotape of the lobby area where the shooting happened. He said that he offered it to the police and they just turned it down and closed the case, calling it a "random mugging" of Tupac.

Panther National spokeswoman Kathleen Cleaver, now a Yale-trained law professor, looked at the accumulated evidence I had that the East/West Panther war was duplicated with Tupac and Biggie and agreed it appeared that the FBI had manufactured it. COINTELPRO documents revealed that the FBI wrote fake letters between people, and wrote anonymous letters to affect the splits between leaders. U.S. Intelligence then used the purported East vs. West war between Panthers to cover up their murders of Panthers. Tupac received anonymous letters saying Biggie set up the New York recording studio shooting. The FBI also used undercover agents in and out of prison to manipulate Panther cofounder Huey Newton regarding this East vs. West war. Tupac said strangers in prison told him his friend Biggie set up his shooting.

An investigating police detective found that Tupac's next record label, Death Row Records, instigated the East vs West hype. Knight also brutalized people at political rap events and committed a vast amount of crimes, but remained untouched by the law, until after Tupac's murder.

You detail some of the key issues in government's murder of Malcolm X. What did you think of Manning Marable's 2011 biography?

I only skimmed that book, but it looked like it had some great evidence on the huge operation U.S. Intelligence was waging against Malcolm X. I only disagreed with Marable about one key point and that pertains to Eugene Roberts. Marable, who was a great scholar and activist, surprised me when he didn't give the full history of Roberts. As I said earlier, one of Malcolm X's closest associates was Saludine "Abbah" Shakur. Abbah's sons, Lumumba Shakur and Zayd Shakur, were part of Malcolm's group. Roberts followed the younger Shakurs into the New York Black Panthers, Lumumba founded the Harlem Chapter and Zayd was Minister of Information for the Bronx chapter. Roberts then came out in court at the NY Panther 21 trial saying he worked for police intelligence. He unsuccessfully tried to frame Lumumba and Tupac's mom Afeni Shakur.

At the scene of Malcolm's murder, Roberts' wife held back Betty Shabazz, a nurse, from running to her wounded husband Malcolm. Undercover agent infiltrator Roberts was the first to arrive. This paralleled how a black undercover agent infiltrator Marrell McCullough was the first to arrive at MLK's slain body. William Pepper (James Earl Ray lawyer and current lawyer for Sirhan Sirhan) said this was to check on MLK's life signs to make sure the U.S. Intelligence assassination was successful, and signal the back up snipers to disband.

The story of Afeni Shakur and the Panther 21 trial is astonishing. My immediate thought, reading that section of your book, is that it would make a terrific Hollywood movie, if Antwon Fuqua directed it. Could this be made in Hollywood? Related question: are there points of view systematically kept out of popular culture, especially films?

Yes, I agree that this would make a great movie. I think that production costs are huge and provided mostly by groups that don't want to reveal this kind of history for fear of it inspiring too much change. I do think there are points of view systematically kept out of mainstream media. I have two chapters in my book, and parts of my film, on how that is accomplished. Part of it references former Cal-Berkeley Journalism School Dean Ben Bagdikian on how media companies share boards of directors with defense contractors, oil companies, banks, etc. Bagdikian says that by corporate law they can't go against their stock shareholders' interests. Another reference is Watergate muckraker Carl Bernstein who quoted a Church Committee finding that well over 400 members of the media, including virtually all the owners, led dual lives in their work for the CIA. Also, just after Fahrenheit 9/11[the Michael Moore documentary] came out, the infamous Bush-linked Carlyle Group bought out 2 of the 3 top movie chains.

Obviously the current state of hip-hop as viewed by radio popularity is atrocious. At the same time, over the last decade or so, artists like Mos Def, Talib Kweli, Immortal Technique, and Dead Prez have released albums aimed directly at the governing state. What is your assessment of these artists? Do you think this helps the movement? Do you see this as a movement?

I think Immortal Technique has excellent lyrics. I quoted some Dead Prez lyrics in my book. I like Mos Def but don't know his stuff that well. I mention incidents of targeting Dead Prez and Mos Def though.

Related to the last question, Malcolm once said we need to "talk right down to Earth in a language that everyone here can easily understand." And NWA famously declared that we were about to "witness the strength of street knowledge." Has revolutionary hip hop failed to reach across to the masses, or is the message one that is never going to take hold of the youth. Is the Tupac murder part of a message being sent to stick to "pimps and hoes" in your lyrics?

I think revolutionary hip hop won't be allowed to reach much of the world since the conservative groups control so much of mainstream media, particularly the means of distribution of media and information. They even have gotten control of much "independent" media through foundations offering struggling media grants, usually with strings attached. One CIA whistleblower, Ralph McGehee, said that he saw a CIA document before his resignation, boasting about the Intelligence agency having a representative in every media organization in the country that could spin, twist or censor content.

Another music artist mentioned in the book is Jimi Hendrix. Most

people are completely unaware of the suspicious nature of his death. I had read about it in Alex Constantine, who in turn I believe got the bulk of his analysis from the great Mae Brussell. Why might the government have had an interest in Hendrix's death?

Constantine's research themes and conclusions overlap mine in a big way and Brussell was great in my mind too. Martin Luther King's assassination helped radicalize Jimi Hendrix. After that, Hendrix spoke openly of the need for The Black Panthers and he dedicated his last album to the Panthers. According to his fiancée, Monika Danneman, Hendrix also started formulating many radical leftist, antiwar projects in his last year. He further had fired his business manager, Mike Jeffrey, that was effectively controlling his career. Jeffrey admitted being an ex-agent of Britain's MI6. I show evidence that he never left MI6. In a drunken state he admitted having Hendrix killed, though he pretended it was for more personal reasons.

So many people are targets of the white power structure and the media working hand-in-hand, as in the cases you cite of the bogus 2006 assault charges against Cynthia McKinney, Allen Iverson, and Jim Brown. These are seemingly very different people doing very different things with their lives. How are they connected? Are we dealing, in your view, with a state that reacts to the same activities in the same way as a reflex action, or are we dealing with a long-term cooperative plan?

We're dealing with anyone who develops the fame and means to reach many poorer people and tries to help them rise up from their poverty and change society for the better of what Occupiers now call the 99%. I only spend a few paragraphs on Iverson and Brown, and about a page or two on McKinney, though I could have possibly covered her more if I came out with the book a year later. I believe Iverson and Brown – particularly Brown – were doing something U.S. Intelligence feared. They were setting an example to other wealthy star athletes that looked up to them, in trying to raise money for neighborhood uplift programs in the poor neighborhoods from which they came. Brown was also trying to convert gang members into productive citizens and activists, similar to Tupac and the Panthers.

I understand you are working on a novel, is that right? Any other current projects?

I decided to delay the novel until after I first published a book on the use of drugs as weapons against the masses, and activists in particular. The novel was originally part of that book, but now I decided to separate the two. The non-fiction book will also cover Tupac and Hendrix, but will have more ink on Kurt Cobain and John Lennon, along with the Students for a Democratic Society (SDS). That's probably part of why I like Peter Dale Scott so much as he covers part of this subject and I reference his work in some chapters. Like the *FBI War on Tupac* book, it also will have over a thousand endnotes.

Peter Dale Scott is a favorite of mine as well, as a writer and a person. I look forward to reading your book.

JAMES SOLOMON

Robert Redford's new film The Conspirator *opened last Friday and concerns the aftermath of the assassination of Abraham Lincoln. There are many fascinating details surrounding the event, relatively unknown by the public, in the one American assassination in which the conspiracy is acknowledged. The film works quite well and serves as a good introduction to many fascinating elements of the case, some of which could not be included for time and plot constraints. (For example, of the four people in Lincoln's box that day in the Ford Theatre, two of them were murdered and the other two died in mental institutions. There are tidbits like that sprinkled throughout the case.)*

In the film, the human drama of the Mary Surratt trial is contrasted with the civil liberties issues that emerged from the military tribunal that determined her fate. On April 21, 2011, I got a chance to speak to the screenwriter of the film, James Solomon, who spent eighteen years working on the project before finally realizing it onto the screen.

GREEN: I had assumed this started with the Weichmann book [*A True History of the Assassination of Abraham Lincoln and of the Conspiracy of 1865* by Louis Weichmann]. Is that actually what happened?

JAMES SOLOMON: The origin of *The Conspirator* actually began, as a writing process for me and in research, in 1993. A former American Film Institute classmate of mine, Gregory Bernstein, and I were looking for a project to do together, and he and I stumbled jointly on a trial transcript of Lincoln's assassins. That caught our attention because we didn't know there had been multiple assassins. Everyone thinks they know the story of the

Lincoln assassination. It turns out they don't. I thought the Lincoln assassination was John Wilkes Booth shoots Abraham Lincoln in the Ford Theatre, Lincoln dies several days later, Booth is later killed in a farmhouse, end of story. I had not known [as dramatized in the film] that there were multiple attacks that night. The Secretary of State was nearly killed, someone was at the residence of the Vice-President to kill him, and hundreds were rounded up. Eight civilians were tried by a military tribunal and one of them was a woman who ran a boarding house named Mary Surratt, who was likely on trial for crimes committed by her own son. None of that I knew, as I suspect most of your readers do not, and that was the starting point.

And once you got into the research part of it, did you – for example – pick up the Eisenschiml book [*Why Was Lincoln Murdered?* by Otto Eisenschmil] or *Blood on the Moon* [by Edward Steers]?

I suspect I looked at every book that has been written on the subject over the course of eighteen years. When I first started writing about this, most of those who wrote about the Mary Surratt portion of the story and of the conspirators tended to portray Mary as very much a martyr. Over the last eighteen years, many books have started to portray her as guilty of having helped conspire against Lincoln, or at least part of the conspiracy in some way, shape, or form. The facts haven't necessarily changed. The testimony certainly hasn't changed, but the interpretation of some of those facts and testimony has changed. Further research and scholarship has also been done – but over the years I looked at a broad spectrum of opinion and the movie portrays this broad spectrum of opinion…The story is told from Mary Surratt's point of view, in the sense that she is describing to her counsel, Frederick Aiken, played by James McAvoy, what she said took place. So we see it through her point of view, but the issues of guilt or innocence are left open.

Yeah, I thought the movie did a good job of portraying this ambivalence; in some ways, what you bring to the story informs the extent to which you think Mary was guilty. Although she clearly knew something.

That's right, I think. The only fact as to Mary Surratt's guilt or innocence in the murder of Lincoln is that it is certain that we don't know. It is one of the enduring mysteries. In my opinion, the story of Mary Surratt and the Lincoln assassination is more of the most remarkable, and hardly known, American stories.

Now at any time was there any thought given to an *Executive Action* version of the story? In other words, actively speculating as to, for example, Stanton's involvement? As I understand it, Mary Lincoln went to her grave believing he had been part of the conspiracy.

The focus was always on Frederick Aiken…I happened to be Frederick Aiken's age at the time this project started. I was 27, and now I am a few years older than Mary Surratt was. What was always the focus for me was this extraordinarily human story about a mother abandoned by her own son and a surrogate son, Frederick Aiken, who comes to her defense. A northern officer defending a southern woman accused of murdered his commander in chief. That is the center of the story and always has been. It's not about the Lincoln assassination in broad general terms, but rather of Aiken's defense of Mary Surratt and this extraordinary story that takes place at the center. That was always my emphasis. There are lots of side stories that undoubtedly interest many, but my focus was always on the mother-son story.

You also have some emphasis in this story on civil liberties, which many critics have jumped on as being a 9/11 analogue. Although I think this view is flawed, because when, for example, Kevin Kline (Stanton) says that civil rights have no meaning if you don't have a country, that was a much more legitimate concern at the time then it is now. In other words, there was really a danger then that you could lose the whole thing.

Keep in mind that when I first started working on *The Conspirator*, President Clinton was in the first few months of his inaugural term. George W. Bush wasn't even yet the governor of Texas. So I would have had to have been clairvoyant to predict the events as they unfolded. All I've tried to do throughout the period I was writing it is to portray as faithfully and accurately as possible the events that took place on April 14, 1865, and in the immediate days and months after. Any parallels to the present are simply history repeating itself, not me trying to deliberately draw those parallels. The issues of safety and security in the script vs. civil liberties were in the script from the outset. I will say that when I was writing those scenes when [for example] Reverdy Johnson was questioning the constitutionality of a military trial, these notions seemed more abstract in the nineties. There wasn't quite the frame of reference – there were historical precedents, certainly, but I essentially had to go the history books and they were less real. After 9/11, these were no longer abstract notions. I – we all had – a deeper understanding of what it must have been like on April 14, 1865 – the fear and anxiety. Context is an extraordinarily important aspect of this story. The challenge for me at the start was to try and portray these feeling for an audience. Now, post-September 11, an audience brings its own understanding of these circumstances.

The past is not a perfect parallel to the present, but there are similarities. An historic act of violence, the fear and confusion as to what was taking place, the roundup of many people, the hooding of detainees, referred to then as "public enemies," and now as "enemy combatants."

You bring up an interesting point. Although the use of a military tribunal was a first in this case, the tension hasn't really gone away. For example, after the Kennedy assassination, local authorities attempted to seize the body while federal authorities flew it out of Dallas. So these issues haven't really been resolved.

Well, first let me correct you. With respect to the conspirators, this was not the first time a military tribunal was used to try civilians. Far from it. It just so happened that took place in Washington City that day was unprecedented in Washington since the local courts were open and functioning. Just as an aside, with regard to conspiracies, the agendas in the movie are, I think, very clear.

Sure.

Personally, we often look for conspiracies that may or may not exist, but here is one that did exist. The objective of Booth and his co-conspirators was to accomplish what they had not accomplished on the battlefield: that is, to win the war. They attempted to decapitate the government by essentially taking out the chain of command: President, Vice-President, Secretary of State. And they came very close. Stanton's objective, as portrayed in the movie, was to ensure that the war stayed won and it is important to note that the trial of the conspirators took place just one month after the assassination and the execution of 4 of the 8 conspirators took place just three months afterward. So there is a real compression of time and Stanton is making decisions within the context of confederate troops still being on the field. As he states in the film, he wants them buried and forgotten and wants the war to stay won. He recognizes that the North may want to avenge their fallen President, that the South may rise again, and so this is his objective.

The other important thing is that had there been a civil trial, the only individuals who would have been able to serve on the jury were white males of a southern city. Most of those white males in Washington who were Northern sympathizers were off fighting the war. That left a city full of Southern men, which would have almost ensured that a jury full of Confederate sympathizers would be ruling on the case. This would have made it very difficult to get the verdict that the War Department wanted. The Attorney General's rationale for why a military tribunal was used was that Washington City was under martial law, 50,000 troops were protecting them less than 100 miles from Richmond, the former capitol of the confederacy, and these were "public enemies." A perfectly justifiable rationale at the time…As to whether it was constitutional or not, in 1866 the Supreme Court ruled (on a different case, not this one) called Ex parte Milligan that civilians are entitled to a trial by jury be it in times of war or peace when the courts are open and functioning.

Yes, that was it exactly…I was not so much talking of the conspiracy but the tension that occurs when you have essentially a domestic crime but the assassination is of a public leader. Whose jurisdiction does it become? And you answered that very well. Moving to Aiken himself, what did you make of the congratulatory letter that Aiken later wrote to Jefferson Davis when Davis was released from prison?

He writes a letter to Jefferson Davis prior to the war [offering his services to the Confederacy]. I am not aware of one afterward. But Aiken then serves so nobly in the Union. He becomes a Union man. When Lincoln died, he authored a remembrance of Lincoln, although he neither voted for him in 1860 nor 1864. Aiken is an interesting character, almost lost to history in many respects. As a journalist, he wrote almost nothing that I can find on the case. And even his obituary, which appears in the *Washington Post*, has a number of factual inaccuracies. And he was the first city editor of the Post! So you're not exactly sure what is true or not about Aiken.

At what point did Redford become involved?

The genesis of that was that in 2008 the script was optioned by a company called the American Film Company, initiated by Joe Ricketts, the founder of Ameritrade. Mr. Ricketts believes that there is an audience for historically accurate and intelligent American films. He and three of the principals went searching for material and read some 300 scripts. Someone – a mutual intermediary – sent my script to them and they responded very favorably. They then approached a number of the talent agencies for recommendations for directors. Robert Redford was on one of the lists. I think they all immediately thought there is just no way Robert Redford will direct our debut film but we may as well give it a shot. But he responded favorably and very quickly to it. That was in the late spring 2009. I met with Redford for the first time in August of 2009. Filming began in Savannah, Georgia that October and wrapped by the end of the year.

Amazing. So you worked on this script for –whatever it is – fifteen or more years – and then it sort of instantly happened.

It's taken eighteen years for my fifteen minutes. I wouldn't quite describe myself as an overnight sensation. (laughs) But if somebody had told me then that it's going to take eighteen years, but Robert Redford will direct your screenplay and Robin Wright, James McAvoy, Tom Wilkinson, Kevin Kline, Evan Rachel Wood, Danny Huston, among other great actors would star in it, I would have taken that.

Sure. Now in the meantime you did write *The Bronx is Burning*, did you not?

That was a much faster track. I had written a script for ESPN that wasn't produced, about Joe DiMaggio and Marilyn Monroe's relationship, and they liked that script. They asked me to create a bible based on a book by Jonathan Mahler called *The Bronx is Burning*. That book focuses on a mayoral election, the Son of Sam crime spree, the blackout, and the Yankees. ESPN was interested in the sports aspect as you know, having seen the show. Daniel Sunjata, John Turturro, and Oliver Platt took the leads, and although it was eight hours, it was directed very much like a feature film. One guy directed the whole thing, Jeremiah Chechik. That was a similar thing in some respects – you take a story that people think they know and show them what they didn't know. My background is as a journalist, so my objective was the same – show what happened. The difference is that the people are much accessible from 1977 than 1865, obviously.

One fascinating thing I took away from it was that DiMaggio comes off better than Mickey Mantle in the show – which is the reverse, I think, of how they are generally viewed. DiMaggio is often depicted as kind of a cold fish but in the show he has a deep connection to Reggie Jackson - because they are both gods.

Yeah, that is an extraordinary moment [DiMaggio going into the Yankee locker room to talk to Jackson] – but DiMaggio was prickly. There was that moment when tickets were not available for him so he got so angry he refused to throw out the first ball. And it's kind of a funny story, they're scrambling, and they end up getting a little kid to toss out the first ball. So yeah, he is portrayed favorably, but he could be prickly.

Well, it was very interesting. Thanks very much for your time.

Thanks for your interest.

PETER BOGDANOVICH

I spoke to Peter Bogdanovich for the San Antonio Current when he came down to San Antonio to speak at the Jewish Community Center. He had just published his wonderful collection of interviews, Who the Devil Made It, *with directors such as Otto Preminger, Alfred Hitchcock, George Cukor, and Howard Hawks. I was tremendously excited to do the interview, being a fan of* Targets, The Last Picture Show, Paper Moon, *and the brilliant* They All Laughed *primarily, but also cognizant of Bogdanovich's connections with older directors and the place he carved out for himself in history as a result.*

When, years later, I met and interviewed Joe McBride, it meant I had interviewed both of the featured players in the lost Orson Welles film, The Other Side of the Wind. *For a film buff like myself, this is about as good as it gets.*

GREEN: What will be the focus of your talk at the JCC?

BOGDANOVICH: I'm going to try and explain the title of my book, *Who the Devil Made It.* Hopefully it will be funny; I don't want it to be a dry talk. It will be an insider's view of directing, drawn from both the experiences of these other directors as well as my own experiences. We'll also be showing clips from *Notorious, Red River, Anatomy of a Murder,* and *The Last Picture Show.*

To what degree do you believe in the auteur theory?

Films reflect a certain personality, at least if they're interesting. Although film is a collaborative medium, directors certainly are able to put their own stamp on them. That's what really interests me — when a director is able to do so.

Would you say Hawks was your biggest influence?

I learned a great deal from many directors: Orson [Welles], Renoir, Hitch, Hawks.

Do you think that a film 'personality' is mainly aesthetic, or thematic?

Personality is not always just about theme, nor is it necessarily about camera placement. How does a film reveal the particular characters that are involved? How do you get a sense of the time and place? This is what interests me. But it's all connected – actors, direction, screenwriting.

What would you say about your own personality?

That's for someone else to analyze. I'm not self-conscious that way.

One thematic tie [for your films] might be the idea of nostalgia. For example, *Picture Show* and *Paper Moon*.

I don't think that's entirely accurate. It's been said of me before, but nostalgia is a sentimental emotion. I think that *The Last Picture Show* and *Paper Moon* are more elegiac. *Paper Moon*, although it has a nostalgic quality, is not so much about that as it is about – what's the phrase? – a dysfunctional relationship.

Where the little girl is the boss.

She's the leader, yes.

Looking at your films, it seems that you're not particularly interested in purely aesthetic experiments. You use a more honest, narrative approach.

Movies that tell stories. I like actors, and I'm interested in people. I enjoy craft and technique, but only in the service of filmmaking. Films that exist just as a kind of experiment don't do it for me. There's a quote I like by

Thomas Hardy: "Character is plot." I like that definition. *Picture Show* is about a ten people in a small town in 1951, just as *They All Laughed* is about a group of people during 4 days in 1980.

Do you find that you prefer the leaner qualities of say, a Hawks film, as opposed to New Wave? Or, just as an example, *Blowup*?

I like Godard's work, especially his earlier stuff. *Contempt* is about people. Truffaut — I enjoy some of it. But you can use technique and still tell a story. Orson Welles used a great deal of technique, but it didn't get in the way. I don't want the narrative is eclipsed by the telling. I want the audience to be unaware the story is being told. I like being swept away.

What about the deliberately antiseptic quality of Kubrick?

He's not one of my favorites. I liked *The Killing* and *Paths of Glory*.

Older films.

Yes. *Barry Lyndon*, at least for awhile. But his later pictures – I admire him a great deal. But not one of my favorites.

Are there any current trends that you find disturbing – or promising?

Well, mindlessness. Mindlessness is the main thing. Special effects to the exclusion of stories about human beings. And I have a real blind spot for science fiction. It just — leaves me cold, I don't get it. And horror movies, which are quite popular right now. So as you can tell, I'm not very "with it." I don't think any special effect can compete with the human face.

I don't know how familiar you are with the new horror films, but they – as well as, it seems, every film these days – tend to be highly self-conscious.

Yes, horribly self-conscious. They're aware of themselves. I like invisible filmmaking. Films that are interested in people.

Do you think it's just cyclical, or is there something in the air that's changed permanently?

I don't know. The thing about movies is, they go where the success is. If the public responds, they will always cater to that response. As far as where I think it's going, I'm a skeptical optimist. Hopefully, things will swing back to more adult concerns. I'm doing more lower-budget films where you're not obliged to have a $40 million opening weekend. If every movie has to open in 3,000 theaters, then you've got to try and make the movie to get the widest possible audience. And not every story has to cater to that.

I read something that Pauline Kael wrote a few years ago about the way films have changed. She said that there has never been a time when so many good actors have been around – but there's nothing for them to star in.

I would agree. Stories just aren't that interesting. And actors get to pick for themselves what they want to make; they're notoriously the worst judges of what they should star in. This is of course a broad comment, but it's always the comedian who wants to be in Hamlet.

That might account for the treacly Robin Williams pictures of late.

Well, you said it, I didn't. Of course, I haven't seen those pictures. But yes, stars used to be under contract – there were no free agents.

The studios took care of them.

Yeah, exactly. Production people, everybody, they were all trying to do their best to get pictures to suit the talent. It's not the same now. It'll never be the same. There's no studio system anymore, the studios are just like investors or producers – they front the money. Since everybody's a free agent, it becomes anarchistic. Stars don't know what they should be in.

How do you approach actors?

I am an actor. I tell them, I understand what some of your problems are.

Think of me as an actor who just happens not to be in this picture. Of course I've been acting recently, in *The Sopranos*.

So they just called you up, hey, would you like to be on *The Sopranos*?

That's it exactly. I knew David Chase from working on *Northern Exposure* – I had done an episode where I played myself – and it was a good experience. And then seven years later, he calls and asks me to play a psychiatrist to a psychiatrist in *The Sopranos*.

You've gotten a chance to write, direct, and act in Hollywood. Not many can say that. How did it all happen?

Well, it's a long story, but here's the short version: I was a theater director who came to Hollywood to make films. I was writing for Esquire at the time, and Roger Corman asked me to rewrite one of his pictures. He found out I could direct, and here we are. It was Roger Corman who broke me in.

JOSEPH MCBRIDE

Joseph McBride has been researching the Kennedy assassination for most of his life. As a twelve-year-old in 1960, he handed out flyers for John F. Kennedy's presidential run and was only sixteen when Kennedy was murdered in Dealey Plaza on November 22, 1963. He found my website and sent his contact info, which led to me reviewing his book INTO THE NIGHTMARE and this interview, and then later his participation in the documentary KING KILL 63, directed by Ryan Page, for which I served as a writer and coproducer. McBride has worn many hats in a long and brilliant career as a journalist, screenwriter, biographer, and investigative researcher. His screenwriting credits include the classic ROCK'N'ROLL HIGH SCHOOL, starring the Ramones; his biographies have included luminaries such as John Ford, Orson Welles, Steven Spielberg, and Frank Capra; and his acting credits include the classic Roger Corman film HOLLYWOOD BOULEVARD as well as the 'lost' Orson Welles film THE OTHER SIDE OF THE WIND, in which he co-starred with Peter Bogdanovich. Not a bad resume. But for all that, he also spent decades working on INTO THE NIGHTMARE, his extraordinary book chronicling his own descent into the Kennedy assassination. When we sat down to do the interview, we ended up having a conversation that touched on many subjects, so much so that I edited it down for its original publication. I include the full interview here for the first time.

JOSEPH McBRIDE: I might recommend a book to you. A friend of mine, Glenn Frankel, head of the journalism department at the University of Texas, just wrote a book on *The Searchers*. He's a Pulitzer-Prize winning author. Have you seen it?

GREEN: No, I have not.

It's a wonderful book. He won a Pulitzer for covering the Middle East conflict for the Washington Post. So he's not a film person per se, but it is a great book and getting great notices. You may know it's based on the story of Cynthia M. Parker.

Yes.

She was kidnapped by the Comanches. It's quite a story. Amazing piece of research. He did a lot of original research and interviews and goes into the novel and the film as well and changed history into myth.

Interesting. I was thinking that you are the second person that I've interviewed that knew Howard Hawks.

Oh really?

I interviewed Peter Bogdanovich many years ago when he came down to San Antonio for his book *Who the Devil Made It*.

Oh yeah.

Anyway, he had great stuff on Hawks. And it's funny because, you mentioning Ford, I think *The Searchers* is basically the only film I like by Ford. In comparison to Hawks especially – there are aspects to Ford's films that I like – the dancing sequences he always puts in, and so on, but they seem stodgy in some way. They seem more rooted in the Old West that Ford ended up repudiating to some extent in *The Searchers*, as opposed to Hawks, whose films aren't very "serious" in that way. They are nominally Westerns because that happens to be the trappings, but they're Hawks films – there are guys, friends with other guys, and there's a girl, and it has those tropes. How do you feel about that?

Well, Hawks is more modern, and Ford is somewhat archaic in that sense, although I actually like that. I can see where Hawks is more popular today. As you say, no matter what is going on in a Hawks film, they are all kind of similar in that it's a bunch of people hanging around bantering, having sexy talk and making puns. I love *Rio Bravo* and *El Dorado* is great too.

Those are really important to me too. And I love his definition of a good movie – "three great scenes, no bad scenes."

Yeah. *(laughs)* Don't offend the audience. Now have you seen Ford's *Fort Apache?*

Yes, I have.

Now that was the film that got me hooked on Ford. I was nineteen years old and already disillusioned by the assassination and here is this revisionist Western that came out in 1948 in which not only do the Indians win, but they are the good guys. I was amazed. It's quite a critique of America, that film.

You know, you're right, and I forgot about *Fort Apache*. With Fonda as the heavy.

Fonda's brilliant as a real bastard and Wayne is the good guy who is sympathetic toward the Indians, which is against people's expectations as well. It has a great visual style. *Liberty Valance* is a great film, too. You're right that Ford eventually rethought his mythology and critiqued it. I think he grew as an artist – and this is a sign of a truly great artist – that he grew to contradict himself. I quote Walt Whitman, "Do I contradict myself? Very well, then I contradict myself. I am large, I contain multitudes." I think of Ford as being big enough to question his own mythology. *Liberty Valance* is sort of that way – you probably like that, it has some Hawksian elements to it.

Sort of. There are certain things – the famous elements of the movie I do like, I like the structure of it, the story, but not the execution very much. I think it's just me and Ford.

Well some people are just Hawksians. It's an interesting debate. But they both liked each other a lot. They recognized their differences and kidded each other about it. Ford was sentimental, for example, and Hawks was quite unsentimental.

Yes, and there's this other thing too – and I think I read this in Bogdanovich – where Ford asks him what he got Wayne for Christmas. "A book." And Ford responds, "He's already got a book."

Oh yeah, that's a great story. Peter loves to tell that one.

There's something inherently controlling about that – maybe I'm taking it too seriously – but sort of inherently dislikable about that.

Ford could be mean. He was really kind of cruel to John Wayne, who loved him and took all kinds of abuse from him. Because Wayne, a smart guy, recognized he was doing his best work with Ford. There's an interesting new book on Wayne that his family put out that has letters no one's ever seen before, and it quotes Wayne as saying that he "never loved any man more than John Ford." He said it was a "fine, manly love" they had. It was almost like an abusive father relationship they had, where Ford could be kind and sweet at times, but he could be incredibly cruel, too, especially to the people he was closest to. For instance, he had this weird relationship with Ward Bond, who seemed like a horrible human being in many ways. Ford used to mock him relentlessly, but he loved him in some crazy way.

Wow. I don't know anything about Ward Bond, personally.

He was one of the leaders of the blacklist, an extreme right-winger. I interviewed Henry Brandon, who played Chief Scar in *The Searchers*, a German, very liberal guy and who was also gay, and he said that Ward Bond and Hedda Hopper ran the blacklist, the way he put it. He said, in Texas, if you tried to take a man's horse away, you'd be hung. Love that line. So he said Bond was a horror, in his words, "Bond was a shit, and a good actor." I always found it a fascinating thing because the tendency is for people to think that if they like an actor or a director that they must be a great guy but it's often not true. You can be a shit and be a great actor. I always thought Bond would be a good subject for research because there hasn't been a lot done, but there's a new book out called *Three Bad Men* which is about the friendship between Wayne, Ford, and Bond. [The author Scott Allen Nollen] puts together a fair amount of new material on Bond, who is hard to research because he wasn't written about much and he's been dead for a long time. But when he died, he was in Dallas. He had become friends – because of his appearances on *Wagon Train* – by these rich oil people like Clint Murchison.

No kidding.

That whole gang there. He would go to Dallas and hobnob with them – [he ended up dying] of a heart attack at a football game in the bathroom. He was overweight and wasn't taking care of himself. Ford was shattered and brought his body back to Hollywood. Ford had this chapel at the Motion Picture Home called the Field Photo Home for the veterans of World War II and he loved to put on big funerals just like he does in his films. They were going to do a big funeral for Bond. John Ford's daughter gave an interview in which she said the night before the funeral, somebody stole Ward Bond's body. They had it lying in state but it came back in time for the funeral.

Amazing.

Apparently these were his enemies who had done that. But he died three days before Kennedy was elected president and that to him would have been a calamity. The last thing he did before he died was write a letter against Communists – he kept it up to the bitter end.

I can imagine. The John Birchers thought Eisenhower was a Communist, so –

Yes. *(laughs)* That's one of the most amazing things. I don't know what Bond thought of Eisenhower, but he was a real stupid guy, too. Lamarr Johnson, the screenwriter of *The Grapes of Wrath*, said that John Huston, to keep working, had to go through this ritual with Ward Bond where Huston had to abase himself and admit all his political beliefs were wrong. "Isn't it terrible that Huston has to humiliate himself to an oaf like Ward Bond?" He took it upon himself to purge Hollywood. He wasn't the only one, obviously, but one of the ringleaders. A terrible thing. He's in *Rio Bravo* too.

He's in my favorite scene, where he tells Wayne "You mean all you've got is a drunk and a crazy old man?" And Wayne says, "That's *what* I've got."

Great scene. And then Bond helps him and ends up getting shot.

Although – and this is totally fascinating – but at some point I should probably ask you about Kennedy. *(laughs)*

Sure. *(laughs)*

Maybe a good place to start – I happened to read Deep Politics Forum and saw that you've been discussing your book there, and there are already little ripples from your opinion of researcher Mary Ferrell.

Yeah, I expected that to be provocative. There are lots of people who think she was wonderful.

But there are also a lot of people who think otherwise.

It's getting some good reactions. Some people are happy that the whistle is being blown on her. Since I'm a longtime journalist, I have a lot of experience in seeing through people fairly well. I smelled a rat with her right away. I write in the book about the Belmont memo – which nobody had ever written about before when I found it in the 1980s – and it is an amazing memo. It talks about how there is a bullet in Kennedy's right temple and this bullet was never entered into evidence. That memo alone destroys the Warren Report.

Sure.

I wanted to make sure that no one had ever written about this before, and I had heard that Mary Ferrell was very helpful. So I contacted her. She said "This is startling information and you're onto something important." And I asked her to please keep it to herself, because I want to print this. And when it was done I sent her the article and she said, "Now I'll feel free to tell anybody about it." And I said, well you told me you wouldn't spread the word. And she said "Now that I've read it, I can't not tell people about it." So that was very duplicitous. But nobody really wrote about that much until Doug Horne did a good analysis in his books. Also, Dale Myers reproduced it in his book *With Malice: Lee Harvey Oswald and the Murder of Officer J. D. Tippit*, but people didn't seem to recognize how important that memo was.

I saw that you mentioned that and I have not read the Myers book.

Just like the Warren volumes, the book ends up being very useful because there are always these nuggets in there to find and follow. In effect, the Warren Commission undercut their own report by putting out the 26 volumes. There's that quote from Allen Dulles who said "The American people don't read." But that actually didn't turn out to be true. In fact, people have been studying it since it came out, like Sylvia Meagher. I still think the best book on the assassination is her *Accessories After the Fact*. [This book is one of the first of the works criticizing the Warren Commission and was reissued in September 2013.] A great book that holds up beautifully. She logically demolished the report using the 26 volumes. Myers's book is very pro-Warren Report and minimizes all the problems and puts a lot of the contrary information in footnotes, but there is a lot of data that is useful in spite of itself.

I'd like to ask you a bit about Penn Jones, who is mentioned a few times in your book. I never knew him – he died really before I even knew he existed, and he is one of the first-generation critics I wish I had met. He was a good friend of my friend John Judge, and if you have any stories I'd love to hear them.

He was an amazing, wonderful character. I grew up in a family of journalists, my parents were journalists, and so I have a certain affection for the old journalistic style. My friend Sam Fuller – whose work you may know –

Oh yeah, of course!

He and I hit it off instantly because we had that newspaper connection.

Fuller was an old journalist and his work as a filmmaker was like an investigative reporter. Like *Shock Corridor* which came out right before the Kennedy assassination, really hits the nail on the head as far as analyzing the sickness of the country. The James Best character in that is somewhat like an Oswald-type character. So when I met Penn, I thought, wow, he's just like Sam Fuller, he's an old newspaper guy like me. And we became friends instantly. We spoke the same language. Penn was a very original, brave maverick in the best tradition of such. He wasn't always right, and he could go off on tangents – sometimes you had to take things with a grain of salt because he could make mistakes. Dave Perry loves to analyze Penn's mistakes. But he broke a lot of ground and he was out there in the early days, pounding the pavement, knocking on doors, getting those doors slammed in his face at times…coming up with leads for all of us and writing very eloquently on the case.

Sure. We all have our foibles, and our blind alleys, but that's much less important to me than being sincere and aggressive about the truth.

He was very passionate about Kennedy and America, a WWII veteran. He was convinced it was a military takeover and I think it's true. I spent a lot of time with him. Met him in 1983 for the 20th anniversary when I went to Dallas. Penn used to lead the ceremonies by giving a little prayer and a talk with his gimme cap [a cap given away by companies to farmers and truckers] on. I liked the way he dressed as a regular working guy.

He was very lucid at that time. Unfortunately, by 1993 when I spent about three months in Dallas, he was mentally almost gone. I spent a lot of time at Penn and Elaine's farm house in Waxahachie and we'd watch movies but he couldn't say very much. All he would say – he would repeat this one phrase over and over – "they like what they got and they ain't never gonna give it back." It was actually a kind of distillation of his whole attitude. Over the years he said many interesting things to me, like pointing out that Johnson was the only who ducked. [This is a reference to the Altgens photograph.]

Before he was gone, Penn asked John to continue that tradition of the

moment of silence on the grassy knoll, so John has been doing that every year and it is part of the COPA conference every November. Although it's questionable whether we're going to be able to do it this year.

Yeah, the whole thing is mishegas, sounds crazy. It's awful that they're trying to keep people out. The police department says they are going to keep out extremists.

Yeah, by their terms.

That fellow in the Dallas Observer – he's been writing good stuff – Jim Schutze. He said the one extremist they should keep out is the mayor.

Yeah, he's been great. We have somebody in Dallas who still likes free speech.

He pointed out it's a sign of insecurity that they have to control it so much. They keep out dissenting voices and it makes the city look bad. They're trying to get beyond the stigma of the tragedy, and perhaps they never will, but there are ways to deal with these things responsibly. Germany has dealt with WWII and the Holocaust by memorializing it and admitting their guilt and teaching it in schools. If Dallas did that, people would respect them for it. But instead they look like they have something to hide.

Which clearly they do.

Yeah. *(laughs)* Well if you read my book you realize that the Dallas police are up to their necks in the assassination, the plotting. There are some people who say it was just unfortunate that it happened in Dallas, there was just some crazy person…but actually it was more pervasive than just one person. The Dallas police and elements of the city were involved and some people in the Dallas establishment know that.

Oh, there's nothing accidental about it.

When Oswald is killed surrounded by several dozen policemen, handcuffed between two detectives and shot, that is enough to tarnish the city forever. But then you find out – and this was a major discovery – that Tippit and another policeman were sent out to find Oswald at the time.

Edgar Lee Tippit, [policeman J. D. Tippit's father] who was 90 years old and sharp as a tack and to whom no one had ever spoken before on the record, told me that Marie Tippit was visited by a policeman after the assassination to tell her what happened. He and J.D. had been told to hunt Oswald and Tippit had gotten there and been shot. The other policeman had apparently been in an auto accident. This was all new information. Although people had speculated – even as early as December 1963 – that Tippit had been sent out to find Oswald and shoot him, or capture him – but this is fresh confirmation from an inside source. Edgar Lee didn't know the name of the other policeman so I tried to explore that. I come out with some names of some policemen who were not where they were supposed to be and may be candidates.

That was a fascinating part of the book and information not available anywhere else.

That's an example of working as a reporter. I've done biographies of Frank Capra and John Ford, for example, and I've learned you have to do a tremendous amount of interviews as well as research into the available documents to get the whole picture. You can't do just one or the other. I spent seven years researching Capra to dot every i and cross every t. And I did the same thing with Tippit. When I did my Spielberg book, no one had ever done a serious biography of him, and no one had ever bothered to look up his friends, the people he had done films with as kids. What they all told me was that they had been waiting 30 years for someone to ring the doorbell.

So when the opportunity arose to talk to Edgar Lee, I went to his home in east Texas and sat down with him. The other key thing he told me was what an uncannily expert shot his son was. There was one document in his personnel file that shows J. D. to be a mediocre shot, but this seems like disinformation.

248

And as you pointed out in the book, the further along you get into Tippit's personnel file, the material grows more and more sparse – the opposite of what you would expect.

Yes, that's suspicious, suggesting it was sanitized. A policeman who served for 11 years would have more than one firing skill evaluation. It's odd that there's only one. After about 1956 the file gets thinner and thinner.

One gets the feeling that this book has been gestating for 50 years. It's relatively "safe" now on the left to write about McCarthy – but JFK remains a hot topic. Were you waiting for a while to put this book out because of that, or did it just take that long to get it right?

It took that long. This was a very difficult book to write about for a lot of reasons. It's a very complex subject and intricate and no one person can do the whole thing. That's why we rely on a community, why people like us form a community to work on this stuff. One of the best pieces of advice Penn gave me – and he also gave it to Larry Ray Harris – was take one part of the case that hasn't been studied enough and research the hell out of it. So I zeroed in on the Tippit part of it. We learned this in Watergate. The hidden part is the most important, the point of maximum psychological resistance is most important.

When you read the Warren Report, one thing that strikes you is how little it talks about Tippit. Sylvia Meagher said [Tippit] was unknown and unknowable, and I took that as a challenge. For Capra, for example, his life was completely different from what people thought, and if you're a reporter you can get the real story if you work hard enough. Of course, in this case it's even more difficult because witnesses have been killed, or they're scared. One of the unfortunate side effects of Penn's mysterious deaths [detailed in his out-of-print book *Forgive My Grief* series] is that it scared some witnesses into hiding.

Now there is an extremely high percentage of violence in the relatively small section of the Tippit case. The high degree of mortality is more than even other areas of the assassination, and there is a high degree of anxiety among those witnesses. That tells you something right there. So it took a lot

249

of time and legwork and research at the National Archives - six million pages came out after [Oliver Stone's movie] *JFK*, although many documents are still being kept secret after all these years. Jefferson Morley is still trying to pry documents out about George Joannides who was supervising the anti-Castro Cubans. After 50 years, they're still withholding documents.

When I told one of my friends I was writing this book, that person asked "So what contemporary issues are you interested in?" I said this is a contemporary issue. Morley is still trying to get documents being hidden for reasons of national security. What is the national security reason for hiding something after 50 years? Army intelligence and Secret Service documents have been purged. The autopsy photos are still hidden. A lot of the evidence was altered and falsified so critical analysis becomes key for evaluation. I have learned not to take things at face value. When I was a kid I was raised Catholic and Democrat and I had my beliefs shattered and I no longer was able to take things at face value.

With Tippit, some witnesses say Oswald did it, and some say the killer didn't look anything like Oswald, and some people say two men did it, and you have to sort all this out and figure out. It's like [the Akira Kurosawa film] *Rashomon* where you have different versions of reality. It took a lot of work to shape this out. I experimented with different approaches and finally decided on a memoir, and the book follows my evolution. I was a skeptic right from the beginning, because at 12:40PM that day, the radio reported shots fired from the overpass at the front, and then at one o'clock, they changed to the Texas School Book Depository and I thought immediately there was something wrong. They didn't bother explaining why the story had changed. I smelled a rat within 20 minutes. And then that evening on television at 7:55PM when Oswald said he hadn't shot anybody and that he was a patsy, I believed him. He seemed honest and credible. He clearly was shocked to be accused of shooting Kennedy. But then like a lot of people I was fooled by the Warren Report until the books started to come out – Mark Lane, Sylvia Meagher – and the media was fairly open about debating it. By about '67 [I felt I was] totally unable to evaluate the case, but I feel now that it was the beginning of wisdom.

Then Watergate opened my eyes, because here was a genuine conspiracy in which everybody recognized it. It validated Peter Dale Scott's deep politics, the hidden aspects of government that lie beneath the surface. We don't know a lot about Obama's government, and when people like Bradley Manning and Edward Snowden come forward, they're getting prosecuted for trying to tell us the truth. As a result of the Kennedy assassination, things changed forever and it still affects the present day.

We should talk about the Hoover memo a bit, and your experiences at *The Nation* magazine, and the issues trying to publish an article about it. The editor [Victor Navasky] had a guy with a CIC (Counterintelligence Corps) background edit your piece.

Yes. Richard Lingeman, who is still at the *Nation* and a distinguished biographer. He recently wrote about his experiences with the Counterintelligence Corps in the 1950s. He specifically denies being a CIA operative but said he had some dealings with them, as you would if you were in the intelligence field. He was stationed in Japan. But the salient facts are that he had a background in intelligence and in 1988 he mentioned doing work for the United States Information Agency, which is part of the propaganda arm of our government. At the same time, he was rewriting my first article. To give full disclosure, I wrote a show called *Let Poland Be Poland* for the Reagan administration. I was against Reagan but at the time I was convinced he was on the right side of supporting Solidarity and it turned out to be a good thing. I have that small connection there.

When I found the Hoover memo, which is dated Nov 29, 1963, it revealed an FBI briefing done with George Bush of the CIA and described how the anti-Castro Cubans were reacting to the Kennedy assassination.

Which – interestingly – was a lie. [The memo indicates that those Cubans were sad about Kennedy's death, which they weren't.]

Yeah. It is a strange cover story of some kind. They were worried about a negative reaction or something coming from the Cubans. It relates to Peter Dale Scott's Phase One/Phase Two analysis. Scott had a big influence on me and helped me understand the political context. He has a theory that the plotters wanted the assassination to trigger an attack on Cuba which

Kennedy had previously denied them. Curtis LeMay and others wanted to obliterate Cuba during the Cuban Missile Crisis. I think Kennedy was very sobered by the Cuban Missile Crisis and so was trying to pull back on that. He was trying to reach out to Castro and work out a reasonable détente.

Via Jean Daniel.

One thing I found out in my research in the analysis of the media is how they have covered up and distorted this case, but also been involved in some of the activities. *Life Magazine* bankrolled a raid against Cuba [using Alpha 66] which might have been part of the attempt to kill Castro, but some of the same players in the JFK assassination were involved in that as well. Then *Time-Life* became one of the leading cover-up agencies following the assassination, They owned the Zapruder film. Why would *Life Magazine* own a key piece of evidence in the case? And they distorted it as well.

I used to be skeptical about Zapruder film alteration. Over the years I had to kind of learn about a few things. I resisted believing that the Zapruder film had been altered apart from the obvious damage that *Life Magazine* did.

The cutting out of the frames, yes.

But Douglas Horne's research proved to me that Zapruder film was altered in various ways. His interview with CIA technician Homer McMahon says that the version of the film he saw that weekend showed Kennedy being hit by 6-8 shots from at least three directions. We don't see that in the film and we don't see the car come to a stop. Senator Ralph Yarborough told me that the car came to a stop and Secret Service men ran out of the vehicle and you don't see this [in the Zapruder film], you see only Clint Hill jumping onto the car.

[Lyndon] Johnson was being investigated and Don Reynolds had been testifying that very day about corruption and bribery. Robert Caro says that this was happening at the exact moment that Kennedy was being shot. Also at that same moment, *Life Magazine* was holding a meeting in which they were about to conduct an investigation into Johnson's finances. Johnson knew he was likely to go to jail, and at the very least be dropped from the ticket, and this provides a powerful motive for him. For a long time I resisted believing that Johnson was involved.

I think he was very blackmailable. It's clear he didn't like Kennedy, he had everything to gain from having Kennedy removed, and it seems pretty clear he knew it was going to happen. I don't think he ran the assassination. Unlike what Philip Nelson and Ed Tatro suggest – whom I really like – I don't think he was the prime mover of the assassination.

One of the things I had to decide was how much to go into certain areas. For a while I was thinking of going into more detail on Johnson and how he was involved exactly, but that would have been a different book. That could be a whole book in itself, which some people have written – not very well, but it's a serious subject. I agree with you that he was not the main instigator. But he was certainly involved. Johnson ran the cover-up, and the Warren Commission was really the Johnson Commission. They called it the Warren Commission because it makes it sounds better, but it was really LBJ controlling that. He was in a position to issue orders for everything, including the autopsy and destruction of evidence.

No, I think that's all correct, I agree on that. Where I stop is the design of the assassination. The assassination is a military operation. Johnson either knows about it beforehand or he is being blackmailed into cooperating because he has a powerful motive to do so. Both for reasons of power and to stay out of jail. Johnson was obviously a very bad guy. I think last year – or maybe the year before – Ed Tatro gave a presentation at COPA where he very entertainingly gave us 50 terrible anecdotes about LBJ. It was funny and appalling at the same time, but…it's hard trying to imagine the mentality of a guy who was taking his genitals out all the time, peeing on his security detail. That guy was running the country for a while.

It is astonishing. Caro does a great number on Johnson, although when it comes to the assassination…I was really hoping he would rise to the occasion. Some years ago, Caro had given a speech in which he said that it was "*literally* a blood feud" between Kennedy and LBJ. He didn't say *figuratively*. This is a man who uses words very carefully. So I had hopes. But when it came down to it, he buckled under because you don't make it to the big dance – the awards – by questioning the Warren Report.

One of the things Yarborough told me was about Johnson's demeanor, because he was riding in the back seat with him. He was tense, very quiet. He wouldn't wave at people. Yarborough said he even told Johnson, "Look at all these people, they're all waving at you, why don't you wave back?" Even though they weren't fond of each other. And Johnson just stared straight ahead, very preoccupied, tense. He attributed that to the Don Reynolds hearing only later, when he found out about it. He also said that Johnson and [Rufus] Youngblood were both listening to the walkie-talkie Youngblood carried on his shoulder.

When Penn Jones said that Johnson was "ducking" – you can see in the Altgens photograph that Johnson is leaning forward - right after the shots were fired, LBJ huddled with Youngblood to listen to the walkie-talkie. But I think they were actually listening in during the shooting. There were two frequencies – one for the motorcade itself but another that connected with the White House situation room and local communication hookup through the Sheraton Hotel. I suspect they were listening to get the bigger picture of what was happening both in Washington and Dallas.

When I read that in your book, the first thing that went through my mind was when Johnson later asks Hoover "were they shooting at me?"

That's fascinating. People wonder whether Johnson was engaging in a sham or if he was really worried. One thing that's very odd that goes against protocol, is for both presidents to be in the same motorcade, especially that close together. It's very strange. So some people think the plotters were sending a message to Johnson by making him witness the assassination.

Johnson is riding in this car and he knows what's going to happen, but maybe this thought goes through his mind – if they can get rid of one, they can get rid of the other. How can he be sure that he is not also being double-crossed?

Some things I didn't go into. After the assassination, LBJ became very suspicious of the Secret Service and refused to have them protect him. He got the FBI to send men instead to provide his protection because he didn't trust the Secret Service. Remarkable.

It is certainly suggestive. He is a gangster who knows he's dealing with other gangsters.

I think Vince Palamara has done great work on the Secret Service side of the case, and he proves something that I also could not have imagined at the time in the 1960's – that the Secret Service was involved in the assassination. If you study political assassinations, you find that almost inevitably the bodyguards are involved. Like Indira Gandhi, who was killed by her bodyguards. It's very hard to kill a head of state without penetrating the security apparatus in some way.

In the book I mention a lead that hasn't been explored enough. As we know, E. Howard Hunt gave a deathbed confession to his son. (Some people think he [Hunt] was one of the three tramps.) Now the guy running the operation was Cord Meyer, Jr. of the CIA. Hunt says that he was running it with Johnson and that LBJ had directed him to do the operational details. He didn't necessarily know who the triggermen were. Such operations have "cut-outs," where one triggerman doesn't know who the other one is, and everything is compartmentalized. But this was a surprise to me. Cord Meyer is a possible candidate for a mastermind of the assassination – and it's interesting to note that he was married to Kennedy's mistress Mary Meyer, who was allegedly killed for being too curious and knowledgeable. It needs more research. The whole issue of Johnson's culpability is a subject that needs more work, as Robert Caro unfortunately didn't do it for us.

One thing that I hadn't mentioned but occurs to me now – I take it you've seen Errol Morris's short film with Josiah Thompson?

Yes, It's disturbing.

For both guys.

Yes. Alex Cox did a short film in response, and he also has a book out on the assassination as well [*The President and the Provocateur: The Parallel Lives of JFK and Lee Harvey Oswald*]. He's great, a maverick film director, does great work.

Absolutely. I also have an intense interest in 1970's film – I'm kind of an *Easy Riders Raging Bulls* kind of guy, love the period with films like *Three Days of the Condor, The Conversation*, and especially *The Parallax View*.

You know, I got to interview Alan Pakula [director of *The Parallax View, Klute, All the President's Men, Sophie's Choice* and many others].

Fantastic.

Wonderful guy, Brilliant man. I had an interview lined up with him when I was on Daily Variety. He was shooting *All the President's Men* and I was supposed to go to his house on Saturday afternoon but somehow the publicist didn't tell him I was coming. So I rang the doorbell at his house and there he was, but completely preoccupied with the shoot. He said "I'm really sorry, I don't have time to talk now." But I threw him a question – I was close to someone who knew the people who had written the book on the Robert Kennedy assassination...

Bill Turner and -

[Jonn] Christian and Turner, right. *The Assassination of Robert F. Kennedy*. My friend had told me that Bob Woodward was CIA. And actually it turns out he was in Naval Intelligence. ONI. But I mentioned it quickly to Pakula: "You're making *All the President's Men* - have you heard the story that Woodward is CIA?" And he responded, "Yeah, I've heard this. But, frankly, I have to not consider that while I'm making this film because if I did, it would drive me crazy."

Wow.

"So maybe it's true, but I can't go into that, it would drive me crazy and I wouldn't know how to make this film." Someone should remake that film. It's a really good film but it's a fairy tale.

When you read [Len Colodny and Robert Gettlin's] *Silent Coup* and [Jim Hougan's] *Secret Agenda*, you realize it was an intelligence operation to bring down Nixon, with the help of Woodward, who was a Naval Intelligence officer posing as a journalist. This is still a big taboo in American journalism because it undercuts the notion of the hero Woodward and the great liberal bastion Washington Post.

Instead of the CIA front that it is.

The Post is a CIA front. One of the interesting things about the *Nation* article I did is that the story was picked up by many different outlets. The media was fascinated with it for about ten days and I was on C-SPAN and Brian Lamb interviewed me. Even Tom Wicker had written an article questioning whether we really wanted a President with an intelligence background, because he might be blackmailed with his dark secrets. That's true, but the fact is that you don't get to be CIA director without some experience in the field. He lied under oath during his hearing when he was being confirmed as CIA director. If the media had followed up on my story, he might have been disqualified from being President. But the media had been interested in my story until the CIA broke their policy and announced that the George Bush from the memo was a different George Bush.

There was one other George Bush at that time working for the CIA and I found him very quickly. He was a low level operative, a young man at the time, George William Bush, a functionary who did not receive the briefing. The media dropped it like a hot potato at that moment and they did not report on my follow up stories in the *Nation*. But the Washington Post didn't cover it at all. They didn't even run a summary instead of the AP story, as some papers will do. They just ignored it. And a friend of mine at one point said, look at the comic strip "Bloom County" around that time. It was a comic strip and it appeared in both the Baltimore Sun and the Washington Post that same day, and in the comic one of the characters is reading a newspaper with the headline "Bush was in the CIA in 1963." In the Baltimore paper, you could read it. In the Post, they had blown up the panel so you couldn't see the headline. They went to the lengths of censoring a comic strip to hide it from their readers. A little indication about how threatened they were. And then later I learned that when Bush was starting his Zapata oil company, one of the investors was Eugene Meyer, who owned the Washington Post and was the father of Katharine Graham.

Bush was also the head of the Republican National Committee at the time of Watergate, which I had pointed out in my original *Nation* article and which Lingeman rewrote and removed. And I said it was significant because…it was possible that Bush was one of the people who helped engineer Nixon's ouster. He was one of the people who convinced him to resign. He may have been working behind the scenes to push Nixon out. The *Nation* didn't like that at all and they said I was paranoid, which I found insulting. I also didn't like them having someone rewrite my articles, but I felt it was more important to get the story out. It was the only time in my career I allowed someone to rewrite my work, although I was able to rewrite his rewrite even though there were certain things I wasn't allowed to put back in.

There is this thing in the Nixon tapes, and I can't recall if Haldeman or Nixon says it, but they are trying to have something done and basically the line is "Well, get George Bush to do that, because he'll do anything."

Ah, yeah. That was one of the odd things, here's this guy who is an obscure congressman from Texas in 1968, but he's already being considered by Nixon as a vice-presidential candidate? It's very weird, because they had so many more ostensibly qualified people. He ended up with Agnew, who was obviously terrible, but why would you even consider a first-term Texas congressman? But this tells you they had a deep connection. Prescott Bush was one of Nixon's first backers, and some people even think that it was Prescott who picked Nixon to run in that first race against Jerry Voorhis.

Yes. Nixon talked about the "Committee of 100."

Nixon's a fascinating character, I wish I had more time to go into him. When you go into the Nixon tapes and the Haldeman memoir, you find out that Nixon is talking about "the Texans" who supplied some of the money for the Watergate burglars. People think that George Bush was possibly one of the people who supplied that money which was being laundered in Mexican bank. Bush was possibly involved in the actual Watergate break-in, which in my opinion and that of Jim Hougan and Colodny & Gettlin, was a CIA operation designed to create a trap for Nixon to walk into. And he walked right in and started committing illegal acts. And I think Oliver Stone's *Nixon* is a brilliant film, especially the uncut version. It's really an accurate representation. They show – have you seen the long version with Helms? [In the film *Nixon*, there is a long scene where Anthony Hopkins, as Nixon, confronts Richard Helms at his CIA office. The scene was cut from the theatrical release but is available on DVD.]

That's the best scene in the picture.

Sam Waterston, playing Helms. It really gets to the heart of darkness, as he speaks to Nixon about the secrets that lie beneath the surface. And critics really missed the point of that movie – Oliver had to make it a subtext ultimately because he was so beaten up about *JFK* – but it was about Nixon's guilty knowledge of the Kennedy assassination.

Penn Jones put out that story about the party at Clint Murchison's home [prior to the assassination, in which Hoover, Lyndon Johnson, and others were alleged to have participated]. I don't believe it.

I don't believe it either.

However, Nixon did have some guilty knowledge, it's clear, and he was in Dallas the day of the assassination. And I found that Bush had been there that day as well. And then Russ Baker in his book found that Bush had been there the night before, which I hadn't known. Baker concludes that Bush and his wife flew to Tyler, Texas on the morning of November 22. Baker told me he believes Bush's wife when she says they then flew to Houston from Dallas on the afternoon of November 22, but – small disagreement here – I think that Bush stayed in Dallas, like he told the FBI that he was going to do. He was checking into the Sheraton hotel which just so happened to be center for the White House communication agency and the Secret Service.

It's interesting how that all ties together. So it turns out that there are four present and/or future U.S. presidents in Dallas [on November 22, 1963]: Kennedy, Johnson, Nixon, and Bush.

JOHN JUDGE

It's fitting that John Judge should take us into this book and leave it, because I have little doubt that I never would have written either of my DISSENTING VIEWS books without his influence.

The Museum will continue, led by his partner Marilyn Tenehoff. See the website at www.museumofhiddenhistory.org.

GREEN: That's an intriguing name. Why the Museum of Hidden History?

JOHN JUDGE: I think most of history, including our own, is hidden from us by various means. As a simple example, the history of the Europeans in America is not the same history as the indigenous people who were nearly eliminated in the process of "civilization" and occupation. History is often intentionally destroyed by conquering cultures and colonizers.

The history we are taught in school is from one perspective, the dominant paradigm of the culture, and omits many other aspects, perspectives and facts as less relevant. Mahatma Gandhi said that history is usually told as the history of war, conflict and military victories, but that the real history of humanity is one of cooperation, which in fact is why the species has survived, but rarely mentioned.

President Truman one said that the only new thing in the world is the history we do not know. The National Archives uses the slogan, "The Past is Prologue," pointing to the fact that our history is important to our present and our possible future.

Especially in the modern era, since the start of WWII, history has increasingly become a commodity of warring nations and their emerging security organizations. Winston Churchill noted that in wartime, "Truth must be surrounded by a bodyguard of lies." Secrecy became the norm with the Manhattan Project and the inception of the nuclear arms race and the Cold War. Since then, nearly one billion records have been classified and kept from public view relating to both military and civilian agencies and operations of the United States, both at home and abroad. Our history is literally buried in underground vaults controlled by undemocratic agencies for the assumed protection of the society and the democracy this thwarts.

Even recent history is being lost and distorted, and we are in danger of entering a post-historical consciousness because so little emphasis is put on history.

People are naturally curious about secrets, about what is hidden or untold. We want to use that curiosity to expose millions of visitors to Washington, DC to three types of history they are not likely to know. We define hidden history as:

- History we don't see because of miseducation and assumptions
- History we can't see because of our paradigms and lack of counter-narratives
- History we are not allowed to see because of the National Security State
- Our core will be the history of America's recent past and the covert operations it has carried out against people around the world as well as its own citizens. But we will also present both national and local history from diverse perspectives, new investigations and released files, and fresh revisions based on unearthed facts.

Where would this be located? Why?

The Museum of Hidden History will be located in Washington, D.C. It will focus on American history, so the nation's capital seems to be the right location for that. Washington is also host to tens of millions of visitors each year from around the world that we hope to introduce to the history Americans do not know, but many others in the world do. The Museum will combine a library, an archive and exhibits. We will locate the initial stage, a Hidden History Research Center, and eventually the Museum, near a Metro for public access, and in an area of community development to engage participation from local residents as well. In addition, we hope to have traveling exhibits displayed at other museums around the country, and possibly a mobile exhibit van that would include examples of local hidden history wherever it stopped, creating an exhibit in D.C. that would highlight those aspects from many different cities and states.

D.C. is of course the heart of our national security state in many ways. Why is it important to have an alternative voice in our nation's capital?

The history presented by the Smithsonian, while often including other perspectives, is still told in the framework of assumptions that distort real or deep historical realities. Much of our buried history resides in the National Archives and Records Administration facilities in and around Washington, and we will promote further transparency and declassification instead. The local International Spy Museum works from a perspective of defending our cover operations and our national security apparatus. The recent creation of museums about Native Americans and African-Americans are welcome new perspectives on the dominant stories. We hope to include even more voices and perspectives including diverse immigrant communities, women, and others. We want to present "people's history," as Howard Zinn put it, the untold story of struggles for civil liberties, civil rights, peace, economic justice and democratic society as well as the government and corporate operations that were created to oppose them. The need to both preserve alternative history and to present it arises from centuries of distortion and decades of miseducation that have made our world so confusing to all but the victims.

Thomas Jefferson once said that, given the choice between a government without a newspaper and a newspaper without a government, he would always choose the latter. He understood that the flow of information and knowledge was more central to a democratic society than the government machinery that functioned to carry it out. Similarly, Jefferson believed that there was no safe repository for the powers of a society but in the people themselves. He knew that if one believed these people "unable to exercise their discretion in a wholesome fashion", the remedy was not to "take the power from them, but to inform their discretion". That is what we hope the museum will help to do.

Why is so much of our history hidden? What does that say about the place we live in?

History carries both lessons and self-identity and realization. Cultures and societies build on and rely on their histories. Oral traditions carried these for many people in pre-literate societies, but we are now entering a post-literate era that threatens the loss of even written history for the current generations. George Orwell's theme in his dystopian future novel, 1984, was that, "Those who control the present control the past and those who control the past control the future." The job of Winston, his protagonist in the novel was to destroy historical records and photographs down the "Memory Hole", to rewrite the past newspapers to reflect the present, and to manipulate the historical reality of wars and state propaganda. His associate at the Ministry of Truth had the task of reducing the number of words in the dictionary so that concepts considered dangerous could be eliminated as well. It has always been in the interest of conquering cultures to destroy and distort the history of the vanquished and of those in power to control the history and image of their ascendency to power. Added to this trend, we now have the demands of the National Security State, which asserts that some concepts are classified at birth, and that our history is better conducted in secret. "History," Henry Kissinger wrote, "to be successful, must be negotiated in absolute secrecy."

However, in a democracy, policies cannot be evaluated or changed without public scrutiny and open and transparent government operations. This commoditization of our history since WWII has put the decisions back into the hands of an elite which perpetuates its control through that secrecy. We are now approaching the event horizon of a black hole of classification, with 15.5 million new records classified each year, searches for one million declassified records to make them secret again since 9/11, and a petabyte of electronic records classified every 18 months. Human readers could not be hired in sufficient numbers to even view such volumes of information in the same time periods to review them for declassification. Meta-tags will now be used to mark the electronic files for classification and for declassification reviews by machines, not humans.

There are some fantastic names attached to the Museum. How did Howard Zinn, for example, come to know and support the idea?

I approached Howard Zinn after a public talk in Washington, D.C. to introduce him to our idea for a Museum of Hidden History and he asked me to send more information. He agreed to sponsor the effort, sending a note before he passed on that he supported what we were planning to do. Other historians, investigative journalists, scientists and academics of note are also on our current sponsor list. We hope to have some of them, as well as others across diverse specialties, be part of an Advisory Committee that will evaluate proposed ideas for exhibits on hidden history, using the best practices of historical research, academic standards, journalistic rules, museum presentation and scientific methods to create thought-provoking exhibits using solid factual evidence. We hope to work closely with the Zinn Education Project, which continues to promote his writings and teaching in public schools, to present a People's History at our museum. We mourn the loss of his insights and historical research and his integrity, personal warmth and spirit.

You spoke at Zinn's memorial.

The event, which was aired on C-SPAN, was held in Washington at the local Busboys & Poets restaurant, run by a progressive local activist who knows me personally. I was added to the agenda at the last minute to say a few words because he knew Zinn had sponsored our work. I took the opportunity to present the idea of the museum and to ask for interested people to contact me directly. Some of the early volunteers that helped to plan the museum's beginning stage were located through that broadcast.

Cynthia McKinney has also continued to support the Museum, is that right?

Yes. Former Congresswoman Cynthia McKinney from Georgia, who spent six terms in Congress, is a sponsor as well. She has a continuing interest in the military-industrial-intelligence complex that came to power in the wake of the assassination of President Kennedy, and that President Eisenhower had warned about. She is also interested in many aspects of hidden history, including COINTELPRO and other operations against popular, democratic movements, as well as political assassinations. She introduced legislation to release tens of thousands of government records still classified regarding the murder of Dr. Martin Luther King, Jr.

In your mind, what would the Museum look like? What might a couple of the exhibits be?

The Museum of Hidden History will combine a library of over 4,000 books, and thousands of articles, clippings, and audio and video recordings. Three libraries have been cataloged already on intelligence history and operations, major political assassinations, and the historical framework, events and response to the attacks of 9/11. These include many government investigations, reports, testimony and documents and related archives. These will form the basis for the first stage of the museum, a Hidden History Research Center. The traveling exhibits on such topics as the JFK assassination, the Pentagon Papers and whistleblowers, and intentional community experiments, will form the permanent exhibits that will highlight all three aspects of our hidden history, as well as local examples. The finished museum will include the research center and will host many public presentations of new books, released files, film documentaries and panel discussions on topics related to our theme.

One interesting thing that would come about as the result of such a Museum is that people would be given a deeper alternative to existing so-called "alternatives." To take an example, the Watergate is still poorly understood by most Americans, although it is often held up as a pillar of investigative journalism. In this case, however, even the "deeper" version is a mask covering the real machinations behind the events. Can you talk about this a little bit?

The day after the Watergate break-in I saw a small UPI article about the people who had been arrested in the local Dayton, Ohio newspaper. I recognized all of them from my research into the assassination of President Kennedy and the Bay of Pigs operation. Some had testified to the Warren

Commission. I called my mother in Washington, D.C. and asked her to clip the newspapers there for any further articles about the arrest. It was significant they had been arrested. Her clipping mailings grew week by week over the next three years and they educated her to some of the hidden history and politics of our country. The true story of Watergate goes much deeper than the illegality of a burglary of the Democratic National Headquarters, and real purpose of the botched attempt was to corner, if not frame, President Nixon. The use of CIA operatives and their army of available covert operations "teams" dating back to the Bay of Pigs in a White House initiated crime reveals much about the government behind the one we see.

Nixon, who had a long history with both the intelligence agencies and organized crime, was intent on covering up parts of his own hidden history and stopping "leaks" with his team of "Plumbers". Deeper still were plans to implement martial law and "Continuity of Government" in a "national emergency" (arising presumably from the rise of powerful social movements for peace, civil rights and justice, movements for change that threatened and challenged an entrenched undemocratic elite in power), to be implemented by a team of 16 in the Office of Emergency Preparedness at the White House which included Watergate burglar and long-time CIA hand Bernard Barker, who placed the "second piece of tape" on the garage door, leading to the arrests. Perceptive investigative researcher Mae Brussell exposed much of what would only emerge in Congressional hearings years later in her article two weeks after the event, "Why Was Martha Mitchell Kidnapped?" in [Paul Krassner's] The Realist.

The lawyer who showed up to defend the Watergate burglars at their arraignment came without any of them making a call, Douglas Caddy, a member of William F. Buckley's Young Americans for Freedom, and who had worked with Tom Charles Houston, author of the infamous plan for martial law created by Nixon's teams. The portions of that plan that were revealed are instructive to the responses and destruction of civil rights and liberties that have followed 9/11. The current plans and protocols for an even more undemocratic Continuity of Government response, drafted after the Senator Frank Church hearings into intelligence community abuses that led to limits and reforms by bitter opponents at the Reagan White House,

Donald Rumsfeld and Richard Cheney, and later by Contragate operative Oliver North, were implemented in part on the day of September 11, 2001, creating a "Shadow Government Operating in Secret" according to the Washington Post headline a month later. The scope of these plans has resisted scrutiny by several Congressional investigations and by members of the oversight committees that approve the intelligence budgets devoted to such plans and their implementation come Code Red.

Fascinating information. I look forward to the day when I can buy a ticket to go in.

APPENDIX A

THE BEST BOOKS ON THE KENNEDY ASSASSINATION

Like anything else, building such a list depends on criteria, but I tried to pick books which covered the most ground, were well-written, and that I go back to often.

This is my list of the 10 best.

JFK AND THE UNSPEAKABLE, Jim Douglass
ACCESSORIES AFTER THE FACT, Sylvia Meagher
THE LAST INVESTIGATION, Gaeton Fonzi
RECLAIMING PARKLAND, Jim DiEugenio
BREACH OF TRUST, Gerald McKnight
HISTORY WILL NOT ABSOLVE US, E. Martin Schotz
THE YANKEE AND COWBOY WAR, Carl Oglesby
JFK AND VIETNAM, John Newman
INTO THE NIGHTMARE, Joseph McBride
JFK: THE BOOK OF THE FILM, Zachary Sklar & Oliver Stone

There are also some enormously important essays that have been written over the years which are accessible either on the net or in archives. Here are a few of the best, in my opinion:

"The Chicago Plot to Kill JFK," Edwin Black
"The Silence of the Historians," Dr. David Mantik
"The Assassinations of the 1960s as 'Deep Events,'" Peter Dale Scott
"The Posner Report: A Study in Propaganda," David Starks
"A Philadelphia Lawyer Analyzes the Shots, Trajectories and Wounds," Vincent Salandria

"John F. Kennedy's Fatal Wounds: Witnesses and the Interpretations from 1963 to the Present," Dr. Gary Aguilar

"The Magic Bullet: Even More Magical than We Knew?," Dr. Gary Aguilar and Josiah Thompson

"Who --- is Ron Rosenbaum?," Edgar F. Tatro

"The Other Murder," Larry Ray Harris

"Exit Strategy - In 1963, JFK ordered a complete withdrawal from Vietnam," James Kenneth Galbraith

"The Posthumous Assassination of John F. Kennedy." Jim DiEugenio

"Why is the Rockefeller Commission so Single-Minded about a Lone Assassin in the Kennedy Case?," Dr. Cyril Wecht

"Assassination as a Tool of Fascism," John Judge

"The Last Words of Lee Harvey Oswald," Mae Brussell

"Nazi Connections to the JFK Assassination," Mae Brussell

"Between the Signal and the Noise," Roger Feinman

"Trajectory of a Lie (I-III)," Milicent Cranor

There are many other fantastic essays at the CTKA site. Other essays, like for example Ed Tatro's takedown of Ron Rosenbaum, can be found at the Poage Legislative Library, run by my friend Ben Rogers. Look up the "Penn Jones collection" on the web at Baylor University for a wealth of material.

A few of my other favorite source books:

DESTINY BETRAYED (2nd edition), Jim DiEugenio

BITING THE ELEPHANT, Rodger Remington

THE ASSASSINATIONS, ed. Jim DiEugenio & Lisa Pease

OSWALD AND THE CIA, John Newman

VIRTUAL JFK, James Blight

THE MAN WHO KNEW TOO MUCH (2nd edition), Dick Russell

THE SEARCH FOR LEE HARVEY OSWALD, Robert Groden

THE KILLING OF A PRESIDENT, Robert Groden

THE KENNEDY TAPES, Ernest May & Philip Zelikow

OSWALD, THE CIA, AND MEXICO CITY: THE LOPEZ-HARDWAY REPORT, Edwin Lopez & Dan Hardway

FORGIVE MY GRIEF, Penn Jones

JFK: ORDEAL IN AFRICA, Richard D. Mahoney

Additionally, there are other vital books on the case that provide either unique research or a unique perspective on the case. I think these all belong in any researcher's library:

THE ECHO FROM DEALEY PLAZA, Abraham Bolden
SURVIVOR'S GUILT, Vince Palamara
THE GIRL ON THE STAIRS, Barry Ernest
HARVEY AND LEE, John Armstrong
THY WILL BE DONE, Gerald Colby Zilg
JFK: THE CIA, VIETNAM, AND THE PLOT TO ASSASSINATE JOHN F. KENNEDY, Fletcher Prouty
ON THE TRAIL OF THE ASSASSINS, Jim Garrison
CONSPIRACY, Anthony Summers (*Summers retitled his book for later publication NOT IN OUR LIFETIME. Don't get that one. Try to find the original.*)
INSIDE THE ARRB, Doug Horne
BLOODY TREASON, Noel Twyman
THE PRESIDENT AND THE PROVOCATEUR, Alex Cox
SIX SECONDS IN DALLAS, Josiah Thompson
RUSH TO JUDGMENT, Mark Lane
DEEP POLITICS AND THE DEATH OF JFK, Peter Dale Scott
PRAISE FROM A FUTURE GENERATION, John Kelin

APPENDIX B

OUTSTANDING WEBSITES

There are excellent resources available online for the researcher.

The website for the Hidden History Museum is at
www.museumofhiddenhistory.org.

There is a large collection of JFK materials at the Poage Legislative Library at Baylor University. The index can be found at
http://www.baylor.edu/lib/poage/jfk/index.php. It contains the work of Penn Jones, Dick Russell, John Armstrong, Gary Shaw, Jack White, and many others, including the amazing drawings and books created by Robert Cutler.

There is a great archive run by Dave Ratcliffe that has incredible amounts of stuff, including a lot of John Judge material. www.ratical.org.

Another priceless archive is run by Rob Falotico and contains Mae Brussell's old radio shows, along with a whole lot more.
www.worldwatchers.info.

The best single answer to Gerald Posner's *Case Closed*, and shorter than Harold Weisberg's *Case Open*, was written by Dave Starks. You can find that and much more at www.assassinationweb.com.

Randy Benson, who wrote the foreword to this book, has a website for his film *The Searchers*, about the original Kennedy researchers, at
www.thesearchersfilm.wordpress.com.

John Potash is one of the most interesting researchers around, and his new book *Drugs as Weapons Against Us* is amazing. The website for his first book can be found at http://www.fbiwarontupac.com.

Another popular site and one I've published at myself several times is run by Jim DiEugenio and represents the work of the former Probe Magazine as well as up-to-the-minute articles and reviews: www.ctka.net.

Black Op Radio has terrific people interviewed every week (including myself a few times). It also has a forum which I used to post at occasionally. It is at www.blackopradio.com.

Gregory Burnham keeps an interesting website at www.assassinationofjfk.com. His emphasis, like Penn Jones and John Judge, is on the military.

There are also forums, such as the Simkins Education Forum, and the Deep Politics Forum. I don't post at these places but read them sometimes.

OUTSTANDING BOOKS

In Appendix A I listed an article called "The Chicago Plot," as one of the best things ever written about the assassination of JFK. It was written by Edwin Black.

A few of his books cited in this volume:

IBM AND THE HOLOCAUST
WAR AGAINST THE WEAK
INTERNAL COMBUSTION

He does excellent work that I endorse wholeheartedly.

A few more books which are excellent for researchers:

Feral House has just published a collection of Mae Brussell's work. I can't recommend her work more highly. It's called THE ESSENTIAL MAE BRUSSELL, edited by Alex Constantine.

Also, read as much John Judge as you can. Most of it is online and all of it is brilliant, especially "Good Americans" and "The Black Hole of Guyana." There are also numerous YouTube videos of his talks.

RFK assassination

THE ASSASSINATION OF ROBERT F. KENNEDY, Bill Turner and John Christian
WHO KILLED BOBBY? Shane O'Sullivan
SHADOW PLAY: THE KILLING OF ROBERT KENNEDY, William Klaber & Phil Melanson
ASSASSINATION: ROBERT F KENNEDY 1925-1968, editors of UPI

MLK assassination

THE MARTIN LUTHER KING ASSASSINATION, Phil Melanson
ORDERS TO KILL, William Pepper
AN ACT OF STATE, William Pepper
MURDER IN MEMPHIS, Mark Lane and Dick Gregory
THE 13TH JUROR, trial transcripts
TRUTH AT LAST, Lyndon Barsten
A MEMOIR OF INJUSTICE, Tamara Carter

MALCOLM X assassination

THE JUDAS FACTOR, Karl Evanzz
MALCOLM X: A LIFE OF REINVENTION, Manning Marable
CONSPIRACYS, Baba Zak Kondo
THE FBI WAR AGAINST TUPAC SHAKUR AND OTHER BLACK LEADERS, John Potash

GENERAL POLITICAL RESEARCH

FOUR ARGUMENTS FOR THE ELIMINATION OF TELEVISION,

Jerry Mander
IN THE ABSENCE OF THE SACRED, Jerry Mander
THE CAPITALIST PAPERS, Jerry Mander
THE POLITICS OF HEROIN, Dr. Alfred McCoy
NEMESIS, Chalmers Johnson
KILLING TRUTH, William Blum
SECRET AGENDA, Linda Hunt
THE MIGHTY WURLIZTER, Hugh Wilford
THE CULTURAL COLD WAR, Frances Stonor Saunders
DARK ALLIANCE, Gary Webb
DRUGS OIL AND WAR, Peter Dale Scott
THE ROAD TO 9/11, Peter Dale Scott
NO LOGO, Naomi Klein
SPOOKS, Jim Hougan
SECRET AGENDA, Jim Hougan
SILENT COUP, Len Colodny & Robert Gettlin
THE HALDEMAN DIARIES, H. L. Haldeman
ABUSE OF POWER: THE NEW NIXON TAPES, Stanley Kutler, ed.
THE OUTLAW BANK, Jonathan Beaty & S.C. Gwynne
SPIDER'S WEB, Alan Friedman
THE SMARTEST GUYS IN THE ROOM, Bethany McLean
IN BANKS WE TRUST, Penny Lernoux
THE UNDERGROUND HISTORY OF AMERICAN EDUCATION,
John Taylor Gatto
A HISTORY OF THE GREAT AMERICAN FORTUNES, Gustavus
Myers
THE HISTORY OF THE STANDARD OIL COMPANY, Ida Tarbell
CONFESSIONS OF AN ECONOMIC HIT MAN, John Perkins
A GAME AS OLD AS EMPIRE, ed., Steven Hiatt
GLOBALIZATION AND ITS DISCONTENTS, Joseph Stiglitz
SECRET AND SUPPRESSED, ed., Jim Keith
THE OCTOPUS, Kenn Thomas & Jim Keith
THE ASSASSINATION OF JULIUS CAESAR, Michael Parenti
DIRTY TRUTHS, Michael Parenti
REARVIEW MIRROR, William Turner
HOOVER'S FBI, William Turner
THE PIED PIPER, Richard Cummings

IN DEFENSE OF FOOD, Michael Pollan
FOOD RULES, Michael Pollan
AMERICAN THEOCRACY, Kevin Phillips
PSYCHIC DICTATORSHIP IN THE U.S.A., Alex Constantine
THE COVERT WAR AGAINST ROCK, Alex Constantine
THE ANGLO AMERICAN ESTABLISHMENT, Carroll Quiqley
A CENTURY OF WAR, William Engdahl
AMUSING OURSELVES TO DEATH, Neil Postman
WHITE LIKE ME, Tim Wise
NICKEL AND DIMED, Barbara Ehrenreich
BAIT AND SWITCH, Barbara Ehrenreich
THE FAMILY, Ed Sanders
PROPAGANDA, Jacques Ellul
COERCION, Douglas Rushkoff
KATHARINE THE GREAT, Deborah Davis
THE MAFIA, THE CIA, AND GEORGE BUSH, Pete Brewton
THE END OF AMERICA, Naomi Wolf
FIRE IN THE MINDS OF MEN, James Billington
THE ANATOMY OF HUMAN DESTRUCTIVENESS, Erich Fromm
PATTY HEARST & THE TWINKIE MURDERS, Paul Krassner

AFRICAN-AMERICAN HISTORY

SOUL ON ICE, Eldridge Cleaver
MALCOLM X SPEAKS, edited by George Breitman
THE BLACK PANTHERS SPEAK, edited by Philip S. Foner
THE BLACK PANTHER PARTY RECONSIDERED, Charles E. Jones
WOMEN, RACE, AND CLASS, Angela Davis
SHACKLED AND CHAINED, Eugene Puryear
THE ASSASSINATION OF FRED HAMPTON, Jeffrey Haas
BAD BLOOD: THE TUSKEGEE SYPHILIS EXPERIMENT, James Jones
MEDICAL APARTHEID, Harriet Washington
REVOLUTIONARY SUICIDE, Huey P. Newton
WAR AGAINST THE PANTHERS, Huey P. Newton
TO DIE FOR THE PEOPLE, Huey P. Newton
SEIZE THE TIME, Bobby Seale

READY FOR REVOLUTION, Kwame Ture (Stokely Carmichael)
BLACK POWER, Stokely Carmichael
THE NEW JIM CROW, Michelle Alexander
FORCED INTO GLORY: ABRAHAM LINCOLN'S WHITE DREAM,
Lerone Bennett, Jr.
EYES ON THE PRIZE, ed. Dr. Clayborne Carson
THE MALCOLM X FBI FILE, ed., Dr. Clayborne Carson
THE NEW JIM CROW, Michelle Alexander

More books of interest in alternative history and viewpoints (with kind assistance from Dr. Faith G. Harper:

HISTORY AND EXPERIENCE OF INDIGENOUS AMERICA

EDUCATION FOR EXTINCTION: AMERICAN INDIANS and the
BOARDING SCHOOL EXPERIENCE, David Wallas Adams
CONQUEST: SEXUAL VIOLENCE AND AMERICAN INDIAN
GENOCIDE, Andrea Smith
UNQUIET GRAVE: THE FBI AND THE STRUGGLE FOR THE
SOUL OF INDIAN COUNTRY, Steve Hendricks
A CENTURY OF DISHONOR, Helen Hunt Jackson
A LITTLE MATTER OF GENOCIDE: HOLOCAUST AND DENIAL
IN THE AMERICAS 1492 TO THE PRESENT, Ward Churchill
PRISON WRITINGS: MY LIFE IS MY SUN DANCE, Leonard Peltier
CUSTER DIED FOR YOUR SINS: AN INDIAN MANIFESTO, Vine
Deloria, Jr.
HOW CHOCTAWS INVENTED CIVILIZATION AND WHY
CHOCTAWS WILL CONQUER THE WORLD, D.L. Birchfield
A PEOPLE'S HISTORY OF THE UNITED STATES, Howard Zinn
THE LONE RANGER AND TONTO FISTFIGHT IN HEAVEN,
Sherman Alexie
THE HOUSE OF PURPLE CEDAR, Tim Tingle

WOMEN'S HISTORY AND EXPERIENCE

ON LIES, SECRETS, and SILENCE, Adrienne Rich
ZAMI: A NEW SPELLING OF MY NAME, Audre Lorde

RECONCEIVING WOMEN: SEPARATING MOTHERHOOD FROM
FEMALE IDENTITY, Mardy S. Ireland
WOMEN'S LIVES, Phyllis Rose
THE CHALICE AND THE BLADE, Riane Eisler
WOMEN'S WAYS OF KNOWING, Mary Field Belenky, et al.
A HISTORY OF WOMEN IN AMERICA, Carol Hymowitz and Michaele
Weissman
FROM REVOLUTION TO REVELATION, Tara Brabazon

LGBTQQIA HISTORY

QUEER STREET, James McCourt
OUT IN ALL DIRECTIONS, Lynn Witt, et al.
TRANSGENDER HISTORY, Susan Stryker
EXCLUDED: MAKING FEMINIST AND QUEER MOVEMENTS
MORE INCLUSIVE, Julia Serano
REDIFINING REALNESS, Janet Mock
A QUEER HISTORY OF THE UNITED STATES, Michael Bronski
THE MAYOR OF CASTRO STREET, Randy Shilts
AND THE BAND PLAYED ON, Randy Shilts

LIBERATION THEORY/TRANSFORMING CULTURE

THE LITTLE BOOK OF STRATEGIC PEACEBUILDING, Lisa
Schirch
SYMBOLIC LOSS: THE AMBIGUITY OF MOURNING AND
MEMORY AT CENTURY'S END, Peter Homans
PEDAGOGY OF THE HEART, Paulo Freire
PEDAGOGY OF THE OPPRESSED, Paulo Freire
CULTURAL ACTION FOR FREEDOM, Paulo Freire
PEDAGOGY OF FREEDOM: ETHICS, DEMOCRACY, and CIVIC
COURAGE, Paulo Freire
WRITINGS FOR A LIBERATION PSYCHOLOGY, Ignacio Martin-
Baro
TOWARD PSYCHOLOGIES OF LIBERATION, Mary Watkins and
Heleme Shulman
CHE GUEVARA, PAULO FREIRE, AND THE PEDAGOGY OF

REVOLUTION, Peter McLaren

RELIGIOUS LITERACY

RELIGIOUS LITERACY, Stephen Prothero
GOD IS NOT ONE, Stephen Prothero
THE CHRIST CONSPIRACY, Acharya S.
THE MYTHMAKER, Hyam Maccoby
THE DEATH OF JESUS, Joel Carmichael
THE BIRTH OF CHRISTIANITY, Joel Carmichael
THE GOLDEN BOUGH, James George Frazier
THE ORIGIN OF THE MITHRAIC MYSTERIES, David Ulansey
THE BOOK YOUR CHURCH DOESN'T WANT YOU TO READ, Tim
Leedom

BIBLIOGRAPHY

Aczel, Amir D., *Pendulum: Leon Foucault and the Triumph of Science* (Washington Square Press: New York 2003).

Ambruster, Howard Watson. *Treason's Peace: German Dyes and American Dupes* (The Beechhurst Press: New York 1947).

James Bacque, "A Truth So Terrible," *Abuse Your Illusions*, Russ Kick, ed., (The Disinformation Company: New York 2003).

Baldwin, James. *The Price of the Ticket: Collected Nonfiction 1948-1985* (St. Martin's Press: New York 1985).

Bardi, Jason Socrates, *The Calculus Wars* (Thunder's Mouth Press: New York 2006).

Black, Edwin, *IBM and the Holocaust: The Strategic Alliance Between Nazi Germany and America's Most Powerful Corporation* (Three Rivers Press: CA 2002).

Black, Edwin, *War Against the Weak* (Basic Books: New York 2003).

Bloom, Howard, *Global Brain* (John Wiley & Sons: New York 2000),

Bloom, Howard, *The Lucifer Principle* (The Atlantic Monthly Press: New York 1995).

Borkin, Joseph and Charles A. Walsh, *Germany's Master Plan* (Duell, Sloan & Pearce: New York 1943).

Brown, Jared, *Alan J. Pakula: His Films and His Life* (Backstage Books: New

York 2005).

Carmichael, Joel, *The Death of Jesus* (Barnes & Noble Books: New York 1995 [1962]).

Casner and Gabriel, *Exploring American History* (Harcourt Brace: New York 1938).

Clarke, Arthur C., *Profiles of the Future* (Phoenix: New York 2000 [1961]).

Cockburn, Alexander & Jeffrey St. Clair, *Whiteout* (Verso: New York 1998).

Colby, Gerard, and Charlotte Dennett, *Thy Will Be Done: The Conquest of the Amazon: Nelson Rockefeller and Evangelism in the Age of Oil* (HarperCollins Publishers: New York 1995).

Constantine, Alex ed., *The Essential Mae Brussell: Investigations of Fascism in America* (Feral House: Port Townsend WA 2014).

Cronley, Major T. J., "Curtis LeMay: The Enduring 'Big Bomber Man,'" (United States Marine Corps Command and Staff College Center, Quantico VA 1986).

Richard Cummings, *The Pied Piper: Allard K. Lowenstein and the Liberal Dream* (InPrint.com, Inc.: New York 1985).

Dawkins, Richard, *The Blind Watchmaker* (W.W. Norton and Co., New York: 1986).

Dennett, Daniel, *Consciousness Explained* (Little, Brown, and Company: Boston 1991).

DiEugenio, James, *Destiny Betrayed: JFK, Cuba, and the Garrison Case* (Skyhorse: New York 2012).

DiEugenio, James, *Reclaiming Parkland: Tom Hanks, Vincent Bugliosi, and the JFK Assassination* (Skyhorse: New York 2013).

DiEugenio, James, and Lisa Pease, *The Assassinations* (Feral House: Los Angeles CA 2003).

Douglass, Jim, *JFK and the Unspeakable* (Orbis Books: NY 2008).

Doyle, Arthur Conan, "The Final Problem," *The Complete Sherlock Holmes Vol. 1* (Barnes & Noble Classics: NY 2003).

Ebert, Roger, *Roger Ebert's Four-Star Reviews, 1967-2007* (Andrews McMeel Publishing LLC: Kansas City 2007).

Eco, Umberto, *Travels in Hyperreality* (Harvest: San Diego 1986).

Fetzer, James ed., *Murder in Dealey Plaza* (Catfeet Press: Peru, Illinois 2000).

Field, Syd, *Screenplay* (Random House: New York 2005).

Finstad, Suzanne, *Warren Beatty: a Private Man* (Harmony Books: New York, NY 2005).

Flinn, Denny Martin, *How Not to Write a Screenplay* (Watson-Guphill Publications: New York 1999).

Fonzi, Gaeton, *The Last Investigation* (Thunder's Mouth Press: NY 1993).

Garland, David, *The Culture of Control* (University of Chicago Press: Chicago 2001).

Garrison, Jim, *On the Trail of the Assassins* (Warner Books: New York 1991).

Gatto, John Taylor, *The Underground History of American Education* (Oxford Village Press: New York 2001).

Goldman, William, *The Big Picture* (Applause Books: New York 2001).

Goldman, William, *Which Lie Did I Tell?* (Random House: New York 2000).

Groden, Robert and Harrison Livingstone, *High Treason* (The Conservatory Press: Baltimore MD 1989).

Haley, Alex, and Malcolm X. *The Autobiography of Malcolm X* (Ballantine Books: New York 1989).

Harris, David, *Dreams Die Hard* (St. Martin's Press: New York 1982).

Higham, Charles, *Trading With the Enemy* (Barnes & Noble Books: 1983).

Hofstadter, Richard, ed., *The Mind's I* (Basic Books: New York 1981

Horgan, John, *The End of Science* (Broadway Books: New York 1997).

Kelin, John, *Praise from a Future Generation* (Wings Press: San Antonio TX 2007).

Kuhn, Thomas S., *The Structure of Scientific Revolutions* (University of Chicago Press: 1962

Lazarus, Tom, *Secrets of Film Writing* (St. Martin's Press: New York 2001).

Levine, Michael & Laura Kavanau-Levine, *The Big White Lie* (Thunder's Mouth Press: New York 1993).

Lifton, David, *Best Evidence* (Macmillan: New York 1980).

Lisagor, Nancy, and Frank Lipsius, *A Law Unto Itself* (William Morrow and Company: New York 1988).

Loftus, John & Mark Aarons, *The Secret War Against the Jews* (St. Martin's Press: New York 1997).

Lopate, Philip ed., *American Movie Critics* (The Library of America: New York 2006).

Lundberg, Ferdinand, *The Rich and the Super-Rich* (Bantam Lyle Stuart, Inc.: New York 1968).

Machiavelli, Niccolo, *The Discourses* (Penguin Books: New York 1998).

Marable, Manning. *Malcolm X: A Life of Reinvention* (Viking: New York 2011).

McGowan, David, *Derailing Democracy* (Common Courage Press: Maine 2000).

McKnight, Gerald, *Breach of Trust* (University Press of Kansas 2005).

Mosley, Leonard, *Dulles* (The Dial Press/James Wade: NY 1978).

Nelson, Phillip F., *LBJ The Mastermind of JFK's Assassination* (Xlibris Corporation: 2010).

Newton, Huey. *To Die For the People* (City Lights Books: San Francisco CA 2009).

Parenti, Michael, *Dirty Truths* (City Lights Books: San Francisco CA 1996).

Parenti, Michael, *History As Mystery* (City Lights Books: San Francisco CA 1999).

Price, Glenn W., *The Polk-Stockton Intrigue*, (The University of Texas Press: 1967).

Prussen, Ronald W., *John Foster Dulles: The Road to Power* (The Free Press: Macmillan: New York 1982).

Raab, Selwyn, *Five Families: The Rise, Decline, and Resurgence of America's Most Powerful Mafia Empires* (St. Martin's Press: New York 2006).

Rampton, Sheldon and John Stauber, *Trust Us, We 're Experts!* (Putnam: New York 2001).

Russell, Bertrand, *A History of Western Philosophy* (Simon & Schuster: 2007 [1945]).

Russo, Gus, *Live By the Sword* (Bancroft Press: 1998).

Sagan, Carl, *The Demon-Haunted World* (Ballantine Books: New York 1996).

Scahill, Jeremy, *Blackwater* (Nation Books: New York 2007).

Schumpeter, Joseph, *Capitalism, Socialism, and Democracy* (HarperPerennial: New York 1942).

Searle, John, *The Construction of Social Reality* (The Free Press: Berkeley CA 1997).

Shermer, Michael, *The Borderlands of Science* (Oxford University Press: 2001).

Sibley, Robert, "The Mysterious, Vanishing Rifle in the JFK Assassination," *The Third Decade* (Volume 6, # 6, September 1990).

Sutton, Anthony, *Wall Street and the Rise of Hitler*

Talbot, David, *Brothers* (Free Press: NY 2007).

Thomas, Don, *Hear No Evil* (Mary Ferrell Foundation Press: Ipswich MA 2010).

Thomas, Kenn & Jim Keith, *The Octopus* (Feral House: Los Angeles CA 2004).

Thompson, Paul. *The Terror Timeline* (Regan Books: New York 2004).

Tryon, Lingley, Morehouse, *The American People and Nation* (Ginn and Company: New York 1943).

Turner, William, and John Christian, *The Assassination of Robert F. Kennedy*

(Carrol & Graf: New York 1993 [1978]).

Weber, Max, *The Protestant Ethic and the Spirit of Capitalism* (Charles Scribner's Sons: New York 1958).

Weber, Max, *The Theory of Social and Economic Organization* (Oxford University Press: New York 1947).

Williams, Robert. *Negroes with Guns* (Wayne State University Press: Detroit 1998).

Zilg, Gerald Colby, *DuPont: Behind the Nylon Curtain* (Prentice Hall. Englewood Cliffs, New Jersey: 1974).

ABOUT THE AUTHOR

Joseph E. Green is the author of five other books: *Dissenting Views*, *A Slew of Unfortunates*, *Clowntime is Over and Other Plays*, *The Very Wrath of Love*, and *The Dull are the Damned*. He is also a co-writer and co-producer of the upcoming documentary *King Kill 63*. He is a member of the Coalition on Political Assassinations and the Dramatists Guild of America.

www.ingramcontent.com/pod-product-compliance
Lightning Source LLC
LaVergne TN
LVHW051253080426
835509LV00020B/2955